THE FATHERS
OF THE CHURCH

A NEW TRANSLATION

VOLUME 36

THE FATHERS OF THE CHURCH

A NEW TRANSLATION

SAINT CYPRIAN

TREATISES

Translated and Edited by

ROY J. DEFERRARI

With The Dress of Virgins, trans., Sister Angela Elizabeth Keenan; S. N. D.; Mortality, trans. Mary Hannan Mahoney; and The Good of Patience, trans. Sister George Edward Conway, S. S. J.

THE CATHOLIC UNIVERSITY OF AMERICA PRESS
Washington, D.C.

Nihil Obstat:

JOHN A. GOODWINE

Censor Librorum

Imprimatur:

✠ FRANCIS CARDINAL SPELLMAN

Archbishop of New York

June 27, 1958

Library of Congress Catalog Card No. 77-081349
ISBN 8132-0036-9

INTRODUCTION

FOR THE PERIOD of Cyprian's life following his conversion we have several important sources. Most reliable and informative are his own writings, namely, his treatises and many letters. For the details leading to his martyrdom and for the martyrdom itself the proconsular acts of St. Cyprian inform us rather fully. These are based on official reports put together with connecting phrases by an editor, and consist of three separate documents covering the following events: the first trial that sent Cyprian to Curubis in exile, the arrest and second trial, and the execution. Finally, there is a short memoir of his life written by his deacon, Pontius. The latter is the first Christian biography that attained popularity. It is by no means a finished literary product, and it is important chiefly because of its originality in the field. Pontius was deeply convinced of the greatness of his master and was anxious to make the world equally conscious of his admirable character. Its chief purpose was to edify. It is historically unreliable. As to the events of Cyprian's life previous to his conversion very little is known. This too has to be gathered usually with difficulty and uncertainty from these same sources, and from St. Jerome's famous *Illustrious Men*.

St. Cyprian (Thascius Caecilius Cyprianus) was a bishop and martyr. He was born, very probably at Carthage, between 200 and 210, of a very wealthy and highly cultivated pagan family. His gift of eloquence, very evident in his writings, won him great fame in Carthage. Unless his treatise *Patience* is a sermon reworked into the form of a treatise, as some believe, we have no example of his preaching and oratory.

In his first writing as a Christian, *Ad Donatum,* he tells how, until the grace of God enlightened and strengthened him, it had seemed impossible to conquer sin. According to St. Jerome,[1] he had gone to live with a priest Caecilius, whose name he adopted, and under his influence determined to become a Christian. He had become, moreover, very much disgusted with the immorality of both the private and public life of the time, and with the corruption in government. Accordingly he sold his property, including his gardens at Carthage, and gave all his proceeds to the poor. Pontius tells us that Cyprian's friends restored this property to him by buying it back, and that Cyprian would have sold them a second time had not the outbreak of persecution made this seem imprudent. Probably in the year 246, on Easter eve, April 18, Cyprian was baptized.

Shortly after his baptism, Cyprian was raised to the priesthood, and toward the end of 248 or at the beginning of 249 he was elected Bishop of Carthage 'by the voice of the people.' Some of the elderly presbyters, including one Novatus, opposed to no avail.

Hardly a year had passed when Decius became emperor (October, 249), and published (January, 250) his cruel edict against Christians. Bishops were to be put to death, and all others were to be punished and tortured until they renounced Christianity. On January 20 of this year Pope Fabian was martyred, but Cyprian withdrew to a safe place of hiding. For the rest of his life Cyprian had to defend himself against the charge of running away in cowardice

---

1 *De vir. ill.* 67.

from his responsibilities. But if he had remained in Carthage he would certainly have been put to death, and, just as at Rome, it would have been impossible to elect a new bishop. This would have left the Church at Carthage without a government and have caused great dangers to others.

At this time the majority of the Christians at Carthage apostatized. Some, to be sure, refused to sacrifice but instead purchased *libelli* or certificates testifying that they had done so, and thus were called *libellatici*. There were several thousand of these at Carthage. Of the fallen or *lapsi* some did not repent and others openly became heretics. The majority, however, begged for forgiveness and reinstatement as Catholics. The policy to be followed in such cases caused much bitterness and dissension, which finally resulted in a schism. The confessors, considering themselves authorities on all religious problems, demanded the immediate reconciliation of the *lapsi*. Cyprian, the leader of the rigorists, refused to conform. He proposed that they be restored, when in danger of death, by a priest or even by a deacon; the rest, however, should await the end of the persecution, at which time councils could be held at Rome and at Carthage and a common policy agreed upon.

Thereupon, the deacon Felicissimus brought together a group of Cyprian's opponents from among the confessors and the fallen. This group was soon joined by the five priests who had opposed Cyprian's election as bishop. One of these last, Novatus, went to Rome and supported Novatian against the new Pope Cornelius.

When Cyprian returned to Carthage from exile in the spring of 251, he excommunicated Felicissimus and his followers, and published two documents dealing with the two great problems of the moment. One, *De lapsis,* dealt with the fallen, and declared that all the fallen without distinction should be admitted to penance, and at least at the hour of death be reconciled with the Church. Moreover, the decision in each case should be determined after considering the individual circumstances involved. The other, *De ecclesiae unitate,* dealt with the schism and is based on Cyprian's theory on the unity of the Church. This in its first form was a letter, but this was elaborated later into a pamphlet. This has been used extensively in support of those who will not accept the chair of Peter as the head of the Church. 'What St. Cyprian really says is simply this, that Christ, using the metaphor of an edifice, founds His Church on a single foundation which shall manifest and ensure its unity. And as Peter is the foundation, binding the whole Church together, so in each diocese is the bishop. With this one argument, Cyprian claims to cut at the root of all heresies and schisms.'[2]

In the problem of the rebaptism of heretics, Cyprian also was in the camp of the rigorists. Pope Stephen definitely pronounced against it, and his successor, Sixtus II, did not contradict him, although he certainly communicated with Cyprian, who was the chief exponent of rebaptism. The question seems to have been tacitly dropped, especially since the East was largely committed to the erroneous practice of rebaptism, and since in any case it was regarded chiefly as a matter of discipline rather than one of doctrine. All seemed to be unaware of the principle so strongly set forth later by St. Augustine, that Christ is always the principal agent (*Ipse est qui baptizat*), and thus the validity of the sacrament is not affected by the unworthiness of him who administers it.

In the very midst of this controversy over the rebaptism of heretics, a terrible plague caused fresh sufferings and persecutions for the Christians who were considered responsible for the troubles by reason of their denial of the pagan gods.

---

2 See "Cyprian," *Catholic Encyclopedia.*

The empire was surrounded by barbarian hordes. All this was a signal for a renewal of persecution by the Emperor Valerian. On August 30, 251, Cyprian was summoned before the proconsul Paternus. The *Acta proconsularia* of his martyrdom are extant and contain the interrogatory. After Cyprian professed to be a Christian and a bishop, and declared that he served one God to whom he prayed day and night for all men and for the welfare of the emperors, Paternus asked: 'Do you persevere in this?' 'A good will which knows God cannot be altered.' 'Can you, then, go into exile at Curubis?' 'I go.' He refused to give the names of the priests, also, on the ground that 'informing' or delation was forbidden by the law. He added, however, that they could easily be found in their respective cities. In the following September he went to Curubis, accompanied by Pontius. Pontius in his biography gives us a detailed description of Cyprian's life there at this time. About a year later, in 258, Cyprian learned that on August 6 of that year Pope Sixtus, together with four of his deacons, had been put to death in the catacombs. This was the immediate result of a new edict which declared that bishops, priests, and deacons should be put to death at once; senators, knights, and others of rank should lose their wealth, and, if still persistent, should die; matrons should be exiled; and officers of the *fiscus* should become slaves. Cyprian was brought back to Carthage on the 14th of September and was beheaded not far from Carthage. He was the first African bishop to become a martyr.

St. Cyprian's works fall naturally into two groups: treatises (*sermones, libelli, tractatus*) and letters.

All of the treatises of St. Cyprian, with the exception of the *Ad Quirinum*, known also as *Testimoniorum libri adversus Judaeos*, are included in this volume. The books of testimonies against the Jews was long disputed as to its authorship, but there is general agreement among scholars today that it certainly belongs to St. Cyprian. By its very nature it is essentially a compilation, and for the polemists of the third and fourth centuries it became a veritable arsenal from which to equip themselves in their literary battles. In the dedication of the work to Quirinus, Cyprian himself describes this treatise: 'The plan of this treatise conforms to your desire: it is a compendium, an epitome. I did not wish to present any developments, but to group and bind together extracts so far as my poor memory can supply them. See in this not a formal treatise, but material for the use of those who might wish to write one. This brevity has great advantages for the reader. Without confusing his mind over too long an explanation, it supplies useful summaries to his memory which it can faithfully preserve.' The work consists of three books, the last of which was probably added later, since in the introduction only two are announced. In the first book, the failure of the Jews and the call of the Gentiles are demonstrated in 24 theses; in the second book, the divinity and the mission of Christ in 30 theses; and in the third the duties of a Christ in the moral and disciplinary order in 120 theses. While the work is of very great value especially for the study of the versions of the Bible read in Carthage toward the middle of the third century, it has little of interest for the general reader of cultivated taste today. It has accordingly been omitted from this volume. The remaining treatises will receive a brief discussion preceding the English translation of each as they are presented here. These treatises in order of their appearance are: *To Donatus* (*Ad Donatum*), *The Dress of Virgins* (*De habitu virginum*), *The Fallen* (*De lapsis*), *The Unity of the Catholic Church* (*De catholicae ecclesiae unitate*), *The Lord's Prayer* (*De Dominica oratione*), *To Demetrian* (*Ad Demetrianum*), *Mortality* (*De mortalitate*), *Work and Alms* (*De opere et eleemosynis*), *The Blessing of Patience* (*De bono patientiae*), *Jealousy and Envy* (*De zelo et livore*), *To Fortunatus* (*Ad Fortunatum*), and *That Idols Are Not Gods* (*Quod idola dii non sint*).

The letters of St. Cyprian as we have received them number 81, of which 65 are from his own hand, and the remainder from others addressed to him. Since it has been planned to include these in a separate volume, only brief remarks regarding them are in order here. All of the extant letters of St. Cyprian were composed during his episcopacy, and may be arranged in the following groups: (1) those which cannot be dated (1-4 and 63) but all of which were probably composed before the persecution of Decius; Letter 63 is an especially precious document, since it confirms the traditional Catholic doctrine of the sacrificial character of the Eucharist; (2) letters sent to Carthage (5-7 and 10-19) while in exile during the first period of the Decian persecution; (3) letters of Cyprian as the representative of the clergy of Carthage (8, 9, 20-22, 27, 28, 30, 31, 35-37) to the clergy in Rome upon whom fell the responsibility of the government of the Church between the death of Fabian and the succession of Cornelius (January 250 to March 251); (4) letters sent to Carthage (23-26, 29, 32-34, 38-43) during the last period of the Decian persecution, in 250 and 251; (5) letters (44-55) of the years 251 and 252, dealing with the troubles caused by the schism of Novatian.

Everything that Cyprian wrote was directly connected with his work as Bishop of Carthage. His works were of a practical nature intended to facilitate and make more effective the administrative functions of his office. All in all, he was very well balanced in his dealing with problems, and very gentle though firm in making his decisions, quite unlike Tertullian upon whom he drew extensively for ideas although never taking over any of the bitterness and excesses of which this source was filled. Moreover, the calm and kindliness of Cyprian's character shine forth from the clear, simple, and nicely balanced style of his works.

St. Cyprian's prestige and influence was great in Christian antiquity. Unfortunately he is not as well known or as widely read in modern times as he deserves. This is probably due to Cyprian's lack of complete orthodoxy in the modern sense of the word regarding the recognition of the see of Peter and the rebaptism of heretics. The modern reader must always bear in mind that the period of the Fathers was the time of the laying of the foundation of so much which today we accept and see so clearly. In any case, both Lactantius (*Dio. Inst.* 5, 1, 24) and St. Augustine (*De bapt. contra Donatistas*), while acknowledging the weaknesses of St. Cyprian's stand on the questions mentioned, do not in the slightest detract from their respect and admiration for their fellow countryman. Prudentius pays St. Cyprian the following tribute in his Peristephanon (13, 5, 6ff):

'As long as Christ will allow the race of men to exist and the world to flourish,

As long as any book will be, as long as there will be holy collections of literary works,

Everyone who loves Christ will read you, O Cyprian, will learn your teachings.'

SELECT BIBLIOGRAPHY

Text:

W. Von Hartel, *Corpus Scriptorum Ecclesiasticorum Latinorum* 3.1-3 (Vienna 1868-1871).

Translations:

C. Thornton, in *Library of the Fathers* 3 (Oxford 1839).
E. Wallis, in *Ante-Nicene Fathers* 5 (New York 1896).

Secondary Works:

E. W. Benson, *Cyprian: His Life, His Times, His Work* (London 1897)
J. H. Fichter, *Saint Cecil Cyprian, Defender of the Faith* (St. Louis 1942).
E. Hummel, *The Concept of Martyrdom according to St. Cyprian of Carthage* (Washington 1946).
W. Muir, *Cyprian: His Life and Teachings* (London 1898).
P. Monceaux, *Saint Cyprien, évêque de Carthage* (Paris 1914).
A. D. Nock, 'The Conversion, Confession, and Martyrdom of St. Cyprian,' *Journal of Theological Studies* 28 (1927) 411ff.
D. D. Sullivan, *The Life of the North Africans as Revealed in the Works of St. Cyprian* (Washington D. C. 1933).

CONTENTS

SAINT CYPRIAN

TREATISES

Translated and Edited by

ROY J. DEFERRARI, Ph.D., LL.D., L.H.D., Litt.D.
The Catholic University of America

TO DONATUS

Translated by

ROY J. DEFERRARI, Ph.D.
The Catholic University of America

TO DONATUS

To DONATUS IS undoubtedly the earliest of Cyprian's treatises. It must be placed very soon after his conversion to Christianity. His baptism probably took place on Easter eve in 246. The new convert, enjoying the marvelous effect of divine grace in his own conversion, writes to his friend Donatus, a Christian but apparently a little less ardent, to share the great spiritual blessings which are now his. In 'confessing' his own fall and at the same time proclaiming the glory of God, Cyprian in this treatise reminds us very much of St. Augustine in the *Confessions*.

Some have tried, by adding some very common place lines at the beginning, to change this enthusiastic monologue into a dialogue. Manuscript tradition, however, does not permit this. Moreover, these lines create obvious inconsistencies with little touches through the rest of the work, which stamp it definitely as a monologue.

While the tone of *To Donatus* is very strongly sincere, yet its style unlike that of all the other works of St. Cyprian, is wordy and affected, and quite wanting in simplicity. It differs much from 'the more dignified and reticent eloquence' of his later works, as St. Augustine himself has observed.[1]

'In the case of a "strong people," such as God has spoken

---

1 *De doctrina Christiana* 4.14.31.

about: "I will praise Thee in a strong people,"[2] there is no
pleasure in that attractiveness of style, which certainly does
not teach falsehoods, but ornaments trifling and perishable
truths with a frothy showiness of style such as would not be
a fitting or dignified adornment for noble and enduring
truths. There is something like this in a letter of the blessed
Cyprian, which I believe either happened accidentally or
was done designedly, that succeeding ages might perceive
how the soundness of Christian teaching has restrained his
style from that redundancy, and restricted it to a more
dignified and more moderate eloquence, such as in his later
writings is safely admired and anxiously sought after, but
imitated only with very great difficulty. He says, for example,
in a certain place:[3] 'Let us seek this abode. The neighboring solitudes offers a place of retirement where, while the
wandering tendrils of the vines creep through the trellis supports with overhanging interlacing, the leafy covering has
formed a colonnade of vines.' This is expressed with a wonderful fluency and luxuriance of style, but, because of its
immoderate profuseness, it is displeasing to the serious reader.
Those who like this style think that those who do not use it,
but express themselves with greater restraint, cannot speak
in that style, not realizing that they avoid it deliberately.
This holy man shows both that he can speak in that way,
because he has done so here, and that he does not prefer
to do so, since he never does so afterward.

It is noteworthy that this treatise and *That Idols Are Not
Gods* contain no quotations from Scripture, which abound
in all of Cyprian's other works. The fact that these are
Cyprian's earliest efforts, composed soon after his conversion,
may at least to some extent account for this.

2 Ps. 34.18
3 *Ad Donatum* 1.

TO DONATUS

Chapter 1

WELL DO YOU REMIND ME, dearest Donatus, for I made the promise, and certainly this season is opportune for fulfilling it, when the mind relieved by the favorable harvest for repose receives the annually recurring respite of the wearying year. The place too benefits the time, and the delightful appearance of the gardens harmonizes with the gentle breezes of a soothing autumn in delighting and animating the senses. Here it is delightful to pass the day in conversation and by diligent discussions to train the understanding of the heart in the divine precepts. And that no profane critic may impede our talk and no unrestrained clamor of a noisy household annoy us, let us seek out this spot. The neighboring thickets furnish seclusion, where the wandering slips of vines, with their pendent interlacing creep over the burden-carrying reeds, and the leafy covering has made a vine-covered portico. Well do we bring our ears to attention here, and as we look upon the trees and the vines, we delight our eyes by the pleasing view, and likewise instruct the soul by what we hear and nourish it by what we see. And yet now your only pleasure and your only concern is with conversation, and, overlooking the enticements of the pleasures of sight, you have fixed your eyes upon me

with that countenance and with that attention by which
you are altogether a listener and with this affection with which
you love me.

Chapter 2

But of whatever nature or however much that is which
comes into your heart from us, (the poor mediocrity of my
meagre talent produces a very sparing harvest, and does not
grow heavy with stalks for a copious rich deposit), nevertheless I shall approach my task as well as I can; for the sub-
ject-matter of my talk is quite to my liking. In courts of justice,
in public assembly before the rostrum let an opulent eloquence be displayed with unrestrained ambition, but when
speech is concerned with the Lord God, the pure sincerity
of speech depends not on the force of eloquence for the
arguments in support of faith but on facts. Therefore, receive
not eloquent words, but forceful ones, not decked out with
cultivated rhetoric to entice a popular audience, but simple
words of unvarnished truth for the proclaiming of God's
mercy. Receive what is felt before it is learned, and what
is gathered not after a long study with much delay, but what
is drawn in by a quickening act of divine grace.

Chapter 3

While I was lying in darkness and in the obscure night,
and while, ignorant of my real life, I was tossing about on
the sea of a restless world wavering and doubtful in my
wandering steps, a stranger to the truth and the light,
I thought it indeed difficult and hard (to believe) according
to the character of mine at the time that divine mercy was
promised for my salvation, so that anyone might be born

again and quickened unto a new life by the laver of the saving water, he might put off what he had been before, and, although the structure of the body remained, he might change himself in soul and mind. 'How,' I said, 'is such a conversion possible, that the innate which has grown hard in the corruption of natural material or when acquired has become inveterate by the affliction of old age should suddenly and swiftly be put aside? These things, deep and profound, have been thoroughly rooted within us. When does he learn thrift, who has become accustomed to lavish banquets and extravagant feasts? And when does he who, conspicuous in costly raiment, has shone in gold and purple, dispose himself to ordinary and simple clothing? He who has been delighted by the fasces and public honors cannot become a private and inglorious citizen. He who has been attended by crowds of clients or has been honored by a crowded assemblage of an officious throng thinks it a punishment to be alone. Of necessity, as in the past, wine-bibbing ever entices with its tenacious allurements, pride puffs up, anger inflames, covetousness disturbs, cruelty stimulates, ambition delights, lust plunges into ruin.'

Chapter 4

This I often said to myself. For as I myself was held enlivened by the very many errors of my previous life, of which I believe that I could not divest myself, so I was disposed to give in to my clinging vices, and in my despair of better things I indulged my sins as if now proper and belonging to me. But afterwards, when the stain of my past life had been washed away by the aid of the water of regeneration, a light from above poured itself upon my chastened and pure heart; afterwards when I had drunk of the Spirit from heaven a second birth restored me into a new man; immediately in a marvelous manner doubtful matters clarified themselves, the closed opened, the shadowy shone with light, what seemed impossible was able to be accomplished, so that it was possible to acknowledge that what formerly was born of the flesh and lived submissive to sins was earthly, and what the Holy Spirit already was animating began to be of God. Surely you know and recognize alike with myself what was taken from us and what was contributed by the death of sins and by that life of virtues. You yourself know; I do not proclaim it. Boasting to one's own praise is odious, although that cannot be a matter of boasting but an expression of gratitude, which is not ascribed to the virtue of man but is proclaimed as of God's munificence, so that now not to sin begins to be of faith, and what was done in sin before to be of human error. Our power is of God, I say, all of it is of God. From Him we have life; from Him we have prosperity; by the vigor received and conceived of Him, while still in this world, we have foreknowledge of what is to be. But let fear be the guardian of innocence, so that the Lord, who of His mercy has flowed into our hearts with the silent approach of celestial tenderness, may be kept in the guest-chamber of a heart that gives delight by its righteous action, lest the security we have received beget carelessness, and the old enemy creep upon us anew.

Chapter 5

But if you hold to the way of innocence, to the way of justice, with the firmness of your step unbroken, if depending upon God with all your strength and your whole heart you only be what you began to be, so much power is given you in the way of freedom to act as there is an increase in spiritual grace. For there is no measure or moderation in receiving of God's munificence, as is the custom with earthly benefits. For the Spirit flowing forth bountifully is shut in by no boundaries, and is checked within the spaces of definite limits by no restraining barriers. It spreads out continually; it overflows abundantly, provided only our hearts are athirst and open for it. According as we bring to it a capacious faith, to this extent do we draw from it overflowing grace. From this source is the power given with modest chastity, with a sound mind, with a pure voice to extinguish the virus of poisons within the marrow of the grieving, to cleanse the stain of foolish souls by restoring health, to bind peace to the hostile, rest to the violent, gentleness to the unruly, by dire threats to force those unclean and vagrant spirits to confess, who have forced their way within men to destroy them, to force them with heavy blows to withdraw, to stretch them out struggling, wailing, groaning with an increase of expanding punishment, to beat them with scourges, and to roast them with fire. There the matter is carried on but is not seen; the blows are hidden but the punishment is manifest. Thus since we have already begun to be, the spirit which we have received possesses its own freedom of action; since we have not yet changed our body and members, our still carnal view is obscured by the cloud of this world. How great is this domination of the mind, how great is its force, not only that it itself is withdrawn from pernicious contacts of the world, so that as one cleansed and pure it is seized by no stain of an attacking enemy, but that it becomes greater and stronger in its might, so that it rules with imperial right over every army of an attacking adversary.

Chapter 6

But in order that the characteristics of the divine munificence may shine forth when the truth has been revealed,
I shall give you light to recognize it, by wiping away the
cloud of evil I shall reveal the darkness of a hidden world.
For a little consider that you are being transported to the
loftiest peak of a high mountain, that from this you are
viewing the appearance of things that lie below you and
with your eyes directed in different directions you yourself
free from earthly contacts gaze upon the turmoils of the
world. Presently you also will have pity on the world, and
taking account of yourself and with more gratitude to God
you will rejoice with greater joy that you have escaped from
it. Observe the roads blocked by robbers, the seas beset by
pirates, wars spread everywhere with the bloody horrors of
camps. The world is soaked with mutual blood, and when
individuals commit homicide, it is a crime; it is called a virtue
when it is done in the name of the state. Impunity is acquired
for crimes not by reason of innocence but by the magnitude
of the cruelty.

Chapter 7

Now if you turn your eyes and face toward the cities
themselves, you will find a multitude sadder than any solitude.
A gladitorial combat is being prepared that blood may delight
the lust of cruel eyes. The body is filled up with stronger
foods, and the robust mass of flesh grows fat with bulging
muscles, so that fattened for punishment it may perish more
dearly. Man is killed for the pleasure of man, and to be able
to kill is a skill, is an employment, is an art. Crime is not
only committed but is taught. What can be called more
inhuman, what more repulsive? It is a training that one

may be able to kill, and that he kills is a glory. What is this, I ask you, of what nature is it, where those offer themselves to wild beasts, whom no one has condemned, in the prime of life, of a rather beautiful appearance, in costly garments? While still alive they adorn themselves for a voluntary death, wretched they even glory in their wicked deeds. They fight with beasts not because they are convincts but because they are mad. Fathers look upon their own sons; a brother is in the arena and his sister near by, and, although the more elaborate preparation of the exhibition increases the price of the spectacle, oh shame! the mother also pays this price that she may be present at her own sorrows. And at such impious and terrible spectacles they do not realize that with their eyes they are parricides.

Chapter 8

Turn your gaze away from this to the no less objectionable contaminations of a different kind of spectacle. In the theatres also you will behold what will cause you both grief and shame. It is the tragic buskin to relate in verse the crimes of former times. The ancient horror of parricide and incest is unfolded in acting expressed in the model of the truth, lest, as time goes by, what was once committed disappear. Every age is reminded by what it hears that what has been done can be done again. Transgressions never die from the passage of the ages; crime is never erased by time; vice is never buried in oblivion. Then in the mimes by the teaching of infamies one delights either to recall what he has done at home or to hear what he can do. Adultery is learned as it is seen, and, while evil with public authority panders to vices, the matron who perchance had gone forth to the spectacle chaste returned from the spectacle unchaste. Then

further how great a collapse of morals, what a stimulus
to base deeds, what a nourishing of vices, to be polluted
by the gestures of actors, to behold the elaborate endurance
of incestuous abominations contrary to the convenant and
law of our birth. Men emasculate themselves; all the honor
and vigor of their sex are enfeebled by the disgrace of an
enervated body, and he gives more pleasure there who best
breaks down the man into woman. He grows into praise
from crime, and he is judged the more skilful, the more
degraded he is. Oh shame! Such a one is looked upon, and
freely so. What cannot one in such a state suggest? He
rouses the senses; he flatters the affections; he drives out
the stronger conscience of a good heart; nor is there lacking
the authority of a seductive vice, that ruin may creep upon
men with less notice. They depict Venus as unchaste, Mars
as an adulterer, and that famous Jupiter of theirs no more
a chieftain in dominion than in vice, burning with earthly
love in the midst of his own thunderbolts, now shining
white in the plumage of a swan, now pouring down in
a golden shower, now plunging forth with ministering birds
for the raping of young boys. Ask now whether he who
looks upon this can be healthy minded or chaste. One
imitates the gods whom he venerates. For these poor wretches
sins become even religious acts.

Chapter 9

Or, if you should be able, standing on that lofty watch-
tower, to direct your eyes into secret places, to unfasten the
locked doors of sleeping chambers and to open these hidden
recesses to the perception of sight, you would behold that
being carried on by the unchaste which a chaste countenance
could not behold; you would see what it is a crime even

to see; you would see what those demented with the fury of vices deny that they have done and hasten to do. Men with frenzied lusts rush against men. Things are done which cannot even give pleasure to those who do them. I lie if he who is such does not accuse others of the same; the depraved defames the depraved, and believes that he while conscious of his guilt has escaped, as if consciousness were not sufficient condemnation. The same persons are accusers in public and the defendants in secret, both their own critics and the guilty. They condemn abroad what they commit at home, which, after they have committed it, they accuse; a daring acting directly with vice and an impudence in harmony with the shameless. Do not marvel at such things as they speak. Whatever sin is committed with the voice is less than that by the mouth.[1]

Chapter 10

But viewing the treacherous highways, the manifold battles scattered over the whole earth, the exhibition either bloody or vile, the infamies of lust offered for sale in brothels or enclosed within domestic walls, whose daring is greater in proportion to the secrecy of the sin, the forum perhaps may seem to you to be devoid of all this, that it is free of harassing outrages and is unpolluted by contacts with evil. Turn your sight in that direction. There you will find more things to abhor; from these you will the more turn aside your eyes. Although the laws are engraved on twelve tables, and the statutes are published on bronze set up in public, there is sin in the midst of the laws themselves, there is wickedness in the midst of the statutes, and innocence is not preserved where it is defended. The madness of those who

---

1 See Rom. 1.26,27. The awful extent of this form of lust is implied by the constant rebukes of the Fathers.

oppose each other rages, and among the togas[1] peace is disrupted and the forum roars madly with law suits. There
the spear and the sword and the executioner are close at
hand, the claw that tears, the rack that stretches, the fire
that burns, for the one body of man more tortures than
it has limbs. Who in such cases gives assistance? One's patron?
But he is in collusion and deceives. The judge? But he sells
his sentence. He who sits to punish crimes commits them,
and in order that the defendant may perish in innocence, the
judge becomes guilty. Everywhere transgressions flourish,
and in every direction by the multiform nature of sinning
the pernicious poison acts through wicked minds. One coun-
terfeits a will, another by a capital fraud gives false testimony; on the one hand children are cheated of their inheritance, on the other strangers are endowed with property;
an enemy makes a charge, a calumniator attacks, a witness
defames. On both sides the venal impudence of the hired
voice proceeds to the falsification of charges, while in the
meantime the guilty perish not with the innocent. There
is no fear of the laws, of the inquisitor, no dread of the judge;
what can be bought is not feared. Now it is a crime for an
innocent man to be among the guilty; whoever does not
imitate the evil gives offence. The laws have come to terms
with sins, and what is public begins to be allowed. What
shame of events can there be here, what integrity, when
those to condemn the wicked are absent, and only those
to be condemned meet with you.

Chapter 11

But perchance we may seem to select the worst examples,
and to lead your eyes through them with a view to dis-

---

1 The toga was the dress of peace.

paragement, whose sad and revolting sight offends the face and gaze of the better conscience. Presently I shall show you those examples which worldly opinion considers good. Among those also you will see things to be shunned. As for what you think to be honors, what you consider the fasces, what affluence in riches, what power in camp, the sight of people among the magistrates, power in the license of rulers, all this is the hidden virus of enticing evils, and the happy appearance of smiling wickedness, but the treacherous disception of hidden calamity. It is like a certain kind of poison, when after sweetness has been spread in its lethal juices and its flavor medicated with cunning to deceive what is consumed seems an ordinary draught, but when the stuff has been swallowed, the destruction which has been drained creeps over you. Surely you see that man who, conspicuous by his rather brilliant cloak seems to himself to be brilliant in purple. With what baseness he has brought this, that he may be brilliant. What acts of contempt did he first endure on the part of the haughty; what proud gates as a courtier did he besiege early in the morning; how many insulting steps of arrogant men, pressed into the throng of clients, first precede, so that afterwards attendants in solemn array might precede him also with salutations, submissive not to the man but to his power. For he has not merited to be cherished for his character but for his fasces. Finally you may see the wretched exits of these men, when the time-serving sycophant has departed, when the deserting follower has defiled the bare side of him now a private citizen.[1] Then the injuries of a mutilated home strike the conscience; then the losses of a bankrupted family-estate are known, by which the favor of the mob was bought, and the people's breath was sought with fleeting and empty entreaties. Surely a foolish and empty expense, to have wished to make ready

---

1 Mentioned by all the Roman satirists; cf. Horace, *Sat.* 6.1.

by the pleasure of a disappointing spectacle that which the people did not accept and the magistrate lost.

Chapter 12

But those also whom you consider rich, as they add forest to forest, and extend the infinite boundless country-side ever wider, excluding the poor from its limits, and who possess the greatest heap of silver and gold, and mighty sum of money either in sturdy ramparts or buried stores, these too fearful in the midst of riches are distraught by the anxiety of vague thought, lest the robber lay them waste, lest the murderer attack, lest the hostile envy of some wealthier neighbor disturb him with malicious law-suits. Neither food nor sleep is had in peace; he sighs at the banquet, although he drinks from a jewelled cup, and when the excessively soft couch hides his body enervated by feasting within its deep folds, he lies awake in the midst of the down, and the wretch does not understand that these gilded things are his torments, that he is held bound by gold, and is possessed by riches rather than possesses them, and—oh detestable blindness of minds, and profound darkness of insane cupidity—when he can unburden himself and relieve himself of his load, he continues to brood still more over his troublesome fortunes; he continues to cling stubbornly to his punishing hoards. From these there is no largess for his dependents, there is no sharing with the needy, and they call it their money, which they guard with solicitous care locked up at home as if it were another's, out of which they impart nothing to friends, nothing to their children, and in short nothing to themselves; they possess it only for this purpose, that another may not possess it, and—how great is the diversity of names!—they call those things good of which they make no use except for evil ends.

Chapter 13

Or do you think that even those are safe, that those at least are secure with firm stability midst chaplets of honor and great wealth, whom as they are resplendent with the splendor of a royal court a guard of vigilant arms surrounds? They have greater fear than others. He is forced to fear just as he is feared. Sublimity exacts punishments in like measure of the more powerful, although hedged in by a band of satellites he guards his side surrounded and protected by a numerous retinue. Just as he does not allow his subjects to be secure, so it is necessary that he also not be secure. Their own power terrifies the very ones whom it advises to be the source of terror. It smiles that it may rage; it cajoles that it may deceive; it raises up, that it may cast down. With a certain usury of mischief the fuller the sum total of dignity and honor, the greater is the interest in punishments which is exacted.

Chapter 14

Therefore, there is one peaceful and trustworthy tranquillity, one solid and firm security, if one withdraws from the whirlpools of a disturbing world and takes anchor in the harbor of the port of salvation. He raises his eyes from earth to heaven, and now admitted to the gift of God and being next to God in mind, whatever to others seems sublime and great in human affairs, he boasts to lie beneath his consciousness. Nothing can he now seek from the world, desire from the world, who is greater than the world. How stable, how unshaken is that protection, how heavenly is that safeguard with its perennial blessings to be released from the snares of the entangling world, to be purged of the dregs of earth for the light of immortality. He would see what a crafty destruction on the part of an attacking enemy formerly proceeded against us. We are compelled to cherish more what we are to be, when it is permitted us to know and to condemn what we were. Nor for this is there need of a price either in the way of bribery or labor, that man's highest dignity or power may be achieved with elaborate effort. It is both a free and easy gift from God. As the sun radiates of its own accord, the ray gives light, the spring waters, the shower moistens, so the heavenly Spirit infuses itself. When the soul gazing upon heaven recognizes its Author, higher than the sun and more sublime than all this earthly power, it begins to be that which it believes itself to be.[1]

Chapter 15

Do you, whom already the heavenly warfare has designated for the spiritual camp, only keep uncorrupted and chastened in religious virtues. See that you observe either constant prayer or reading. Speak now with God; let God now speak with you. Let Him instruct in His precepts; let Him dispose you in them. Whom He shall make rich, no one will make poor. There can be no want, when once the celestial food has filled the breast. Now ceilings enriched with gold and houses decorated with slabs of precious marble will seem of no account when you realize that you are to be cherished more, that you rather are to be adorned, that this house is of more importance for you, where God dwells in a temple, in which the Holy Spirit begins to live. Let us embellish this house with the colors of innocence; let us illuminate it with the light of justice. This house will never fall into ruin by the decay of age, nor will it be disfigured by the

1 A most eloquent testimony to regeneration.

tarnishing of the color and gold of its walls. Whatever has been falsely beautified is destined to perish, and what possesses no reality of possession offers no stable confidence to those who possess it. This abides in a beauty perpetually vivid, in complete honor, in everlasting splendor. It can neither be destroyed nor blotted out. It can only be fashioned for the better, when the body returns.

Chapter 16

These things, dearest Donatus, in the meantime are in brief. For although what is profitably heard delights the patience easy by reason of its goodness, the mind strong in the Lord, a sound faith, and nothing is so pleasing to your ears as what is pleasing to the Lord, yet we ought to temper our speech, being at once close and likely to speak to each other frequently, and since now is the quiet of a holiday and a time of leisure, whatever is left of the day as the sun slopes toward evening, let us spend this time in gladness, and let not even the hour of repast be void of heavenly grace. Let a temperate repast resound with psalms, and as you have a retentive memory and a musical voice, approach this task as is your custom. You sustain your dearest friends the more, if we listen to something spiritual, if the sweetness of religion delights our ears.[1]

---

1 While this section savors strongly of Horace, Cyprian greatly surpasses him by adding the Christian flavor.

THE DRESS OF VIRGINS

translated by

SISTER ANGELA ELIZABETH KEENAN, S. N. D.
Emmanuel College

THE DRESS OF VIRGINS

YPRIAN'S TREATISE, *De habitu virginum,* is something more than a homily on the dress of virgins, as St. Augustine noted in his reference to the work in the *De doctrina Christiana.*[1] It is an encomium of the virtue of chastity, directed to a group of women who have consecrated their lives in a special way to Christ. The work is particularly significant because it is one of the first treatises of this nature found in Christian literature and hence is invaluable for the contribution it makes to the history of the religious life for women in the early Church. The paucity of material available in early writings on the subject of the ascetical life gives added importance to Cyprian's treatise.

Before Cyprian's time we know simply of the existence of groups of Christians who aimed to lead a more perfect life; beyond this our knowledge is extremely limited. Clement of Alexandria[2] notes that in addition to the faithful there are the 'elect of the elect who draw themselves, like ships to the strand, out of the surge of the world to a place of safety'—those whom the 'Word calls the "light of the world" and the "salt of the earth." ' Origen,[3] in his enumeration of dignitaries, mentions first the bishop, the priest, the deacon,

---

1 See *De doctrina Christiana* 4.21.48.
2 *Quis dives salvetur* 36.
3 *In numer. II Homil.* n. 1.

and the sacerdotal orders, and from these passes to the virgins and the continent. Hippolytus[4] introduces the ascetics in an enumeration of the seven divine orders which sustain the society of the faithful, thus ranking them as a distinct body among the prophets, martyrs, priests, saints, and the just.

It is not until the third century that the details of the picture begin to take more definite shape. Most of the information on the subject is contained in the several extant discourses which were directed in particular to this class of Christians—*De habitu virginum* of Cyprian, *Convivium decem virginum* of Methodius of Olympus, and the Pseudo-Clementine letters *Ad virgines*. Of these the treatise of Cyprian is probably the earliest,[5] and assuredly the most important, coming as it does from the pen of the greatest known bishop of the third century. Herein are crystallized all the facts known through incidental references in earlier Church literature of the degree of development of the ascetical life for women in the first three centuries. It is plain that the position of consecrated virgins in the Church is a lofty one. They are the 'flower of the Church, the beauty and adornment of spiritual grace, the pure and untarnished work of praise and honor, the image of God reflecting the holiness of God, the more distinguished part of Christ's flock.'[6] They have made to God a definite vow, for they are 'virgins of Christ'[7] who have renounced the concupiscences of the flesh, consecrated their lives to Christ, and dedicated themselves to God in body as well as in spirit.[8]

---

4 *Fragmenta in proverbia, PL* 10.627.
5 The exact dates of these treatises are unknown. The general opinion seems to be that Cyprian wrote his work before 250 and that the remaining two belong to the latter part of the third century. Cf. Bardenhewer, *Gesch. d. altkirchl. Lit.* I 130, and Puech II 44.
6 *De habitu virginum* 3.
7 *Ibid.* 9.
8 *Ibid.* 4.

Careful investigation of the nature of the vow signified in this discourse has led to the conclusion that it was distinctly a private resolution, and that it concerned chastity alone. There is no evidence to substantiate the belief that it was received publicly by a bishop in the name of the Church.[9] That this private vow involved definitely the renunciation of marriage is clear from Cyprian's recommendation to virgins not to attend wedding festivities. It is equally certain that it did not include the surrender of property—the vow of poverty as it is practiced among religious today. The ground was prepared even for this, however, in the exhortation to the wealthy to live simply, and to give alms generously to the poor.[10] There is no question of community life, nor of a vow of obedience as we understand it. Consecrated virgins sought to attain their ideal, a life of close union with God, without resigning either home or liberty; but the rudiments, at least, of organization are apparent in the suggestion made to the older women to teach the younger, and to the younger to stimulate one another by mutual acts of virtue.[11] Furthermore, in recommending a life of great seclusion and in restricting the freedom of women to seek worldly pleasures that were incompatible with a profession of virginity, Cyprian is doubtless paving the way for the total surrender of the will, which is the essence of the vow of obedience in the religious life today. In a similar way there is a forecast of the adoption in the fourth century of a uniform habit and veil, in the appeal of the Bishop for greater simplicity of attire and the renouncement of elaborate apparel and adornment.

The reproofs that Cyprian finds it necessary to administer

---

9 See Koch, *Virgines Christi* 76-86; Cabrol-Leclercq, article 'Cenobitisme,' Vol. 22, cols. 3081-3085.
10 *De habitu virginum* 11.
11 *Ibid.* 24.

in regard to worldly extravagance in dress and immodest deportment at wedding festivities and at the public baths indicate that the virginal life at Carthage in the third century had its shadows as well as its consolations. Not all lived true to the chosen ideal. It was too difficult for some to abide by the promises first made. Consequent withdrawals from this manner of life and even actual profanations of the vow were problems for the attention of the Bishop. The attitude of the Church toward such failures is expressed by Cyprian with deep feeling. She mourns over the 'secret disgrace,' considering the maidens who have been unfaithful to their original promises 'widows before they are brides, adulteresses —not to a husband, but to Christ.'[12]

There is little originality of thought in this work of Cyprian. For the most part it is a composite of extracts from the Bible and paraphrases of portions of the treatises of Tertullian which are concerned with a similar theme—*De pudicitia, De virginibus velandis, De exhortatione castitatis,* and more particularly, *De cultu feminarum.*

It is in the matter of expression, in diction and style, that Cyprian shows greatest independence in the use of his sources. This is to be expected in consideration of his superior literary and rhetorical training. Tertullian is undoubtedly the more forceful, the more realistic and colorful, perhaps, and certainly the more imaginative of the two. Cyprian, on the other hand, is the cultured, discreet, and tactful artist. He rejects the overbold, grandiloquent thoughts, the brusque, clumsy, often ambiguous expressions, the colloquialisms, the newly-coined words, and the bitter, satirical tone so characteristic of Tertullian. He gives far more attention than his predecessor to the adornment of his expression, to the perfection of rhetorical figures, of clausulae and other artifices of style cultivated

12 *Ibid.* 20.

in the literary schools of his day. The result is a clearer presentation of his subject, and that smoothness of style which caused Jerome[13] to make the comparison: *'beatus Cyprianus instar fontis purissimi dulcis incedit et placidus;'* and Cassiodorus:[14] *'uelut oleum decurrentem in omnem mansuetudinem.'*

The influence of Cyprian's brief treatise on virginity on Christian treatises of a later day is evidenced in references made to the work by St. Jerome and St. Augustine. In the case of St. Jerome, the interest centers particularly about the content of the discourse. He found the work sufficiently important to be recommended as a manual of instruction for the virgins who were under his direction.[15] St. Augustine, while not disregarding the subject matter, deems the style especially worthy of comment. It is no mean tribute to the eloquence of St. Cyprian and to his skill in the use of the Latin language that the learned Bishop of Hippo has selected from this work passages to illustrate the various modes of appeal which may be used effectively in oratory.[16]

One of the most interesting examples of the influence of Cyprian's treatise on later writers is to be found in *De laude virginitatis,* a work of St. Aldhelm, Bishop of Malmesbury, which was written in the seventh century. In counseling virgins to make beautiful their souls rather than their bodies, Aldhelm quotes generously from *De habitu virginum,* as if to strengthen his exhortation by appealing to St. Cyprian as one of the recognized authorities on the subject of virginity.[17] By the seventh century, then the treatise had gained some historical importance and had already taken its place in the great tradition of treatises on the virginal life, of which it has the distinction of being among the first.

---

13 *Epist.* 58.10.
14 *Instit. Div. Litt.* 19.
15 *Epist.* 22.22; 107.12; 107.4.
16 *De doctrina Christiana* 4.21.47,49.
17 Cf. *De laude virginitatis* 5; 12; 9; 14.

THE DRESS OF VIRGINS

Chapter 1

Discipline, the guardian of hope, the bond of faith, the guide of the way of salvation, the incentive and nourishment of natural endowment, the teacher of virtue, causes us to abide always in Christ and to live continually for God, to attain to the heavenly promises and divine rewards. To pursue it is salutary, and to avoid and neglect it is fatal. In the Psalms the Holy Spirit says: 'Embrace discipline, lest perchance the Lord be angry and you perish from the just way, when His wrath shall be kindled quickly upon you.'[1] And again: 'But to the sinner God says: Why dost thou declare my justices and take my covenant in thy mouth? Seeing thou hast hated discipline and hast cast my words behind thee.'[2] And again we read: 'He that rejecteth discipline is unhappy.'[3] And from Solomon we have received the mandates of Wisdom admonishing: 'My son, contemn not the correction of God, and do not faint when thou art chastised by Him; for whom God loveth He chastiseth.'[4] Now if God chastises whom He loves, and chastises that He may correct, brethren also, and

1 Ps. 2.12.
2 Ps. 49.16,17.
3 Wisd. 3.11.
4 Prov. 3.11,12.

priests particularly, do not hate but love those whom they chastise that they may correct, since God also prophesied before through Jeremias and pointed to our own time saying: 'I will give you pastors according to my own heart, and they shall nourish you, feeding you with discipline.'[5]

Chapter 2

But if repeatedly throughout the holy Scripture discipline is enjoined, and the whole foundation of religion and of faith proceeds from obedience and fear, what should we seek with greater earnestness, what should we desire and hold to more, than that we should stand unshaken by the winds and storms of the world, our roots firmly fixed and our homes set upon a rock, on a strong foundation, and that we should attain to the rewards of God by observing His divine commands, reflecting as well as knowing that our members are the temples of God, cleansed from all impurity of the old corruption by the sanctifying waters of life, and that we are under obligation not to dishonor nor to defile them, since he who dishonors the body is himself dishonored? Of these temples we are the keepers and the high priests. Let us serve Him whose possession we have already begun to be. Paul says in his Epistles, by which he has formed us for life's course through divine teachings: 'You are not your own; for you have been bought at a great price. Glorify and bear God in your body.'[1] Let us glorify God and bear Him in a pure and spotless body and with more perfect observance, and let us who have been redeemed by the blood of Christ submit to the rule of our Redeemer with the absolute obedience

---

5 Jer. 3.15.

---

1 1 Cor. 6.19,20.

of servants, and let us take care not to bring anything unclean or defiled into the temple of God, lest He be offended and leave the abode where He dwells. We have the words of God, our Protector and our Teacher, alike our Physician and our Counsellor: 'Behold, He says, thou art made whole; sin no more lest some worse thing happen to thee.'[2] He instils the fear of living. He gives the law of innocence after He has restored health; and He does not permit us presently to wander about with free and loosened rein, but rather He threatens with greater severity the man who has delivered himself up to those very ills of which he has been cured, because without doubt it is less blameworthy to have transgressed before you have yet a knowledge of the discipline of God, but there is no excuse for further sin after you have begun to know God. And, indeed, men as well as women, boys as well as girls, every sex and every age should give heed to this and be concerned about it, in keeping with the religious obligation and the faith which are due to God, lest what is received pure and holy through the benevolence of God be not guarded with anxious fear.

Chapter 3

Now our discourse is directed to virgins, for whom our solicitude is even the greater inasmuch as their glory is the more exalted. They are the flower of the tree that is the Church, the beauty and adornment of spiritual grace, the image of God reflecting the holiness of the Lord, the more illustrious part of Christ's flock. The glorious fruitfulness of Mother Church rejoices through them, and them she flowers abundantly; and the more a bountiful virginity adds to its numbers, the greater is the joy of the Mother. To these

2 John 5.14.

do we speak, these do we exhort, rather through affection than authority, and not because we, who are the last and least, and fully conscious of our lowliness, arrogate to ourselves any liberty to censure, but because the more provident we are in our solicitude, the more we fear from the attack of the devil.

Chapter 4

Nor is this an empty precaution and a vain fear which takes thought of the way of salvation, which guards the life-giving precepts of the Lord, so that those who have consecrated their lives to Christ, and, renouncing the concupiscences of the flesh, have dedicated themselves to God in body as well as in spirit, may perfect their work, destined as it is for a great reward, and may not be solicitous to adorn themselves nor to please anyone except their Lord, from whom in truth they await the reward of virginity, since He Himself says: 'All men take not this word but those to whom it is given; for there are eunuchs who were born so from their mother's womb, and there are eunuchs who were made so by men, and there are eunuchs who have made themselves eunuchs for the kingdom of heaven.'[1] Again, too, by these words of the angel the gift of continence is made clear, virginity is extolled: 'These are they who were not defiled with women, for they have remained virgins. These are they who follow the Lamb whithersoever He goeth.'[2] And indeed not to men only does the Lord promise the grace of continence, disregarding women; but since woman is a part of man and was taken and formed from him, almost universally in the Scriptures God addresses the first formed because they are two in one flesh, and in the man is signified likewise the woman.

---

1 Matt. 19.11,12.
2 Apoc. 14.4.

Chapter 5

But if continence follows Christ, and virginity is destined for the kingdom of God, what have such maidens to do with worldly dress and adornments, whereby in striving to please men they offend God, not reflecting that it has been said: 'Those who please men have been confounded, because God has brought them to nought;'[1] and that Paul has declared in his glorious and sublime way: 'If I should please men, I would not be the servant of Christ.'[2] But continence and chastity consist not alone in the purity of the body, but also in dignity as well as in modesty of dress and adornment, so that, as the Apostle says, she who is unmarried may be holy both in body and in spirit. Paul instructs us saying: 'The unmarried man thinketh on the things that belong to the Lord, how he may please God. But he that hath contracted a marriage thinketh on the things that are of the world, how he may please his wife. So the unmarried woman and the virgin thinketh of the things of the Lord, that she may be holy both in body and in spirit.'[3] A virgin should not only be a virgin, but she ought to be known and considered as such. No one on seeing a virgin should doubt whether she is one. Let her innocence manifest itself equally in all things, and her dress not dishonor the sanctity of her body. Why does she go forth in public adorned, why with her hair dressed, as if she either had a husband or were seeking one? Let her rather fear to be attractive, if she is a virgin, and not desire her own ruin who is keeping herself for higher and divine things. She who has not a husband whom she may pretend to please should persevere in innocence and purity of mind

1 Ps. 52.6.
2 Gal. 1.10.
3 1 Cor. 7.32-34.

as well as of body. And in truth it is not right for a virgin to adorn herself to set off her charms, nor to glory in her body and its beauty, since there is no struggle greater for such maidens than that against the flesh, and no battle more obstinate than that of conquering and subduing the body.

Chapter 6

Paul cries out in a strong and lofty voice: 'But far be it from me to glory save in the cross of our Lord Jesus Christ, whom the world is crucified to me and I to the world.'[1] But a virgin in the Church glories in the appearance of her flesh and in the beauty of her body! Paul says, moreover: 'And they that are Christ's have crucified their flesh with the vices and concupiscences.'[2] But she who professes to have renounced the concupiscences and vices of the flesh is found in those very things which she has renounced! You are discovered, O virgin, you are exposed; you boast of being one thing and you are striving to be another. You defile yourself with the stains of carnal concupiscence, although you are a candidate for innocence and modesty. Cry, says God to Isaias, 'All flesh is grass, and all the glory thereof as the flower of the field. The grass is withered and the flower is fallen, but the word of the Lord endureth forever.'[3] It is not becoming for any Christian, and especially is it not becoming for a virgin to take any account of the glory and honor of the flesh, but rather it becomes her to seek only the word of God, to embrace blessings that will endure forever. Or if she must glory in the flesh, then truly let her glory when she suffers in the confession of the Name, when a woman is found

---

1 Gal. 6.14.
2 Gal. 5.24.
3 Isa. 40.6,7.

stronger than the men who are inflicting the torture, when she endures fire, or the cross, or the sword, or beasts, that she may be crowned. These are the precious jewels of the flesh; these are the better ornaments of the body.

Chapter 7

But there are some women who are wealthy and rich in the abundance of their possessions, who display their riches and who argue that they ought to use the blessings that are theirs. Let them know, first of all, that she is rich who is rich in God; that she is wealthy who is wealthy in Christ; that those things are blessings which are spiritual, divine, heavenly, which lead us to God, which remain with us in everlasting possession with God. But the things that are earthly, that have been acquired in the world and will remain here with the world, should be despised just as the world itself is despised, whose pomps and pleasures we already renounced at the time that we came to God by passing to a better way. John stimulates and encourages us, and affirming in a spiritual and heavenly voice says: 'Love not the world nor the things which are in the world. If any man hath loved the world, the charity of the Father is not in him. For all that is in the world is the concupiscence of the flesh, and the concupiscence of the eyes, and the vanity of the world, which is not of the Father, but is of the concupiscence of the world. And the world shall pass away and the concupiscence thereof; but he that hath done the will of God shall abide forever, even as God also abideth forever.'[1] Eternal and divine things therefore must be sought, and all things must be done in accordance with the will of God, that we may follow the footsteps and instructions of our Lord,

---

1 1 John 2.15-17.

who has warned us and said: 'I have not come down from heaven to do my own will, but the will of Him who sent me.'[2] But if the servant is not greater than his master, and the freedman owes allegiance to his deliverer, we who desire to be Christians ought to imitate what Christ has said. It has been written, it is read, and it is heard, and it is proclaimed for our instruction by the mouth of the Church: 'He that sayeth he abideth in Christ ought himself also to walk even as He has walked.'[3] We must keep step with Him; we must strive to emulate His pace. Then shall our striving for truth correspond to our faith in His name, and a reward is given to the believer, if he practices also what he believes.

Chapter 8

You say that you are wealthy and rich. But Paul objects to your wealth, and with his own voice gives directions for keeping your apparel and adornments within right limits: 'Let women, he says, array themselves with modesty and sobriety, not with plaited hair, nor gold, nor pearls, nor costly attire, but as it becometh women professing chastity in good conversation.'[1] Peter also agrees with these same precepts and says: 'Let there be in woman not the outward wearing of ornament or gold or the putting on of apparel, but the ornamentation of the heart.'[2] But if Paul advises that married women also, who are accustomed to make their husbands the excuse for their costly attire, should be restrained and kept within bounds by a scrupulous observance

---

2 John 6.38.
3 1 John 2.6.

---

1 1 Tim. 2.9,10.
2 1 Peter 3.3,4.

of church discipline, how much greater is the obligation of a virgin to render such obedience, who may claim no forbearance for her adornment, and who cannot attribute to another the deception in her fault, but remains herself alone accountable.

Chapter 9

You say that you are wealthy and rich. But not everything that can be done ought also to be done, nor should desires that are immoderate and that are born of worldly vanity overstep the bounds of virginal honor and modesty, since it is written: 'All things are lawful, but all things are not expedient. All things are lawful, but all things do not edify.'[1] But if you adorn yourself too elaborately and appear conspicuous in public, if you attract to yourself the eyes of the youth, draw after you the sighs of young men, foster the desire of concupiscence, enkindle the fire of hope, so that, without perhaps losing your own soul, you neverthless ruin others and offer yourself a sword and poison, as it were, to those who behold you, you cannot be excused on the ground that your mind is chaste and pure. Your shameless apparel and your immodest attire belie you, and you can no longer be numbered among maidens and virgins of Christ, you who so live as to become the object of sensual love.

Chapter 10

You say that you are wealthy and rich. But it does not become a virgin to boast of her riches, since holy Scripture says: 'What hath pride profited us? Or what advantage hath the boasting of riches brought us? All those things are passed

---

1 1 Cor. 10.23.

away like a shadow.'[1] And the Apostle again warns us, and says: 'And they that buy, let them be as though they possessed not; and they that use this world, as if they used it not; for the fashion of this world passeth away.'[2] Peter also, to whom the Lord commends his sheep to be fed and guarded, upon whom He established and founded His Church, says that gold, in truth, and silver he has not, but that he is rich in the grace of Christ, that he is wealthy in His faith and power, wherewith he wrought miraculously many great works, wherewith he possessed in abundance spiritual blessing unto the reward of glory. These possessions, this wealth she cannot have who prefers to be rich in the world rather than in Christ.

Chapter 11

You say that you are wealthy and rich and you think that you must use the things that God has wished you to possess. Use them, but for your salvation and for good works; use them for what God has ordained, for what the Lord has pointed out. Let the poor feel that you are rich; let the needy feel that you are wealthy; through your patrimony make God your debtor; feed Christ. That you may preserve to the end the glory of virginity, that you may succeed in attaining the rewards of God, pray with the prayers of many; lay up your treasures there where no thief digs them up, where no treacherous robber breaks in; acquire possessions for yourself, but rather possessions in heaven, where rust does not wear away, nor the hail strike down, nor the sun burn, nor the rain corrupt your fruits, which are eternal and never failing and free from every touch of the blight of the world. For you are offending God even in this very

---

1 Wisd. 5.8,9.
2 1 Cor. 7.30,31.

point, if you believe that wealth has been given to you by Him for the express purpose of enjoying it without thought of salvation. For God has indeed given man a voice, and yet he should not sing love songs and songs that are coarse; and God ordained that iron should be used for cultivating the land, but murders should not be committed on that account; or because God has made incense and wine and fire, should they be used in offering sacrifice to idols? Or because the flocks of sheep are numerous in your fields, should you slay them as victims and sacrifices? Nay truly, a large patrimony is a temptation unless the income is devoted to good purposes, so that through his fortune every wealthy man should atone for his faults rather than increase them.

Chapter 12

Showy adornments and clothing and the allurements of beauty are not becoming in any except prostitutes and shameless women, and of none, almost, is the dress more costly than those whose modesty is cheap. Thus in holy Scripture, by which the Lord has wished us to be instructed and admonished, a harlot city is described, beautifully attired and adorned, and with her adornments, and rather because of those very adornments, destined to perish. 'And there came,' it says, 'one of the seven angels having vials, and addressed me, saying: Come, I will show thee the condemnation of the great harlot, who sitteth upon many waters, with whom the kings of the earth have committed fornication. And he led me away in spirit, and I saw a woman sitting upon a beast; and the woman was clothed in a cloak of purple and scarlet, and was adorned with gold, and precious stones, and pearls, having a golden cup in her hand full

of malediction, filthiness, and fornication of the whole earth.'[1]
Let chaste and modest virgins shun the attire of the unchaste,
the clothing of the immodest, the insignia of brothels, the
adornments of harlots.

Chapter 13

Isaias also, filled with the Holy Spirit, cries out and chides
the daughters of Sion who have been defiled by gold and
raiment, and reproves those who have an abundance of
harmful riches, and who withdraw from God for the sake
of the pleasures of time. 'The daughters of Sion,' he says,
'are haughty, and have walked with high necks, and wanton
glances of the eyes, and sweeping their tunics in the tread
of their feet, and mincing their steps. And God will humble
the royal daughters of Sion, and the Lord will uncover their
vesture; and God will take away the glory of their attire,
and their adornments, and hair, and curls, and little moons,
and their head dress, and bracelets, and the clusters of grapes,
and armlets, and rings, and earrings, and silks woven with
gold and sapphire. And instead of the odor of sweetness there
shall be dust, and in place of a girdle you shall be bound
with a rope, and instead of golden ornaments for the head,
you shall have baldness.'[1] This, God blames; this, He brands
with reproach. By this He declares that they have been
defiled; by this they have departed from the true adornment
that merited disgrace and shame. Having put on silk and
purple, they cannot put on Christ; adorned with gold and
pearls and necklaces, they have lost the adornments of the
heart and soul. Who would not detest and shun what has

---

1 Apoc. 17.1-5.

---

1 Isa. 3.16-24.

caused another's ruin? Who would seek and take what has served as a sword and weapon for the death of another? If, on draining the cup, he who had taken the potion should die, you would know that what he drank was poison; if, after taking food, he who had taken it should perish, you would know that what could kill, when taken, was deadly, and you would not eat nor would you drink whence you saw beforehand that others had perished. Now what ignorance of the truth it is, what madness of mind to wish for what has always been and still is harmful, and to think that you yourself will not perish from the same causes from which you know that others have perished!

Chapter 14

For God has not made sheep scarlet or purple, nor has He taught how to tint and color with the juices of herbs and with shell fish, nor has He made necklaces of precious stones set in gold, or of pearls arranged in chains with numerous joinings, wherewith to hide the neck which He has made so that what God has created in man may be covered, and what the devil has invented may be exposed to view. Has God wished that wounds be inflicted on the ears, by which childhood still innocent and without knowledge of the evil of the world may be tortured, so that later from the incisions and holes in the ears precious stones may hang—heavy, although not by their own weight but by their high prices? All these things the sinful and apostate angels brought into being by their own arts, when, haven fallen into earthly contagion, they lost their heavenly power. They also taught how to paint the eyes by spreading a black substance around them, and to tinge the cheeks with a counterfeit blush, and to change the hair by false colors, and to drive out all truth from the countenance and head by the assault of their corruption.

Chapter 15

And indeed at this point in my address, because of the fear of God which faith excites in me, and the affection which brotherhood demands, I think that not only virgins and widows but married women also, and all women in general should be warned that the work of God and His creature and image should in no way be falsified by employing yellow coloring or black powder or rouge, or, finally, any cosmetic at all that spoils the natural features. God says: 'Let us make man to our own image and likeness.'[1] And someone dares to change and transform what God has made! They are laying hands on God when they strive to remake what He has made, and to transform it, not knowing that everything that comes into existence is the work of God; that whatever is changed, is the work of the devil. If some painter had depicted in color rivaling nature's the countenance and form and outward appearance of anyone, and after the portrait had been painted and finished, another should lay hands on it, as if, thinking himself more skilful, to improve what was already represented and finished, grievous would seem to be the insult to the first artist, and righteous his indignation. And you—do you think that you will perpetrate such wicked and rash insolence, an offence against the Artist, God, without being punished? Although you may not be immodest toward men and unchaste through your alluring cosmetics, in corrupting and dishonoring the things that are God's, you are counted a worse adulteress!

1 Gen. 1.26.

As for your thinking that you are adorned, that you are beautifully dressed, this is an assault upon the divine work, a violation of the truth.

Chapter 16

The voice of the Apostle gives the warning: 'Purge out the old leaven that you may be a new paste, as you are unleavened; for Christ, our Pasch, is sacrificed. Therefore, let us celebrate a festival not with the old leaven, nor with the leaven of malice or wickedness, but with the unleavened bread of sincerity and truth.'[1] Do sincerity and truth abide when the things that are genuine are corrupted by meretricious colors, when truth is changed to falsehood by lying dyes? Your Lord says: 'You cannot make one hair white or black.'[2] But you, in order to triumph over the word of your Lord, wish to be more powerful than He; in your wanton attempt and sacrilegious insolence you dye your hair; with an evil foreboding of the future you begin now to have flame—colored hair, and you sin—oh the wickedness of it!—with your head, that is, in the nobler part of the body. And although it is written of the Lord: But His head and hair were white as wool or snow,[3] you abominate grey hair; you loathe whiteness, which is like unto the head of the Lord.

Chapter 17

Do you not fear, I ask, being such as you are, that when the day of resurrection comes, your Maker may not recognize

1 1 Cor. 5.7.
2 Matt. 5.36.
3 Apoc. 1.14.

you, that He may set you aside when you come for His rewards and promises, and may exclude you and, reproving you with the severity of a censor and judge, may say: 'This work is not mine nor is this our image.' You have defiled your skin with lying cosmetics; you have changed your hair with an adulterous color; your face is overcome by falsehoods; your appearance is corrupted; your countenance is that of another. You cannot see God since your eyes are not those which God has made, but which the devil has infected. Him you have followed; the red and painted eyes of the serpent have you imitated; adorned like your enemy, with him you shall likewise burn. Should not the servants of God reflect on these matters, I ask? Should they not meditate on them always, day and night, with fear? Married women should consider to what extent they are deceiving themselves with regard to the comfort that they give to their husbands through their efforts to please them; for in putting them forward as their excuse, they are making them cooperate in a guilty agreement. Assuredly, virgins, to whom this does not pertain, who have adorned themselves by devices of this sort, should not be numbered among virgins, in my opinion, but, like tainted sheep and diseased cattle, they should be keept apart from the pure and holy flock of virgins, lest while they are together they corrupt others by their contact, lest they who have themselves perished ruin others.

Chapter 18

And since we are seeking the blessing of continence, let us avoid whatever is dangerous and hostile to it. I shall not pass over certain things which, in coming into use through carelessness, have acquired liberty for themselves by usurpation, to the detriment of modest and sober manners. Some are not ashamed to attend weddings and, in the freedom of the wanton discourse there, to take part in the unchaste conversation, to hear what is unbecoming, to say what is not allowed, to look on and to be present in the midst of disgraceful talk and drunken feasts, by which the flame of passion is enkindled, and the bride is incited to tolerate and the bridegroom to become emboldened in lust. What place is there at weddings for one who has no thought of marriage, or what can be pleasant and enjoyable in those occasions wherein desires and interests are so different? What is learned there? What is seen? To what a degree does a virgin abandon her own purpose! How much more immodest does she go away who had gone there modest? She may remain a virgin in body and mind, but by her eyes, ears, and tongue she has diminished the purity that she possessed.

Chapter 19

But what is to be said of those who go to the common baths and who prostitute to eyes that are devoted to lust bodies consecrated to chastity and modesty? Do not those who, in the presence of men, and naked, with no sense of shame behold men and are seen by them, offer of themselves an inducement to vice? Do they not excite and arouse the desire of those present to their own dishonor and harm? 'Let another,' you say, 'look to his motive in coming here; as for me, my only concern is to refresh and bathe my poor little body.' Such a defence does not justify you, nor does it excuse the sin of lust and wantonness. Such a bath sullies; it does not purify and it does not cleanse the limbs, but stains them. You gaze upon no one immodestly, but you yourself are gazed upon immodestly. You do not corrupt your eyes with foul delight, but in delighting others you yourself are corrupted. You transform the bath into a public show; the places where you go are more shameful than the theatre. There, all reserve is cast off; the honor and modesty of the body are laid aside together with the clothing; virginity is unveiled to be marked out and contaminated. Now then, consider whether, when she is clothed, such a one is modest among men who has grown in immodesty by the boldness of her nakedness.

Chapter 20

Hence, then, the Church frequently bewails her virgins; hence, she groans over the notorious and detestable gossip about them; hence the flower of virginity is destroyed, the honor and modesty of continence are killed, all glory and dignity are profaned. Hence the conquering enemy insinuates himself by his wiles; hence by snares that deceive through secret ways the devil creeps in; hence virgins in desiring to be adorned more elegantly, to go about more freely, cease to be virgins, being corrupted by a hidden shame, widows before they are brides, adulteresses not to a husband but to Christ. Just as they had been destined as virgins for wonderful rewards, so now will they suffer great punishments for their lost virginity.

Chapter 21

Listen, therefore, virgins, as to a father; listen, I pray you, to one who fears for you and at the same time warns you; listen to one who is faithfully watching over your advantages and interests. Be such as God, the Creator, has made you; be such as the hand of the Father has fashioned you. Let your countenance remain uncorrupted, your neck pure, your beauty genuine; let no wounds be inflicted on your ears, nor let a costly chain of bracelets and necklaces confine your arms or your neck; let your feet be free from golden fetters, your hair colored with no dye, your eyes worthy to behold God. Let the baths be attended with women whose bathing among you is modest. Let indecent weddings and their wanton banquets be avoided, contact with which is dangerous. Conquer your dress, you who are a virgin; conquer gold, you who conquer the flesh and the world. It is not natural for one to be invincible before greater things and to be found unequal to lesser. Straight and narrow is the way which leads to life; hard and steep is the path which ascends to glory. By this pathway the martyrs proceed, the virgins go, all the just advance. Avoid wide and broad roads. In them are deadly allurements and death-bringing pleasures; in them the devil flatters that he may deceive, smiles that he may harm, entices that he may kill. The first fruit, that of a hundred-fold, belongs to martyrs; the second, sixty-fold, is yours. Just as with the martyrs there is no thought of the flesh and of the world, and no slight and trivial and dainty struggle, so also in you, whose reward is second in the order of grace, let the power of endurance be next to theirs. The ascent to great things is not easy. What toil we must endure, what fatigue, while we are attempting to climb hills and the summits of mountains! What, that we may ascend to heaven! If you consider the promised reward, what you endure is less. Immortality is given to the one who perseveres; everlasting life is offered; the Lord promises His Kingdom.

Chapter 22

Persevere, virgins, persevere in what you have begun to be. Persevere in what you will be. A great recompense is reserved for you, a glorious prize for virtue, a most excellent reward for purity. Do you wish to know from what misery the virtue of continence is free, what advantage it possesses? 'I will multiply,' said God to the woman, 'thy sorrows and thy groans, and in sorrow shalt thou bring forth thy children, and thy desire shall be to thy husband, and he shall have dominion over thee.'[1] You are free from this sentence; you do not fear the sorrows of women and their groans; you have no fear about the birth of children, nor is your husband your master, but your Master and Head is Christ, in the likeness of and in place of the man; your lot and condition are in common. This is the voice of the Lord that says: 'The children of this world beget and are begotten; but they who shall be accounted worthy of that world, and of the resurrection from the dead, neither marry nor are given in marriage; neither will they die any more, for they are equal to the angels of God since they are the children of the resurrection.'[2] What we shall be, already you have begun to be. The glory of the resurrection you already have in this world; you pass through the world without the pollution of the world; while you remain chaste and virgins, you are equal to the angels of God. Only let your virginity remain and endure entire and unwounded; and as it began courageously let it persevere unceasingly, and not seek necklaces and clothing as adornments, but right conduct. Let it look upon God and heaven and not lower to the concupiscence of the flesh and of the world eyes that have been raised aloft; let it not turn them to earthly things.

---

1 Gen. 3.16.
2 Luke 20.34-36.

Chapter 23

The first pronouncement gave the command to increase and multiply; the second counselled continence. While yet the world was uncultivated and empty, we, begetting large numbers in our fecundity, propagated ourselves and increased for the extension of the human race. Now, when the earth is filled and the world is peopled, those who can take continence, living in the manner of eunuchs, make themselves eunuchs for the kingdom. And God does not order this, but encourages it; nor does He impose the yoke of necessity, since the choice of the will remains free. But when He says that in His Father's house there are many mansions, He points to the homes of a better habitation. Those better dwellings you are seeking; by cutting away the desires of the flesh you are obtaining the reward of greater grace in heaven. All indeed who attain to the divine and paternal gift by the sanctification of baptism put off therein the old man by the grace of the saving waters, and, renewed by the Holy Spirit, they are cleansed from the impurities of the old contagion by a second birth. But the greater sanctity and truth of the second birth belong to you who no longer have desires of the flesh and of the body. Those things alone in you which pertain to virtue and the spirit have remained unto glory. This is the voice of the Apostle whom God called the vessel of His election, whom God sent to announce the mandates of heaven: 'The first man,' he said, 'was made of the slime of the earth; the second, of heaven. Such as is the earthly, such also are the earthly, and such as is the heavenly, such also are the heavenly. As we have carried the image of him who is of the earth, so let us bear also the image of Him Who is of heaven.'[1] Virginity bears this image, purity bears it, sanctity and truth bear it, those who are mind-

1 1 Cor. 15.47-49.

ful of the discipline of God bear it, who observe justice
scrupulously, who are steadfast in faith, humble in fear, brave
in enduring all suffering, mild in sustaining injuries, ready
in showing mercy, of one mind and heart in fraternal peace.

Chapter 24

Each one of these things, O good virgins, you ought to
observe, to love, to fulfill, you who, devoting yourselves to
God and to Christ, are advancing toward the Lord, to whom
you have consecrated yourselves as the greater and better
part. You who are advanced in years, give instruction to the
younger; you who are younger, give an incentive to those
of your own age. Stimulate one another by mutual words
of encouragement; summon to glory by rival proofs of virtue.
Persevere bravely, proceed spiritually, attain the goal happily.
Only remember us when virginity shall begin to be honored
in you.

THE LAPSED

Translated by

ROY J. DEFERRARI, Ph.D.
The Catholic University of America

THE LAPSED

THE TREATISE ON THE LAPSED was composed soon after Cyprian's return to Carthage, after the persecution of Decius, in the spring of 251. During the persecution, when the problem of the reconciliation of the many who had apostasized became acute, Cyprian had promised to treat the subject in writing as soon as a cessation of hostilities permitted. This promise he fulfills in this work.

The problem of the lapsed was a most serious one. The chief sources of information which are available to us today on the subject are, in addition to the present treatise, Letters 15-19, 25, 27, 30, 33, 35, 36, 39, 55, and 56.

There were two categories of the lapsed: those who had actually performed pagan sacrifice, the *sacrificati*, and those who had been certified as having sacrificed but actually had not, having avoided it by bribery or other such means. Obviously, all were obliged to do penance. Some of the questions raised were: what should be the nature of this penance; should it be a mere formality or a serious process of some difficulty; should it be the same for all, or varied according to the degree of wilfulness and viciousness involved. Some actually had sacrificed to the gods before they were forced to do so; others had even brought their children to take part in these rites; still others, out of blind love of their property, openly denied the faith.

The so-called 'confessors' played an important role in this controversy. From early Christian times, even before Tertullian, it was felt that those who had suffered for the faith had a certain right of intercession in behalf of sinners. Several of these confessors at this time had perished under torture or in prison.[1] Most of them were subjected to prolonged imprisonment under very severe conditions. The great majority of the lapsed soon conceived the idea of taking advantage of the privilege of intercession conceded to the confessors. Moreover, not all of the confessors were of high moral character. Some of them took great joy and pride in playing the part of intercessor and liberator for their weaker brethren. Without requiring any guarantee of repentance or of doing penance they granted reconciliations at random. People obtained pardon *en bloc*. This abuse which involved the complete ignoring of the bishop naturally pained Cyprian greatly, and represented a serious difficulty in the settlement of the general problem.

Cyprian faced the problem with his usual firmness and efficiency. His action, as set forth in the present treatise, may be summarized as follows. He warned the confessors against interceding for the lapsed, noting that such leniency would only interfere with their making due atonement. Those who had become weak only under great tortures were deserving of greater mercy. But all, without exception, had to submit to penance, even the *libellatici,* since, although they had not actually participated in pagan sacrifice, they had defiled their conscience.

This treatise on the lapsed was read at the council which met in Carthage in the spring of 251. It has been described as a work of surprising unction, profundity of sentiment, and tact. All that Cyprian had to say was said but with the utmost regard for Christian charity. It became the basis for uniform action with regard to the lapsed for the entire Church in North Africa.

---

1 See *Ep.* 22.2.

THE LAPSED

Chapter 1

BEHOLD, BELOVED BRETHREN, peace has been restored to the Church, and, what recently seemed difficult to the incredulous and impossible to the perfidious, our security has by divine aid and retribution been re-established. Our minds are returning to gladness, and with the passing of the cloud and storm of oppression tranquility and serenity have shone forth again. Praises must be given to God, and His blessings and gifts must be celebrated by the giving of thanks, although not even in the persecution did our voice cease to give thanks. For it is not possible even for an enemy to prevent us, who love God with our whole heart and soul and power, from proclaiming His blessings and praises always and everywhere with glory. The day longed for by the prayers of all of us has come, and after the horrible and loathsome darkness of a long night the world has shone forth illuminated by the light of the Lord.

Chapter 2

With happy countenances we look upon the confessors illustrious by the proclaiming of a good name and glorious in the praise of virtue and the faith; clinging to them with holy kisses we embrace them whom we have desired with a divine and insatiable eagerness. The white-robed cohort of Christ's soldiers is at hand, who by a steadfast formation have broken the turbulent ferocity of an attacking persecution, prepared to suffer imprisonment, armed to endure death. Bravely have you opposed the world, a glorious spectacle have you furnished God, you have been an example to your brethren who will follow you. Your religious voice uttered the name of Christ, in whom it has once confessed that it believed; your illustrious hands, which had been accustomed only to divine works, have resisted the sacrilegious sacrifices; your mouths sanctified by heavenly food after (receiving) the body and blood of the Lord have rejected the profane contagion of the leavings of the idols; your head has remained free from the impious and wretched veil[1] with which the captive heads of those performing the sacrifices were there veiled; your brow pure with the sign of God could not endure the crown of the devil, it reserved itself for the crown of the Lord. With what a joyful bosom does the Mother Church receive you as you return from heaven! How happily, with what rejoicing does she open her gates that with united forces, you may enter bringing back trophies from a prostrate enemy! With the man in triumph women too come, who in their struggle with the world have also overcome their sex. Virgins come with the double glory of their warfare and boys surpassing their years in virtue. Furthermore, the rest of the multitude of those who stand follow your glory, accompany your footsteps with marks of praise very close and almost joined with your own. The same sincerity of heart is in these, the same integrity of a tenacious faith. Relying on the unshaken foundation of heavenly precepts, and strengthened by the evangelical traditions, no prescribed exiles, no destined

---

1 The veiled head was the sign of Roman worship.

torments, no penalties as to property or body terrified them. The day for examining their faith was set, but he who is mindful that he has renounced the world knows no day in the world, nor does he now compute the earthly seasons who hopes for eternity from God.

Chapter 3

Let no one, brethren, let no one cut short this glory, let no one by malicious detraction weaken the uncorrupted firmness of those who stand. When the time appointed for the recanters had passed, whoever had not professed in that time to be a Christian confessed that he was. The first title to victory is for him who has fallen in the hands of the Gentiles to confess the Lord; the second step to glory is to make a cautious withdrawal and then to keep himself for God. The one is a public confession; the other private. The former conquers the judge of the world; the latter satisfied with God as his judge guards a conscience pure by integrity of heart. In the former case fortitude is quicker; in the latter solicitude is more secure. The one, as his hour approached, was then found ready; the other perhaps was delayed because he had left his estate and had withdrawn, for he would not deny; surely he would have confessed, had he also been seized.

Chapter 4

One grief saddens these heavenly crowns of the martyrs, these spiritual glories of the confessors, these very great and illustrious virtues of the brethren who stand—the violent enemy has torn away a part of our vitals and has thrown it away in the ruin of his destruction. What shall I do in this situation, dearest brethren? As I waver in the varying tide of emotion, what or how shall I speak? There is need of tears rather than words to express the grief with which the blow to our body is to be mourned, with which the manifold loss of our once numerous people is to be lamented. For who is so hard and without feeling, who so forgetful of brotherly love that as he stands in the midst of the manifold destruction of his people and their sad remains deformed by great squalor he can keep his eyes dry and with a sudden burst of weeping not express his lamentations with tears rather than with words? I grieve, brethren, I grieve with you nor does my own integrity and sanity beguile me to soothe my own grief, since the shepherd is wounded more by the wound of his flock. I join my heart with each one; I share in the grievous burden of sorrow and death. I wail with those who wail; I weep with those who weep; I believe myself to be cast down with those who are cast down. At the same time my limbs were pierced by the darts of the raging enemy; their cruel swords have passed through my vitals. My mind was not able to remain immune and free from the attacks of persecution; among my prostrate brethren, my compassion has also prostrated me.

Chapter 5

Nevertheless, most beloved brethren, the cause of truth must be kept, and the gloomy darkness of the cruel persecution ought not have so blinded our senses that nothing of light and clarity has remained whereby the divine precepts can be perceived. If the cause of the disaster is known, the remedy for the wound also is found. The Lord wished his family to be proved, and, because a long peace had corrupted

the discipline divinely handed down to us, a heavenly rebuke
has aroused a prostrate and, I might say, sleeping faith, and,
although we deserved more on account of our sins, the most
merciful Lord has so moderated all things, that all that has
happened seemed an examination rather than a persecution.

Chapter 6

Everyone was eager to increase his estate, and, forgetful
of what the believers in apostolic times either had done
before or always should have done, with the insatiable ardor
of covetousness they applied themseves to increasing their
possessions. Among the priests there was no devout religion;
in their ministries[1] no sound faith, in their works no mercy,
in their morals no discipline. Among men the beard was
defaced; faces were painted among women,[2] eyes were falsified after God's hands had completed them, hair was colored
in deception. There were crafty frauds to deceive the hearts
of the simple, subtle schemes for circumventing the brethren.
They joined with infidels in the bond of matrimony; they
prostituted the members of Christ to the Gentiles. They not
only swore rashly, but committed perjury also; they looked
down with haughty arrogance upon those placed over them;
they maligned one another with an envenomed tongue; they
quarreled with one another with stubborn hatred. Many
bishops,[3] who ought to be a source of encouragement and
an example to the rest, contemning their divine charge came
under the charge of secular kings; after abandoning their

---

1 The manuscripts strongly support this translation, and not 'ministers'
as this passage has been regularly rendered in the past.
2 This section savors strongly of Tertullian.
3 A delicate reference to conditions in Rome under Pope Callistus and
his predecessors.

thrones and deserting the people, they wandered through foreign provinces and sought the market places for gainful business; while their brethren in the Church were starving, they wished to possess money in abundance; they seized estates by crafty deceits; they increased their capital by multiplying usuries. What do not such as we deserve to suffer for such sins, when already long ago divine censure warned us and said: 'If they forsake my law and walk not in my precepts, if they violate my statutes, and keep not my commandments, I will punish their crimes with a rod, and their sins with stripes.'[4]

Chapter 7

These things were foreshadowed to us and predicted before. But we, unmindful of the law handed down and of its observation, have brought it about by our sins that while we contemn the mandates of the Lord we have come by severer remedies to the correction of our sins and a probation of our faith, and not indeed have we at last turned to the fear of the Lord so as to undergo this reproof and divine probation of ours patiently and bravely. Immediately at the first words of the threatening enemy a very large number of the brethren betrayed their faith, and were laid low not by the attack of persecution, rather they laid themselves low by their own voluntary lapse. What so unheard of, I ask, what so new had come, that, as if with the rise of unkown and unexpected circumstances, the pledge[1] to Christ should be dissolved with headlong rashness? Did not both the prophets first and the apostles afterwards announce these events? Have not they,

4 Ps. 88.31.33.

1 *Christi sacramentum,* a reference to the *sacramentum* or pledge taken by soldiers in the army.

filled with Holy Spirit, predicted the oppressions of the just, and the injuries of the Gentiles always? Does not holy Scripture ever arming our faith and strengthening the servants of God with its heavenly voice say: 'The Lord thy God shalt thou worship and him only shalt thou serve'?[2] Does it not say again, pointing out the wrath of the divine indignation and forewarning of the fear of punishment: 'They have adored those whom their fingers have made, and man hath bowed himself down, and man hath been debased, and I shall not forgive them.'[3] And again God speaks, saying: 'He that sacrificeth to gods shall be put to death, save only to the Lord.'[4] Later in the gospel also did not the Lord, a teacher in words and a consummator in deeds, teaching what would be done and doing whatever He had taught, forewarn us first of what is now taking place and will take place? Did He not before establish eternal punishments for those who deny Him and salutary rewards for those who confess Him?

Chapter 8

For some, ah misery! all these things have fallen away and have receded from memory. They did not wait at least to ascend when apprehended, to deny when questioned. Many were conquered before the battle, were prostrated without a conflict, and they did not leave this for themselves —to seem to sacrifice to idols unwillingly. Moreover they ran to the market place, of their own accord they hastened to death, as if they formerly desired it, as if they were embracing an occasion granted to them, which they had cheerfully desired. How many on that occasion were put off by the

2 Deut. 6.13.
3 Isa. 2.8,9.
4 Exod. 22.20.

magistrates as evening came on, how many also begged that their destruction be not put off! What violence can such a one plead as an excuse, with which to purge his crime, when he himself rather performed the violence that brought about his ruin? When of their own accord they came to the capitol, when they freely approached yielding to the dire crime, did not their footsteps falter, their sight darken, their vitals tremble, their limbs fail, their senses become dull, their tongues cleave, their speech fail? Could the servant of God, who had already renounced the devil and the world, stand there and speak and renounce Christ? Was that altar, which he had approached to die, not a funeral pyre for him? And as for the altar of the devil, which he had seen smoke and smell with a foul fetor, ought he not to have shuddered at it as if the funeral and sepulchre of his own life and to have fled from it? Why, oh wretch, do you bring a sacrificial offering with you, why a victim for supplication? You yourself have come to the altars as a sacrificial offering, you yourself as a victim; you have immolated your salvation there, your hope; there you have cremated your faith in those fires.[1]

Chapter 9

But for many their own destruction was not enough. By mutual exhortations people were driven to their destruction. Death was proposed for one and another in the lethal cup. And that nothing might be lacking to cap the crime, infants also, placed in the arms of parents or led by them, lost as little ones what they had gained at the very first beginning of their nativity.[1] When the day of judgment comes, will

---

1 Cf. Mark 8.36.

---

1 The baptism as well as the communion of infants seems to be general at this time.

they not say: 'We have done nothing; we have not abandoned the Lord's bread and cup and of our own accord
hastened to profane contaminations. The perfidy of others
has ruined us; we have found our parents parricides. They
have denied us the Church as Mother, God as Father, so
that, while we still small and improvident and unaware of
so great a crime were joined through others into a sharing
in the crimes, we were caught in the deceit of others'?

Chapter 10

There is not, alas, any just and serious reason which ex-
cuses so great a crime. The fatherland should have been
abandoned, the loss of personal property suffered. For what
man, who is born and dies, does not at some time have to
abandon his fatherland and suffer the loss of personal property? Let not Christ be abandoned; let not the loss of one's
salvation and one's eternal home be the object of fear. Behold, the Holy Spirit through the prophet cries out: 'Depart,
depart, go ye out from thence, touch no unclean thing, go
out of the midst of her, be ye apart, you that carry the
vessels of the Lord.'[1] And do not those who are the vessels
of the Lord and the temple of God, lest they be forced to
touch the unclean thing and be polluted and corrupted by
deadly foods, go out from the midst and withdraw? In
another place also a voice from heaven is heard admonishing
what the servants of God should do and saying: 'Go out
from her, my people, that you may not share in her sins,
and that you may not receive of her plagues.'[2] He who goes
out and withdraws does not become a sharer in the sin but
he indeed who is discovered as a companion in the crime

---

1 Cf. Isa. 52.11.
2 Apoc. 18.4.

is himself also seized by the plagues. And so the Lord commanded to withdraw and flee in time of persecution, and He both taught that it should be done and did it. For since the crown descends upon us according to the good pleasure of God, and cannot be received unless the hour for assuming it has come, whoever abiding in Christ withdraws for a time does not deny the faith, but awaits the time; but he who, when he did not withdraw, fell, remained to deny it.

Chapter 11

The truth, brethren, must not be concealed, nor must the matter and cause of our wound be kept silent. Blind love of one's personal property has deceived many; nor could they have been prepared or ready for departing, when their possessions bound them like fetters. Those fetters were for those who remained, those chains by which virtue was retarded, and faith hard pressed, and mind bound, and the soul imprisoned, so that they who clung to earthly things became as booty and food for the serpent who, according to the words of God, devours the earth. Therefore, the Lord, the teacher of good things, warning for the future, says: 'If thou wilt be perfect, sell all thy possessions and give to the poor and thou shalt have treasure in heaven; and come, follow me.'[1] If the rich did this, they would not perish by their riches; laying up a treasure in heaven they would not now have an enemy and a domestic conqueror; their heart and mind and feeling would be in heaven, if their treasure were in heaven; nor could he be conquered by the world, who had nothing in the world with which to be conquered. He would follow the Lord, loosed and free, as the Apostles and many in apostolic times, and some others often did, who,

---

1 Cf. Matt. 19.21.

abandoning their possessions and their parents, clung to the undivided ties of Christ.

Chapter 12

But how can they follow Christ who are held back by the chain of their personal property? Or, how can they seek heaven, and ascend to the sublime and lofty, who are weighed down by earthly desires? They think that they possess, who rather are possessed, slaves of their own property, not lords as regards their money but rather the bond-slaves of their money. The Apostle refers to this time, to these men, when he says: 'But those who seek to become rich fall into temptation and a snare and into many harmful desires which plunge men into destruction and damnation. For covetousness is the root of all evils, and some seeking riches have strayed from the faith and have involved themselves in many troubles.'[1] But with what rewards does the Lord invite us to contempt of personal wealth? With what wages does He compensate for these small and trifling losses of this present time? 'There is no one,' He says, 'who has left house, or land, or parents, or brothers, or wife, or sons for the kingdom of God's sake who does not receive a seven-fold[2] in this present time, and in the world to come life everlasting.'[3] Since these things are known and have been ascertained from the truth of God who makes the promise, not only is a loss of this kind not to be feared but even to be desired, for the Lord Himself again proclaims and gives warning: 'Blessed shall you be when men persecute you, and separate you and

---

1 Cf. 1 Tim. 6.9,10.
2 The Cyprianic manuscriut tradition definitely has 'seven-fold' here and not a 'hundred-fold.'
3 Cf. Mark 10.29-31.

shut you out and reject your name as evil because of the Son of man. Rejoice on that day and exult, for behold your reward is great in heaven.'[4]

Chapter 13

But later torments had come, and severe sufferings threatened those who resisted. He can complain about torments who was overcome by torments; he can offer the excuse of pain who has been overcome by pain. Such a one can ask and say: 'Surely I wished to contend bravely, and mindful of my oath I took up the arms of devotion and faith; but as I found in the contest the various tortures and extended punishments overcome me. My mind stood firm and faith strong, and my soul struggled long and unshaken with the excruciating pains. But when, as the cruelty of a most severe judge broke forth afresh, fatigued as I was, the scourges now for the first time slashed me, the cudgels now bruised me, the rack now stretched me, the claw now dug into me, the flame now scorched me, my flesh deserted me in the struggle, the weakness of my vitals gave way, not my soul but my body yielded in the suffering.' Such a plea can quickly advance to forgiveness; an excuse of this kind can be worthy of pity. Thus in these circumstances the Lord once forgave Cestus and Aemilius; thus, although conquered in the first encounter, he made them victorious in the second battle, so that they became stronger than the fires who previously had yielded to the fires, and in what they had been overcome, in this they overcame. They made their entreaties by pity not of tears but of wounds, not with a wailing voice alone, but with laceration and pain of body. Blood instead

---

4 Luke 6.22.23.

of lamentations came forth, and instead of tears gore poured out from their half burnt vitals.

Chapter 14

But now, what wounds can the conquered show, what injuries to gaping vitals, what tortures of the limbs, when faith did not fail in combat, but perfidy arrived before the combat? Nor does the necessity of the crime excuse him who was caught, where the crime is of the will. I do not say this to burden the cases of the brethren, but rather to stimulate the brethren to prayers of satisfaction. For since it is written: 'They that call you blessed, send you into error, and destroy the way of your steps,'[1] he who consoles the sinner with flattering blandishments furnishes the means for sinning, and does not check transgressions but nourishes them. But he who rebukes at the same time that he instructs with firmer counsels urges a brother on to salvation. 'Whom I love,' says the Lord, 'I rebuke and chastise.'[2] Thus also ought the priest of the Lord not to deceive by deceptive submissions but to provide with salutary remedies. A physician is unskilled who handles the swelling folds of wounds with a sparing hand, and increases the poison inclosed within the deep recesses of the vital organs as he cares for it. The wound must be opened and cut and treated by a sterner remedy, by cutting out the corrupting parts. Although the sick man, impatient by reason of his pain, cries out, shrieks, and complains, he will give thanks afterwards, when he has experienced good health.

---

1 Cf. Isa. 3.12.
2 Apoc. 3.19.

Chapter 15

For, very beloved brethren, a new kind of devastation has emerged and, as if the storm of persecution had raged too little, there has been added to the heap, under the title of mercy, a deceiving evil and an alluring destruction. Contrary to the rigor of the Gospel, contrary to the law of the Lord and God because of the temerity of certain persons communion with the rash is related, an empty and false peace, dangerous to those who grant it and of no benefit to those who receive it. They do not seek the patience important for health, nor the true medicine derived from satisfaction. Penance is excluded from their hearts; the memory of a most serious and extreme sin is removed. The wounds of the dying are concealed, and the deadly blow fixed in the deep and secret vitals is concealed by dissimulated pain. Returning from the altars of the devil they approach the holy place of the Lord with hands befouled and reeking with smell; still almost belching forth the death-bearing food of idols, even now with jaws breathing forth their crime and redolent with the fatal contagion they invade the body of the Lord, when the divine Scripture stands in their way, and cries out, saying: 'Everyone that is clean shall eat of the flesh, and whatever soul shall eat of the flesh of the saving sacrifice which is the Lord, and his uncleanness is upon him, that soul shall perish from his people.'[1] Let the Apostle likewise bear witness, saying: 'You cannot drink of the cup of the Lord and the cup of devils; you cannot be partakers of the table of the Lord and of the table of devils.'[2] He likewise threatens the stubborn and the perverse, and denounces them, saying: 'Whoever eats the bread and drinks the cup of the

---

1 Cf. Lev. 7.20.
1 1 Cor. 10.21.

Lord unworthily will be guilty of the body and blood of the Lord.'[3]

Chapter 16

Spurning and despising all these warnings, before their sins have been expiated, before confession of their crime has been made, before their conscience has been purged by the sacrifice and hand of the priest, before the offence of an angry and threatening Lord has been appeased, violence is done to His body and blood, and they sin more against the Lord with their hands and mouth than when they denied the Lord. They think that to be peace which some truck with deceiving words. That is not peace but war, nor is he joined with the Church who is separated from the Gospel. Why do they call an injury a kindness? Why do they refer to impiety by the term 'piety'? Why do they interrupt the lamentation of penance and pretend to communicate with those who ought to weep continually and to entreat their Lord? This is of the same nature to the lapsed as hail to the harvests, a violent storm to the trees, a destructive pestilence to cattle, a raging tempest to ships. They destroy the solace of hope, they pull up the roots, with their unwholesome words they creep on to deadly contagion, they dash the ship upon rocks lest it arrive within the harbor. That kind of facility does not grant peace but takes it away, nor does it bestow communion but stands in the way of salvation. This is another persecution and another temptation, by which a subtle enemy attacking the lapsed still further approaches with a concealed devastation, so that lamentation is hushed, grief is made silent, the memory of sin vanishes, the groaning of the heart is repressed, the weeping of the eyes is halted, nor is the Lord implored with a long and full penitence,

3 1 Cor. 11.27.

although it is written: 'Remember whence thou hast fallen and do penance.'[1]

Chapter 17

Let no man betray himself; let no man deceive himself. The Lord alone can have mercy. He alone can grant pardon for sins which were committed against Him, who bore our sins, who grieved for us, whom God delivered up for our sins. Man cannot be greater than God, nor can the servant by his own indulgence remit or forego what has been committed against the Lord by a more serious sin, lest to him still lapsed this too be added to his crime, if he does not know that it has been proclaimed: 'Cursed be the man that hath hope in man.'[1] The Lord must be implored; the Lord must be placated by our own satisfaction, who said that He denied him who denied [Him], who alone received every judgment from the Father. We believe indeed that the merits of the martyrs and the works of the righteous have very great power with the Judge, but [this will be] when the day of judgment shall come, when after the end of this age and of the world His people shall stand before the tribunal of Christ.

Chapter 18

But if anyone with precipitate haste rashly thinks that he can grant remission of sins to all or dares to rescind the precepts of the Lord, not only is this of no advantage to the lapsed but it is even a hindrance. Not to have observed the judgment of the Lord, and to think that His mercy is not

---

1 Apoc. 2.5.

1 Jer. 17.5.

first to be implored, but after contemning the Lord to presume on one's own power, is to have provoked His wrath. Under the altar of God the souls of the slain martyrs cry out with a loud voice saying: 'How long, O Lord holy and true, does Thou refrain from judging and from avenging our blood on those who dwell on earth.'[1] And they are ordered to be quiet and to continue to have patience. Does someone think that anyone can wish to become good by remitting and pardoning sins at random or that he can defend others before he himself is vindicated? The martyrs order something to be done;[2] if just, if lawful, if not contrary to the Lord Himself, they are to be done by the priest of God; let the agreement be ready and easy on the part of the one obeying, if there has been religious moderation on the part of him asking. The martyrs order something to be done. If what they order is not written in the law of the Lord, we must first know, that they have obtained from the Lord what they ask, then do what they order. For what has been assured by man's promise cannot be seen at once to have been granted by the divine majesty.

Chapter 19

For Moses also sought pardon for the sins of the people and yet did not receive it when he sought it for those sinning. 'I beseech Thee, O Lord,' he said, 'this people hath sinned a heinous sin, and now, if you forgive their sin, forgive; but if not, strike me out of the book that thou hast written. And the Lord said to Moses: If anyone hath sinned against me, him will I strike out of my book.'[1] That friend of God, that

---

1 Apoc. 6.10.
2 The martyrs or witnesses or confessors awaiting martyrdom.

1 Cf. Exod. 32.31-33.

one who had often spoken face to face with the Lord was unable to obtain what he sought, nor did he placate the displeasure of an indignant God by his intercession. God praises Jeremias, and proclaims, saying: 'Before I formed thee in the womb, I knew thee; and before thou comest forth out of the womb, I sanctified thee, and made thee a prophet unto the nations,'[2] and He said to him as he frequently interceded and prayed for the sins of the people: 'Do not pray for this people and do not take up praise and prayer for them, for I will not hear them in the time of their cry to me, in the time of their affliction.'[3] Who was more righteous than Noe, who, when the earth was replete with sins was alone found righteous upon the earth? Who more glorious than Daniel? Who stronger in firmness of faith for enduring martyrdom, happier in God's favors, who when he fought so often conquered and when he conquered survived? Who was more diligent in good works than Job, stronger in temptations, more patient in suffering, more submissive in fear, more true in faith? And yet God said that, if they should ask, He would not grant. When the prophet Ezechiel interceded for the sins of the people, God said: 'Whatever land shall sin against me, so as to transgress grievously, I will stretch forth my hand upon it, and will break the staff of bread thereof, and will send famine upon it, and will destroy man and beast out of it. And if these three men, Noe, Daniel, and Job, shall be in it, they shall deliver neither sons nor daughters, but they only shall be delivered.'[4] Therefore, not all that is sought is in the prejudgment of the seeker, but in the decision of the giver, and human opinion takes or assumes nothing to itself unless the divine pleasure also assents.

---

2 Jer. 1.5.
3 Jer. 11.14; Cf. 7.16.
4 Ezech. 14.13,14,16.

Chapter 20

In the Gospel the Lord speaks saying: 'Everyone who acknowledges me before men, him will I also acknowledge before my Father who is in heaven; but whoever denies me, even I shall deny him.'[1] If he does not deny him who denies, neither does he acknowledge him who acknowledges. The Gospel cannot be firm in part and waver in part. Either both must be strong or both must lose the force of truth. If those who deny will not be guilty of a crime, neither do those who acknowledge receive the reward of virtue. Furthermore, if the faith which has conquered is crowned, the perfidy also which has been conquered must be punished. Thus the martyrs either can be of no avail, if the Gospel can be broken, or if the Gospel cannot be broken, they who become martyrs according to the Gospel cannot act contrary to the Gospel. Let no one, most beloved brethren, no one defame the dignity of the martyrs; let no one destroy their glories and crowns. The strength of an uncorrupted faith remains sound, and no one can say or do anything against Christ whose hope and faith and virtue and glory is entirely in Christ, so that they who have performed the mandates of God Himself cannot be the authors of anything being done by the bishops contrary to the mandate of God. Is anyone greater than God or more merciful than divine goodness, who either wishes that undone which God suffered to be done, or, as if He had too little power to protect His Church, thinks that we can be saved by his own help?

---

1 Cf. Luke 12.8,9.

Chapter 21

But if these things have been accomplished with God's knowledge or all these have come to pass without His permission, let divine Scripture teach the unteachable and admonish the forgetful as it speaks in these words: 'Who hath given Jacob for a spoil and Israel to those who plundered him? Hath not God against whom they have sinned and were unwilling to walk in His ways and to hear His law? And He hath poured out upon them the indignation of fury.'[1] And elsewhere it testifies saying: 'Indeed does not the hand of God prevail to save, or, has He burdened His ear that He does not hear? But your sins make a division between you and your God, and because of your sins he hath turned away His face from you lest He have pity.'[2] Let us consider our sins, and reviewing the secrets of our action and mind let us weigh the merits of our conscience. Let it return to our hearts that we have not walked in the ways of the Lord, have rejected the law of God, have never been willing to keep His precepts and saving counsels.

Chapter 22

What good do you feel with respect to him, what fear, what faith do you believe there was in him whom fear was unable to correct, whom persecution itself has not reformed. His high and erect neck has not been bent because he has fallen; his puffed up and proud mind has not been broken because he has been conquered. On his back and wounded he threatens those who stand and are sound, and because he does not immediately receive the Lord's body in his sullied

---

1 Cf. Isa. 42.24,25.
2 Isa. 59.1,2.

hands or drink of the Lord's blood with a polluted mouth, he rages sacrilegiously against the priests. And, oh that excessive madness of yours, frenzied one, you rage at him who struggles to avert God's anger from you; you threaten him who beseeches the Lord's mercy for you, who feels your wound which you yourself do not feel, who pours forth tears for you which you yourself perhaps do not pour forth. You pile up and increase your crime still more, and, when you yourself are implacable towards the bishops and priests of God, do you think that the Lord can be placated about you?

Chapter 23

Accept and admit what we say. Why do your deaf ears not hear the salutary precepts which we advise? Why do your blind eyes not see the way of penitence which we place before you? Why does your closed and insane mind not perceive the vital remedies which we both learn and teach from the heavenly Scriptures? If certain incredulous ones have less faith in the future events, let them at least have fear for the present. Behold, what punishments we perceive of those who have denied, what sad deaths of those do we mourn! Not even here can they be without punishment, although the day of punishment has not yet come. Meanwhile certain ones are punished, that the rest may be guided aright. The torments of a few are examples for all.

Chapter 24

One of these who of his own accord went up to the capital to deny became mute after he had denied Christ. The punishment began there where the crime also began, so that he could no longer ask who did not have words for prayers of mercy. Another was stationed in the baths—for this was lacking to her crime and evils, so that she proceeded at once even to the baths, who had lost the grace of the lifegiving laver—but there she who was unclean being seized by an unclean spirit lacerated with her teeth the tongue which had either fed or spoken impiously. After the polluted food had been consumed, the madness of the mouth worked its own destruction. She herself was her own executioner and was not able to survive long thereafter; being tortured by the pain of her belly and vitals she died.

Chapter 25

Hear what took place in my very presence and with me as a witness. Some parents in hasty flight, with little consideration because of their fear, left their little daughter in the care of a nurse. The nurse handed the abandoned girl over to the magistrates. There before the idol where the people were gathering, because she was unable as yet to eat meat because of her age, they gave her bread mixed with wine, which itself had been left over from the immolation of those who were being destroyed. Afterwards the mother recovered her daughter. But the girl was unable to mention and point out the crime that had been committed as she was unable previously to understand and prevent it. Through ignorance, therefore, it came about that the mother brought the child with her to us as we were offering the Sacrifice. Moreover, the girl having mingled with the holy people, being impatient of our supplication and prayer, was now shaken with weeping and was now tossed about by the vacillating motion of her mind; as if under the compulsion of a torturer the soul of the girl still of tender years was trying to confess with such signs as she was able a consciousness of the deed. But when the solemnities were completed and the deacon began to offer the cup to those present, and when, as the rest were receiving, her turn came, the little girl with an instinct of divine majesty turned her face away, compressed her mouth with tightening lips, and refused the cup.[1] The deacon, however, persisted and poured into the mouth of the child, although resisting, of the sacrament of the cup. Then there followed sobbing and vomiting. In the body and mouth which had been violated the Eucharist could not remain; the draught consecrated in the blood of the Lord burst forth from the polluted vitals. So great is the power of the Lord, so great His majesty. The secrets of the shades are detected under His light, nor did hidden crimes deceive the priest of God.

Chapter 26

So much about the infant who as yet did not have the years of speaking of a crime committed by others against herself. But that lady of advanced age and settled in more advanced years, who crept stealthily upon us as we sacrificed, taking food and a sword for herself, and admitting, as it were, a kind of deadly poison, within her jaws and body, began presently to be tormented by frenzy of soul, and suffering the misery no longer of presecution but of her sin, fell quivering and trembling. The crime of her hidden conscience was not long unpunished and concealed. She who had deceived man felt God as an avenger. And when a certain women tried with unclean hands to open her box, in which was the holy [body] of the Lord, thereupon she was deterred by rising fire from daring to touch it. And another man who, himself defiled, after the celebration of

1 Infant communion.

the sacrifice dared secretely to take a part with the rest, was unable to eat or handle the holy of the Lord, and found when he opened his hands that he was carrying a cinder. By the evidence of one it was shone that the Lord withdraws when He is denied, and that what is received is of no benefit to the undeserving, when the grace of salvation is changed as the holy escapes into a cinder. How many are daily filled with unclean spirits; how many are shaken out of their minds by the fury of madness even to insanity! It is not necessary to go over the death of each one, when over the varied ruins of the world the punishment of sins is as varied as the multitude of sinners is numerous. Let everyone consider not what another has suffered but what he himself deserves to suffer, and let him not believe that he has escaped, if in the meantime punishment has put him off, since he should fear the more whom the wrath of God the Judge has reserved for Himself.

Chapter 27

Let them not persuade themselves that they should not do penance, who, although they have not contaminated their hands by impious sacrifices, yet have defiled their consciences with certificates. That profession is of one who denies; the testimony is of a Christian who rejects what he had been. He said that he had done what another actually did, and, although it is written: 'You cannot serve two masters,'[1] he served a secular master, he submitted to his edict, he obeyed human authority rather than God. He should have seen whether he published what he committed with less scandal or less guilt among men; however, he will not be able to escape and avoid God as his judge, for the Holy Spirit says in the Psalms: 'Thine eyes have seen my imperfection and

---

1 Matt. 6.24.

all will be written in thy book,'[2] and again: 'Man looks upon the face, but God upon the heart.'[3] Let the Lord Himself also forewarn and instruct you with these words: 'And all the churches shall know that I am He who searches the desires and hearts.'[4] He perceives the concealed and the secret, and considers the hidden, nor can anyone evade the eyes of God who says: 'Am I a God at hand, and not a God afar off? Shall a man be hid in secret places and I not see him?[5] He sees the hearts and breasts of each one, and, when about to pass judgment not only on our deeds but also on our words and thoughts, He looks into the minds and the wills conceived in the very recess of a still closed heart.

Chapter 28

Finally, of how much greater faith and better fear are they who, although bound by no crime of sacrifice or of certificate, since however they have even thought of this, confessing this very thing with grief and simply before the priests of God, make a conscientious avowal, remove the weight of their souls, seek the saving remedy for their wounds however small and slight knowing that it is written: 'God is not mocked.'[1] God cannot be mocked and deceived, nor can He be deluded by any treacherous cunning. Rather does he sin more who, thinking of God as if human, believes that he is escaping the punishment of his crime, if he has not admitted the crime openly. Christ in His precepts says: 'Whoever is ashamed of me, of him shall the Son of man

2 Cf. Ps. 138.16.
3 Cf. 1 Kings 16.7.
4 Cf. Apoc. 2.23.
5 Jer. 23.23,24.

1 Gal. 6.7.

be ashamed.'[2] Does he think himself a Christian who is either
ashamed or fears to be a Christian? How can he be with
Christ, who either blushes or fears to belong to Christ?
Clearly he might have sinned less by not looking upon idols,
and by not profaning the sanctity of the faith under the
eyes of a populace that stood about and cast insults, by not
polluting his hands with the deadly sacrifices, and by not
defiling his mouth with the wretched food. This is of benefit
to this extent, that the fault is less, not that the conscience
is without guilt. He can more easily arrive at a forgiveness
of his crime, but he is not free from crime. Let him not
cease doing penance and beseeching the mercy of the Lord,
lest what seems less in the quality of his sin be increased
by his failure to give satisfaction to it.

Chapter 29

Let each one confess his sin, I beseech you, brethren, while
he who has sinned is still in this world, while his confession
can be admitted, while the satisfaction and remission effected
through the priest is pleasing with the Lord. Let us turn to
the Lord with our whole mind, and, expressing repentance
for our sin with true grief, let us implore God's mercy. Let
the soul prostrate itself before Him; let sorrow give satisfaction to Him; let our every hope rest upon Him. He Himself
tells how we ought to ask. He says: 'Be converted to me
with all your hearts, in fasting and in weeping, and in mourning, and rend your hearts and not your garments.'[1] Let us
return to the Lord with a whole heart; let us placate His
wrath and displeasure by fastings, weepings, and mournings,
as He Himself admonishes.

---

2 Mark 8.38.

---

1 Joel 2.12,13.

Chapter 30

Do we think that he laments with a whole heart, implores the Lord with fastings, weepings, and mournings, who from the first day of his crime daily frequents the baths, who, feeding on rich banquets and distended by fuller dainties, belches forth the undigested food on the next day, and does not share his food and drink with the needy poor? How does he, who goes forth joyous and happy, weep over his death, and, although it is written: 'You shall not change the form of your beard,'[1] plucks his beard and adorns his face? And is he eager to please anyone who displeases his God? Or does she groan and moan who has time to put on the elegance of pricely garments but not to think of the robe of Christ which she has lost; to receive precious ornaments and costly necklaces, but not to weep over the loss of the divine and heavenly ornament? Although you put on foreign robes and silken dresses, you are naked. Although you decorate yourself with gold and pearls and gems, without the adornment of Christ you are unsightly. And you who dye your hair, now at least cease in the midst of your sorrows, and you who paint the edges of your eyes by lines of black powder, now at least wash your eyes with tears. If you had lost any dear one of yours by his passing away in death, you would grieve and mourn sorrowfully; with a disordered countenance, changed dress, unkempt hair, gloomy countenance, dejected face you would show the signs of sorrow. Wretched woman, you have lost your soul; spiritually dead you have begun to live on here, and although yourself walking about you have begun to carry your own death. And do you not groan bitterly; do you not mourn continually; do you not go in hiding either because of the shame of your crime or for the continuing of your lamentation? Behold still worse

1 Lev. 19.27.

are the wounds of sinning, behold, greater the transgressions
—to have sinned and not to give satisfaction, to have transgressed and not to bemoan transgressions.

Chapter 31

Ananias, Azarias, and Misahel, illustrious and noble youths,
did not refrain from making confession to God not even midst
the flames and fires of a raging furnace. Although possessed
of a good conscience and often well deserving of the Lord
by obedience of faith and fear, they did not cease to retain
their humility and to give satisfaction to God not even midst
the glorious martyrdoms themselves of their virtues. Divine
Scripture speaks in these words: 'Azarias standing prayed
and opened his mouth and made confession to God together
with his companions in the midst of fire.'[1] Daniel also after
the manifold grace of his faith and innocence, after the
esteem of the Lord often repeated with regard to his virtues
and praises, strives still further by fastings to merit God;
wraps himself in sackcloth and ashes as he sorrowfully makes
confession, saying: 'Lord God, great and strong and terrible
who keepest the covenant and mercy to them that love thee
and keep thy commandments, we have sinned, we have committed iniquity, we have been ungodly, we have transgressed
and gone aside from thy precepts and thy judgments, we
have not hearkened to thy servants in what they have spoken
in thy name to our kings and to all the nations and to the
whole world. To thee, O Lord, to thee is justice, but to us
confusion.'[2]

---

1 Dan. 3.25.
2 Cf. Dan. 9.4-7.

Chapter 32

These things the meek, these the simple, this the innocent have done in meriting well of the majesty of God; and those who have denied the Lord refuse to satisfy the Lord and to entreat Him! I beseech you, brethren, acquiesce in the remedies of salvation, obey the better counsels, join your tears with our tears, write your groans with ours. We implore you that we may be able to implore the Lord for you; we turn our very prayers to you first, with which we pray to God for you, that He may be merciful. Do full penance, prove the sorrow of a soul that sorrows and laments.

Chapter 33

Let neither the imprudent error nor the vain stupidity of some move you, who, although they were involved in so grave a crime were struck by such blindness of soul that they neither realized their sins nor lamented them. This is the greater plague of an angry God, as it is written: 'And God gave them a spirit of rebellion,'[1] and again: 'For they have not received the love of truth that they might be saved. Therefore, God sends them a misleading influence that they may believe falsehood, that all may be judged who have not believed truth, but have taken pleasure in injustice.'[2] Taking pleasure unjustly and mad by the alienation of a damaged mind, they contemn the precepts of the Lord, neglect the medicine of their wound, are unwilling to do penance. Improvident before their sin was committed, obstinate after their sin, neither steadfast before nor suppliant afterwards, when they ought to have stood fast, they fell, when they ought

1 Cf. Isa. 29.10.
2 Cf. 2 Thess. 2.10-12.

to fall down and prostrate themselves before God, they think that they stand. Of their own accord they assumed peace for themselves, although no one granted it, seduced by false promises and linked with apostates and infidels they accept error for truth; they regard communion with those who are not communicants as valid; they believe men against God, who have not believed God against men.

Chapter 34

Flee from such men with all your power; and with wholesome caution those who cling to pernicious contacts. Their speech spreads like a cancer;[1] their speech leaps over barriers like a pestilence; their harmful and poisoned persuasion kills worse than persecution itself. Repentance remains there for giving satisfaction. Those who do away with repentance for crime, close the way to satisfaction. So it happens that, when by the rashness of some a false salvation is either promised or believed, the hope of true salvation is taken away.

Chapter 35

But do you, brethren, who are inclined toward fear of the Lord and whose minds, although set in destruction, are mindful of their evils, repenting and grieving view your sins, recognize the very serious crime of your conscience, open the eyes of your hearts to an understanding of your shortcomings, neither despairing of the mercy of the Lord nor yet already laying claim to pardon. As God by reason of His affection as father is always indulgent and good, so by reason of His majesty as judge He is to be feared. Let us weep as greatly as the

---

1 Cf. 2 Tim. 2.17.

extent of our sinning. For a deep wound let there not be lacking a careful and long cure; let the repentance be no less than the crime. Do you think that God can be easily placated, whom you denied with perfidious words, above whom you set your property, whose temple you violated with sacrilegious contamination? Do you think that He easily has mercy on you, whom you have said was not yours? You ought to pray and beseech more intently, to pass the day grieving, to spend your nights in wakefulness and weeping, to spend all your time in mournful lamentation, to cling to ashes prone on the ground, to wallow in sackcloth and squalor, to wish for no garment now after losing the cloak of Christ, to prefer fasting after the food of the devil, to devote yourself to just works by which sins are purged, to enter frequently upon alms—giving, by which souls are liberated from death. What the adversary tried to take away, let Christ receive; your property ought not to be retained now or to be cherished, by which one has been both deceived and conquered. Wealth is to be avoided as an enemy, as a thief to be fled, as a sword to be feared by those who possess it, and as a poison. To this extent only might that which has remained be of benefit, that by means of it crime and sin may be redeemed. Let your works be done without delay and in abundance; let every means be evoked for the healing of the wound; let the Lord, who is to be our judge, be put in our debt by our resources and faculties. Thus did faith flourish under the Apostles; thus did the first people of the believers keep the mandates of Christ—they were ready; they were generous. They gave all to be distributed by the Apostles and they were not redeeming such sins.

Chapter 36

If anyone performs prayer with his whole heart, if he groans with genuine lamentations and tears of repentance, if by continuous just works he turns the Lord to the forgiveness of his sin, such can receive His mercy, who has offered His mercy with these words: 'When you turn and lament, then you shall be saved and shall know where you have been';[1] and again: I desire not the death of the dying, says the Lord in the Lord's own words: 'Turn,' he says, 'to the Lord your God, for He is gracious and merciful, patient and rich in mercy and who turns his thought toward the evil that has been done.'[3] He can grant mercy; He can turn aside His judgment. He can with indulgence pardon him who is repentant, who performs good works, who beseeches; He can regard as acceptable whatever the martyrs have sought and the priests have done for such. Or, if anyone has moved Him more by his own atonements, has placated His wrath, His rightful indignation by just supplication. He gives arms again with which the vanquished may be armed. He repairs and invigorates his strength so that his restored faith may flourish. The soldier will seek his contest again; he will repeat its fight; he will provoke the enemy; he has become indeed stronger for the battle through suffering. He who has thus satisfied God, who by repentance for his deed, who by shame for his sin has conceived more of both virtue and faith from the very sorrow for his lapsing, after being heard and aided by the Lord, will cause the Church to rejoice, which he recently had saddened, and will merit not alone the pardon of God but a crown.

---

1 Cf. Isa. 30.15.
2 Cf. Ezech. 33.11.
3 Cf. Joel 2.13.

THE UNITY
OF THE CHURCH

Translated by

ROY J. DEFERRARI, Ph.D.
The Catholic University of America

THE UNITY OF THE CHURCH

T HE CHIEF SOURCES for Cyprian's views on the subject of the unity of the Church are his Letter 43 and his treatise on the subject which is being presented here. As a matter of fact, the present treatise represents merely a feebler treatment of the subject than that contained in Letter 43. Thus the most accurate understanding of Cyprian's convictions on the unity of the Church is to be obtained by a careful reading of his own discussion of the matter, which follows.

A brief summary of Cyprian's views, however, may well be of profit here. His attitude on the baptism of heretics was closely bound up with his convictions about the unity of Church. He says (Letter 70.3): 'Baptism is one, just as the Holy Spirit is one, *just as the Church is one.*'[1]

This famous pamphlet was read by Cyprian to the council which met in April, with a view to obtaining the support of the bishops against the schism which was started by Felicissimus and Novatus,[2] and which had a large following. The unity conceived by Cyprian is not so much the unity of the whole Church, the necessity of which he assumes, as the unity to be preserved in each diocese by the union with the bishop. The great problem of the day was unity with and loyalty to the individual bishops within their dioceses,

---

1 Letter 70.3.
2 Letter 53.

especially since so many responsibilities of doctrine as well of administration rested on them by reason of the lack of close and speedy contact with the bishop of Rome, caused by the existing modes of communication. The unity of the whole Church is maintained by the close union of the bishops who are 'glued to one another.' Thus whoever is not united with his bishop is cut off from the unity of the Church, and cannot be united with Christ. The type of the bishop, according to Cyprian, is St. Peter, the first bishop. St. Cyprian nowhere specifically declares the primacy of the see of Rome and complete obedience to it except in the fourth section of the present treatise, accepting the longer version of that section as alone authentic and written by Cyprian himself.

In general, Cyprian seems to feel that there is no serious need of focusing attention on this phase of the unity of the Church. Where the great danger to Church lay at this time was in rebellion against individual bishops and in the fragmentation of the diocese. What Cyprian wishes to stress is simply this, that Christ, using the metaphor of an edifice, founded His Church on a single foundation which shall manifest and insure its unity. And as Peter is the foundation, binding the whole Church together, so in each diocese is the bishop. With this one argument Cyprian claims to cut at the root of all heresies and schisms.

The fourth chapter of *The Unity of the Church* has come down to us in a twofold version, one of which contains 'additions' which stress the primacy of Peter. Long controversy has been waged on the question of their origin. Hartel, the editor of the works of St. Cyprian in the *Corpus Scriptorum Ecclesiasticorum Latinorum* vigorously denounced them as spurious, and his opinion was generally accepted until the turn of the century. Dom Chapman[3] was the first to suggest

---

3 'Les interpolations dans le traité de S. Cyprien sur l'unité de l'Eglise,' *Revue Bénédictine,* 19 (1902) , 246-254, 357-373; 20 (1903) , 20-51.

another theory. He attempted to prove that the variations were not due to a corruption of the text but to a revision of the text made by Cyprian himself. This belief seems to have been firmly established by later investigators, such as D. van den Eynde, O. Perler, and M. Bénevot. The latter, however, differ from Dom Chapman in one important respect. They insist that the version with the additions is the earlier, and the other the final form, revising the opinion of Dom Chapman in this matter. Dom Jean Le Moyne[4] not only substantiates van den Eynde, Perler, and Bénevot but goes even further. On the basis of strong and convincing evidence he concludes that the version without the so-called interpolations is *not* by Cyprian; only the longer form including the 'additions' is the authentic version by Cyprian himself.

In our translation we have followed the text in Chapter 4 as established by Dom Le Moyne.

---

4 'Saint Cyprien est- il bien l'auteur de la rédaction brève du "De unitate" chapitre 4?' *Revue Bénédictine,* 63 (1953), 70-115.

THE UNITY OF THE CATHOLIC CHURCH

Chapter 1

SINCE THE LORD warns us in these words: 'Ye are the salt of the earth,'[1] and since He bids us to be simple unto harmlessness, and yet to be prudent with our simplicity, what else, most beloved brethren, befits us than to have foresight and watching with an anxious heart alike to perceive the snares of the crafty enemy[2] and to beware lest we, who have put on Christ the wisdom of God the Father, seem to be less wise in guarding our salvation. For persecution alone is not to be feared, nor the advances which are made in open attack to overwhelm and cast down the servants of God. To be cautious is easier when the object of fear is manifest, and the soul is prepared for the contest beforehand, when the adversary declares himself. The enemy is more to be feared and guarded against when he creeps up secretly, when deceiving us under the appearance of peace he steals forward by hidden approaches, from which too he receives the name of serpent (creeper, crawler, stealer). This is always his cunning; this is his blind and dark deceit for circumventing men. Thus from the very beginning of the

---

1 Matt. 5.13.
2 St. Cyprian refers to the devil as *adversarius, diabolus,* even *serpens,* but never as *Satan* or *daemon.*

world did he deceive and, flattering with lying words, mislead the inexperienced soul with its reckless incredulity. Thus trying to tempt the Lord himself, as if he would creep up again and deceive, he approaches secretly. Yet he was understood and driven back and so cast down, because he was discovered and unmasked.

Chapter 2

In this an example has been given us to flee the way of the old man; to walk in the footsteps of the conquering Christ, that we may not heedlessly be turned back again unto the snare of death, but that, on guard against the danger, we may receive and possess immortality. But how can we possess immortality, unless we keep those commandments of Christ by which death is overcome and conquered, He Himself warning us in these words: 'If thou wilt enter into life, keep the commandments,'[1] and again: 'If you do what I command you, I no longer call you servant but friends.'[2] These, finally, He calls strong and steadfast, these grounded upon a rock of firm foundation, these firmly established against all the tempests and storms of the world with an unmoveable and unshaken firmness. 'He who hears my words,' He says, 'and does them, I shall liken him to a wise man who built his house upon a rock. The rain descended and the floods came, the winds blew and beat upon that house, but it did not fall, for it was founded upon a rock.'[3] Therefore, we ought to stand firm upon His words, and to learn and do whatever He taught and did. But how does he say that he believes in Christ who does not do what

---

1 Matt. 19.17.
2 John 15.14,15.
3 Matt. 7.24,25.

Christ ordered him to do? Or, whence shall he attain the reward of faith, who does not keep the faith of the commandment? He will necessarily waver and wander, and caught up by the breath of error will be blown as the dust which the wind stirs up, nor will he make any advance in his walk toward salvation, who does not hold to the truth of the saving way.

Chapter 3

But not only must we guard against things which are open and manifest but also against those which deceive with the subtlety of clever fraud. Now what is more clever, or what more subtle than that the enemy, detected and cast down by the coming of Christ, after light had come to the Gentiles, and the saving splendor had shone forth for the preservation of man, that the deaf might receive the hearing of spiritual grace, the blind open their eyes to the Lord, the weak grow strong with eternal health, the lame run to the church, the dumb supplicate with clear voices and prayers, seeing the idols abandoned and his shrines and temples deserted because of the great populace of believers, devise a new fraud, under the very title of Christian name to deceive[1] the incautious? He invented heresies and schisms with which to overthrow the faith, to corrupt the truth, to divide unity. Those whom he cannot hold in the blindness of the old way, he circumvents and deceives by the error of a new way. He snatches men from the Church itself, and, while they seem to themselves to have already approached the light and to have escaped the night of the

---

1 Cyprian distinguishes between heresy and schism. Heresy is a voluntary choice of a false doctrine. Schism implies rather a split in the unity of the Church. Synonyms for the Latin *schisma* are *scissura, discidium, discordia,* and *dissensio.*

world, he again pours forth other shadows upon the unsus-
specting, so that, although they do not stand with the Gospel
of Christ and with the observation of Him and with the
law, they call themselves Christians, and, although they
walk in darkness, they think that they have light, while the
adversary cajoles and deceives, who, as the Apostle says,
transforms himself into an angel of light, and adorns his
ministers as those of justice who offer night for day, death
for salvation, despair under the offer of hope, perfidy[2] under
the pretext of faith, antichrist under the name of Christ, so
that while they tell plausible lies, they frustrate the truth
by their subtlety. This happens, most beloved brethren,
because there is no return to the source of truth, and the
Head is not sought, and the doctrine of the heavenly Master
is not kept.

Chapter 4

If anyone considers and examines these things, there is no
need of a lengthy discussion and arguments. Proof for faith
is easy in a brief statement of the truth. The Lord speaks
to Peter: 'I say to thee,' He says, 'thou art Peter, and upon
this rock I will build my church, and the gates of hell shall
not prevail against it. And I will give thee the keys of the
kingdom of heaven; and whatever thou shalt bind on earth
shall be bound also in heaven, and whatever thou shalt loose
on earth shall be loosed also in heaven.'[1] Upon him, being
one, He builds His Church, and although after His resurrection He bestows equal power upon all the Apostles, and
says: 'As the Father has sent me, I also send you. Receive

2 Latin *perfidia,* here translated 'perfidy,' is in Cyprian always the
opposite of *fides,* 'faith'; hence, lack of faith.

1 Matt. 16.18,19.

ye the Holy Spirit: if you forgive the sins of anyone, they will be forgiven him; if you retain the sins of anyone, they will be retained,'[2] yet that He might display unity, He established by His authority the origin of the same unity as beginning from one. Surely the rest of the Apostles also were that which Peter was, endowed with an equal partnership of office and of power, but the beginning proceeds from unity, that the Church of Christ may be shown to be one. This one Church, also, the Holy Spirit in the Canticle of Canticles[3] designates in the person of the Lord and says: 'One is my dove, my perfect one is but one, she is the only one of her mother, the chosen one of her that bore her.' Does he who does not hold this unity think that he holds the faith? Does he who strives against the Church and resists her think that he is in the Church, when too the blessed Apostle Paul teaches this same thing and sets forth the sacrament of unity saying: 'One body and one Spirit, one hope of your calling, one Lord, one faith, one baptism, one God'?[4]

Chapter 5

This unity we ought to hold firmly and defend, especially we bishops who watch over the Church, that we may prove that also the episcopate itself is one and undivided. Let no one deceive the brotherhood by lying; let no one corrupt the faith by a perfidious prevarication of the truth. The episcopate is one, the parts of which are held together by the individual bishops. The Church is one which with increasing fecundity extend far and wide into the multitude, just as the rays of the sun are many but the light is one,

2 John 20.21,23.
3 Cant. 6.8.
4 Cf. Eph. 4.4-6.

and the branches of the tree are many but the strength is one founded in its tenacious root, and, when many streams flow from one source, although a multiplicity of waters seems to have been diffused from the abundance of the overflowing supply nevertheless unity is preserved in their origin. Take away a ray of light from the body of the sun, its unity does not take on any division of its light; break a branch from a tree, the branch thus broken will not be able to bud; cut off a stream from its source, the stream thus cut off dries up. Thus too the Church bathed in the light of the Lord projects its rays over the whole world, yet there is one light which is diffused everywhere, and the unity of the body is not separated. She extends her branches over the whole earth in fruitful abundance; she extends her richly flowing streams far and wide; yet her head is one, and her source is one, and she is the one mother copious in the results of her fruitfulness. By her womb we are born; by her milk we are nourished; by her spirit we are animated.

Chapter 6

The spouse of Christ cannot be defiled; she is uncorrupted and chaste. She knows one home, with chaste modesty she guards the sanctity of one couch. She keeps us for God; she assigns the children whom she has created to the kingdom. Whoever is separated from the Church and is joined with an adulteress is separated from the promises of the Church, nor will he who has abandoned the Church arrive at the rewards of Christ. He is a stranger; he is profane; he is an enemy. He cannot have God as a father who does not have the Church as a mother. If whoever was outside the ark of Noe was able to escape, he too who is outside the Church escapes. The Lord warns, saying: 'He who is not with me is against me, and who does not gather with me, scatters.'[1] He who breaks the peace and concord of Christ acts against Christ; he who gathers somewhere outside the Church scatters the Church of Christ. The Lord says: 'I and the Father are one.'[2] And again of the Father and Son and the Holy Spirit it is written: 'And these three are one.'[3] Does anyone believe that this unity which comes from divine strength, which is closely connected with the divine sacraments, can be broken asunder in the Church and be separated by the divisions of colliding wills? He who does not hold this unity, does not hold the law of God, does not hold the faith of the Father and the Son, does not hold life and salvation.

Chapter 7

This sacrament of unity, this bond of concord inseparably connected is shown, when in the Gospel the tunic of the Lord Jesus Christ is not at all divided and is not torn, but by those who cast lots for the garment of Christ, who rather might have put on Christ, a sound garment is received, and an undamaged and undivided tunic is possessed. Divine Scripture speaks and says: 'Now of the tunic, since it was woven throughout from the upper part without seam, they said to one another: "Let us not tear it, but let us cast lots for it, whose it shall be." '[1] He bore the unity that came down from the upper part, that is, that came down from heaven and the Father, which could not all be torn by him

1 Matt. 12.30.
2 John 10.30.
3 1 John 5.7.

1 John 19.23,24.

who received and possessed it, but he obtained it whole once for all and a firmness inseparably solid. He cannot possess the garment of Christ who tears and divides the Church of Christ. Then on the other hand when at the death of Solomon his kingdom and people were torn asunder, Ahias the prophet met King Jeroboam in the field and tore his garment into twelve pieces, saying: 'Take to thee ten pieces, for thus saith the Lord: "Behold I rend the kingdom out of the hand of Solomon, and will give thee ten sceptres, but two sceptres shall remain to him for the sake of my servant David and for the sake of Jerusalem the city which I have chosen, that I may place my name there." '2 When the twelve tribes of Israel were torn asunder, the prophet Ahias rent his garment. But because the people of Christ cannot be torn asunder, His tunic woven and united throughout was not divided by those who possessed it. Undivided, joined, connected it shows the coherent concord of us who have put on Christ. By the sacrament and sign of His garment, He has declared the unity of the Church.

Chapter 8

Who then is so profane and lacking in faith, who so insane by the fury of discord as either to believe that the unity of God, the garment of the Lord, the Church of Christ, can be torn asunder or to dare to do so? He Himself warns us in His Gospel, and teaches saying: 'And there shall be one flock and one shepherd.'1 And does anyone think that there can be either many shepherds or many flocks in one place? Likewise the Apostle Paul insinuating

2 Cf. 3 Kings 11.31,32,36.

1 John 10.16.

this same unity upon us beseeches and urges us in these words: 'I beseech you, brethren,' he says, 'by the name of our Lord Jesus Christ, that you all say the same thing, and that there be no dissensions among you: but that you be perfectly united in the same mind and in the same judgment.'[2] And again he says: 'Bearing with one another in love, careful to preserve the unity of the Spirit, in the bond of peace.'[3] Do you think that you can stand and live, withdrawing from the Church, and building for yourself other abodes and different dwellings, when it was said to Rhaab, in whom the Church was prefigured: 'You shall gather your father and your mother and your brethren and the entire house of your father to your own self in your house, and it will be that everyone who goes out of the door of your house shall be his own accuser';[4] likewise, when the sacrament of the Passover contains nothing else in the law of the Exodus than that the lamb which is slain in the figure of Christ be eaten in one house? God speaks, saying: 'In one house it shall be eaten, you shall not carry the flesh outside of the house.'[5] The flesh of Christ and the holy of the Lord cannot be carried outside, and there is no other house for believers except the one Church. This house, this hospice of unanimity the Holy Spirit designates and proclaims, when He says: 'God who makes those of one mind to dwell in his house.'[6] In the house of God, in the Church of Christ, those of one mind dwell; they persevere in concord and simplicity.

---

2 1 Cor. 1.10.
3 Eph. 4.2.
4 Cf. Josue 2.18,19.
5 Exod. 12.46.
6 Cf. Ps. 67.7.

Chapter 9

So the Holy Spirit came in a dove. It is a simple and happy animal, not bitter with gall, not cruel with its bites, not violent with lacerating claws; it loves the hospitalities of men; when they give birth they bring forth their offspring together; when they go and come they cling together; they spend their lives in mutual intercourse; they recognize the concord of peace by the kiss of the beak; they fulfill the law of unanimity in all things. This is the simplicity which ought to be known in the Church; this the charity to be attained, that the love of the brethren imitate the doves, that their gentleness and tenderness equal that of the lambs and the sheep. What is the savagery of wolves doing in the breast of a Christian, and the madness of dogs and the lethal poison of snakes and the bloody cruelties of beasts? Congratulations are due, when such as these are separated from the Church, lest they prey upon the doves and sheep with their cruel and venemous contagion. Bitterness cannot cling and join with sweetness, darkness with light, rains with clear weather, fighting with peace, sterility with fecundity, drought with running waters, storm with calm. Let no one think that the good can depart from the Church; the wind does not ravage the wheat, nor does the storm overturn the tree strongly and solidly rooted; the light straws are tossed about by the tempest; the feeble trees are thrown down by the onrush of the whirlwind. The Apostle Paul execrates and strikes at these, when he says: 'They have gone forth from us, but they were not of us. For if they had been of us, they would have continued with us.'[1]

---

1 1 John 2.19.

Chapter 10

Hence heresies have both frequently arisen and are arising, while the perverse mind has no peace, while discordant perfidy does not maintain unity. Indeed the Lord permits and suffers these things to happen, while the choice of one's own liberty remains, so that, while the norm of truth examines our hearts and minds, the sound faith of those who are approved may become manifest in a clear light. Through the Apostle the Holy Spirit forewarns and says: 'For there must be factions, so that those who are approved among you may be made manifest.'[1] Thus the faithful are approved; thus the perfidious are disclosed; thus also before the day of judgment, already here too the souls of the just and the unjust are divided and the chaff is separated from the wheat. From these are those who of their own accord set themselves over daring strangers without divine appointment, who establish themselves as prelates without any law of ordination, who assume the name of bishop for themselves, although no one gives them the episcopacy; whom the Holy Spirit in the psalms designates as sitting in the chair of pestilence, the plague and disease of the faith, deceiving with a serpent's tongue and masters in corrupting truth, vomiting lethal poisons from their pestilential tongues, whose speech creeps about like cancer, whose discussions inject a deadly virus within the breast and heart of everyone.

---

1 1 Cor. 11.19.

Chapter 11

Against such people the Lord cries out; from these He restrains and recalls His wandering people saying: 'Hearken not to the words of false prophets, since the visions of their hearts frustrate them. They speak, but not from the mouth of the Lord. They say to them who reject the word of God: Peace shall be to you and to all who walk in their own desires. To everyone who walks in the errors of his own heart [they say]: 'Evil shall not come upon you.' I have not spoken to them, yet they have prophesied. If they had stood in my counsel and had heard my words, and if they had taught my people, I would have turned them from their evil thoughts.'[1] These same people does the Lord again designate and point out, when He says: 'They have abandoned me to the fountain of living water, and have dug for themselves broken cisterns which cannot hold water.'[2] Although there cannot be another baptism than the one, they think that they baptize; although the fountain of life has been deserted, they promise the grace of the life-giving and saving water. There men are not washed but rather are made foul, nor are their sins purged but on the contrary piled high. That nativity generates sons not for God but for the devil. Being born through a lie they do not obtain the promises of truth; begotten of perfidy they lose the grace of faith. They cannot arrive at the reward of peace who have broken the peace of the Lord by the madness of discord.

---

1 Cf. Jer. 23.16-17, 21-22.
2 Jer. 2.13.

Chapter 12

Let not certain ones deceive themselves by an empty interpretation of what the Lord has said: 'Whenever two or three have gathered together in my name, I am with them.'[1] Corrupters and false interpreters of the Gospel quote the last words and pass over earlier ones, being mindful of part and craftily suppressing part. As they themselves have been cut off from the Church, so they cut off a sentence of one chapter. For when the Lord urged unanimity and peace upon His disciples, He said: 'I say to you that if two of you agree upon earth concerning anything whatsoever that you shall ask, it shall be granted you by my Father who is in heaven. For wherever two or three have gathered together in my name, I am with them,'[2] showing that the most is granted not to the multitude but to the unanimity of those that pray. 'If two of you,' He says, 'agree upon earth'; He placed unanimity first; He set the concord of peace first; He taught that we should agree faithfully and firmly. But how can he agree with anyone, who does not agree with the body of the Church herself and with the universal brotherhood? How can two or three be gathered in the name of Christ, who it is clear are separated from Christ and His gospel? For we did not withdraw from them, but they from us, and when thereafter heresies and schisms arose, while they were establishing diverse meeting places for themselves, they abandoned the source and origin of truth. The Lord, moreover, is speaking of His Church, and He is speaking to those who are in the Church, that if they are in agreement, if, according to what He has commanded and admonished, although two or three are gathered together, they pray with unanimity, although they are two or three, they can obtain

---

1 Cf. Matt. 18.20.
2 Cf. Matt. 18.19,20.

from the majesty of God, what they demand. 'Wherever two
or three have gathered, I,' He said, 'am with them,' namely,
with the simple and the peaceful, with those who fear God
and keep the commandments of God. He said that He was
with these although two or three, just as also He was with
the three children in the fiery furnace, and, because they
remained simple toward God and in unanimity among themselves, He animated them in the midst of flames with the
breath of dew; just as he was present with the two apostles
shut up in prison, because they were simple, because they
were of one mind, He opened the doors of the prison and
returned them again to the market-place that they might
pass on the word to the multitude which they were faithfully
preaching. When then He lays it down in His commandments
and says: 'Where there are two or three, I am with them,'
He who established and made the Church did not separate
men from the Church, but rebuking the faithless for their
discord and commanding peace to the faithful by His word,
He shows that He is with two or three who pray with one
mind rather than with a great many who are in disagreement,
and that more can be obtained by the harmonious prayer
of a few than by the discordant supplication of many.

Chapter 13

So too when He gave the law of prayer, He added, saying: 'And when you stand up to pray, forgive whatever you
have against anyone, that your Father also who is in heaven
may forgive you your offenses.'[1] And He calls back from the
altar one who comes to the sacrifice with dissension, and
He orders Him first to be reconciled with his brother and
then return with peace and offer his gift to God, because

---

1 Mark 11.25.

God did not look with favor upon the gifts of Cain; for he could not have God at peace with him, who through envious discord did not have peace with his brother. What peace then do the enemies of the brethren promise themselves? What sacrifices do the imitators of priests believe that they celebrate? Do they who are gathered together outside the Church of Christ think that Christ is with them when they have been gathered together?

Chapter 14

Even if such men are slain in confession of the Name that stain is not washed away by blood; the inexpiable and serious fault of discord is purged not even by martyrdom. He cannot be a martyr who is not in the Church. He will not be able to arrive in the kingdom who deserted her who is to rule. Christ gave us peace; He ordered us to be in agreement and of one mind; He commanded us to keep the bonds of love and charity uncorrupted and inviolate. He cannot display himself a martyr who has not maintained fraternal charity. The Apostle Paul teaches and bears witness to this when he says: 'If I have faith so that I remove mountains, but not so that I have charity, I am nothing; and if I distribute all my goods for food, and if I hand over my body so that I am burned, but not so that I have charity, I accomplish nothing. Charity is noble, charity is kind, charity envieth not, is not puffed up, is not provoked; does not act perversely, thinks no evil, loves all things, believes all things, hopes all things, bears all things. Charity never will fall away.' 'Never,' he says, 'will charity fall away.'[1] For she will always be in the kingdom and will endure forever in the unity of the brotherhood clinging to it. Discord cannot

---

1 Cf. 1 Cor. 13.2-5,7,8.

come to the kingdom of heaven; to the rewards of Christ who said: 'This is my commandment that you love one another, even as I have loved you.'[2] He will not be able to attain it who has violated the love of Christ by perfidious dissension. He who does not have charity does not have God. The words of the blessed Apostle John are: 'God,' he says, 'is love, and he who abides in love, abides in God and God abides in him.'[3] They cannot abide with God who have been unwilling to be of one mind in God's Church. Although they burn when given over to flames and fire, or lay down their lives when thrown to the beasts, that crown of faith will not be theirs, but the punishment of perfidy, and no glorious ending of religious valor but the destruction of desperation. Such a man can be slain; he cannot be crowned. Thus he professes himself to be a Christian, just as the devil often falsely declares himself to be even Christ, although the Lord forewarned of this saying: 'Many will come in my name saying: "I am the Christ," and will deceive many.'[4] Just as He is not Christ, although he deceives in His name, so he cannot seem a Christian who does not abide in His Gospel and in the true faith.

Chapter 15

For both to prophesy and to drive out demons, and to perform great miracles on earth is certainly a sublime and admirable thing, yet whoever is found in all this does not attain the kingdom of heaven unless he walk in the observance of the right and just way. The Lord gives warning and says: 'Many will say to me in that day: "Lord, Lord, have

2 John 15.12.
3 1 John 4.16.
4 Mark 13.6.

we not prophesied in Thy name and cast out devils in thy name and worked great miracles in thy name?" And then I will say to them: "I never knew you. Depart from me ye workers of iniquity." '[1] There is need of righteousness that one may deserve well of God as judge; His precepts and admonitions must be obeyed that our merits may receive their reward. The Lord in the Gospel, when he was directing the way of our hope and faith, in a brief summary said: 'The Lord thy God is one Lord,' and 'Thou shalt love the Lord thy God with thy whole heart, and with thy whole soul and with thy whole strength. This is the first, and the second is like unto it: Thou shalt love thy neighbor as thyself. On these two commandments depend the whole law and the prophets.'[2] He taught at the same time unity and love by the authority of His teaching; He included all the prophets and the law in two commandments. But what unity does he preserve, what love does he guard or consider, who mad with the fury of discord splits the Church, destroys the faith, disturbs the peace, dissipates charity, profanes the sacrament?

Chapter 16

This evil, most faithful brethren, began long ago, but now the dangerous destruction of the same evil has increased, and the venemous plague of heretical perversity and schisms has begun to rise and to spread more, because even so it was to be at the decline of the world, for the Holy Spirit proclaimed it to us and forewarned us through the Apostle: 'In the last days,' he says, 'dangerous times will come, men will be lovers of self, haughty, proud, covetous, blasphemous, disobedient to parents, ungrateful, impious, without affection,

---

1 Matt. 7.22,23.
2 Mark 12.29-31; Matt. 22.37-40.

without law, slanderers, incontinent, merciless, not loving the good, treacherous, stubborn, puffed up with pride, loving pleasure more than God, having a semblance of piety, but denying its power. Of such are they who make their way into houses and captivate silly women who are sin-laden and led away by various lusts; ever learning, yet never attaining knowledge of the truth. Just as Jannes and Mambres resisted Moses, so these resist the truth. But they will make no further progress, for their folly will be obvious to all, as was that of those others.'[1] Whatever things were foretold are being fulfilled and, as the end of the world now approaches, have come with the testing of men and the times alike. More and more, as the adversary raves, error deceives, stupidity raises its head, envy inflames, covetousness blinds, impiety depraves, pride puffs up, discord exasperates, anger rushes headlong.

Chapter 17

Yet let not the extreme and precipitous perfidy of many move or disturb us, but rather let it strengthen our faith by the truth of things foretold. As certain ones begin to be such, because these things were predicted beforehand, thus let other brethren beware of matters of a similar sort, because these also were predicted, as the Lord instructed us saying: 'Be on your guard therefore; behold I have told you all things beforehand.'[1] I beseech you, avoid men of this sort, and ward off from your side and from your hearing their pernicious conversation as the contagion of death, as it is written: 'Hedge in thy ears with thorns, and hear not a wicked tongue.'[2] And again: 'Evil communications corrupt good

---

1 Cf. 2 Tim. 3.1-9.

1 Mark 13.23.
2 Eccli. 28.24.

manners.'[3] The Lord teaches and admonishes that we must withdraw from such. 'They are blind guides,' He says, 'of the blind. But if a blind man guide a blind man, both shall fall into a pit.'[4] Such a one is to be turned away from, and whoever has separated himself from the Church is to be shunned. Such a man is perverted and sins and is condemned by his very self. Does he seem to himself to be with Christ, who acts contrary to the priests of Christ, who separates himself from association with His clergy and His people? That man bears arms against the Church; he fights against God's plan. An enemy of the altar, a rebel against the sacrifice of Christ, for the faith faithless, for religion sacrilegious, a disobedient servant, an impious son, a hostile brother, despising the bishops and abandoning the priests of God, he dares to set up another altar, to compose another prayer with unauthorized words, to profane the truth of the Lord's offering by false sacrifices, and not to know that he who struggles against God's plan on account of his rash daring is punished by divine censure.

Chapter 18

Thus Core, Dathan, and Abiron, who tried to assume for themselves in opposition to Moses and Aaron the freedom to sacrifice, immediately paid the penalty for their efforts. The earth, breaking its bonds, opened up into a deep chasm, and the opening of the receding ground swallowed up the standing and the living, and not only did the anger of the indignant God strike those who had been the authors [of the revolt], but fire that went out from the Lord in speedy revenge also consumed two hundred and fifty

3 1 Cor. 15.33.
4 Matt. 15.14.

others, participants and sharers in the same madness, who had been joined together with them in the daring, clearly warning and showing that whatever the wicked attempt by human will to destroy God's plan is done against God.[1] Thus Ozias the king also, when, carrying the censer and violently assuming to himself the right to sacrifice contrary to the law of God, although Azarias, the priest, resisted him, he was unwilling to give way and obey, was confounded by the divine indignation and was polluted on his forehead by the spot of leprosy, being marked for his offense against the Lord where they are signed who merited well of the Lord.[2] And the sons of Aaron, who place a strange fire on the altar, which the Lord had not ordered, were immediately extinguished in the sight of the avenging Lord.

Chapter 19

These, certainly, they imitate and follow, who despise God's tradition and seek after strange doctrines and introduce teachings of human disposition. These the Lord rebukes and and reproves in His Gospel when He says: 'You reject the commandment of God that you may establish your own tradition.'[1] This crime is worse than that which the lapsed seem to have committed, who while established in penance for their crime beseech God with full satisfactions. Here the Church is sought and entreated, there the Church is resisted; here there can have been necessity, there the will is held in wickedness; here he who lapsed harmed only himself, there he who tried to cause a heresy or schism deceived many by

1 Cf. Num. 16.25-35.

2 Cf. 2 Par. 26.16-19.
1 Cf. Mark 7.9.

dragging them with him; here there is the loss of one soul, there danger to a great many. Certainly this one knows that he has sinned and bewails and laments; that one swelling in his sin and taking pleasure in his very crimes separates children from their Mother, entices sheep from their shepherd, and disturbs the sacraments of God. And whereas the lapsed has sinned once, the former sins daily. Finally, the lapsed later, after achieving martyrdom, can receive the promises of the kingdom; the former, if he is killed outside the Church, cannot arrive at the rewards of the Church.

Chapter 20

Let no one marvel, most beloved brethren, that even certain of the confessors proceed to these lengths, that some also sin so wickedly and so grievously. For neither does confession [of Christ] make one immune from the snares of the devil, nor does it defend him who is still placed in the world, with a perpetual security against worldly temptations and dangers and onsets and attacks; otherwise never might we have seen afterwards among the confessors the deceptions and debaucheries and adulteries which now with groaning and sorrow we see among some. Whoever that confessor is, he is not greater or better or dearer to God than Solomon, who, however, as long as he walked in the ways of the Lord, so long retained the grace which he had received from the Lord; after he had abandoned the way of the Lord, he lost also the grace of the Lord. And so it is written: 'Hold what you have, lest another receive thy crown.'[1] Surely the Lord would not make this threat, that the crown of righteousness can be taken away, unless, when righteousness departs, the crown also must depart.

---

1 Apoc. 3.11.

Chapter 21

Confession is the beginning of glory, not already the merit of the crown; nor does it achieve praise, but it initiates dignity, and, since it is written; 'He that shall persevere to end, he shall be saved,'[1] whatever has taken place before the end is a step by which the ascent is made to the summit of salvation, not the end by which the topmost point is held secure. He is a confessor, but after the confession the danger is greater, because the adversary is the more provoked. He is a confessor; for this reason he ought to stand with the Gospel of the Lord, for by the Gospel he has obtained glory from the Lord. 'To whom much is given, of him much is required';[2] and to whom the more dignity is allotted, from him the more service is demanded. Let no one perish through the example of a confessor, let no one learn injustice, no one insolence, no one perfidy from the habits of a confessor. He is a confessor; let him be humble and quiet, in his actions let him be modest with discipline, so that he who is called a confessor of Christ may imitate the Christ whom he confesses. For since he says: 'Everyone that exalts himself shall be humbled, and everyone that humbles himself shall be exalted,'[3] and since he himself has been exalted by the Father, because He, the Word and the Power and the Wisdom of God the Father humbled Himself on earth, how can He love pride who even by His law enjoined humility upon us and Himself received from the Father the highest name as the reward of humility? He is a confessor of Christ, but only if afterwards the majesty and dignity of Christ be not blasphemed by him. Let not the tongue which has confessed Christ be abusive nor boisterous; let it not be heard

---

1 Matt. 10.22.
2 Cf. Luke 12.48.
3 Luke 18.14.

resounding with insults and contentions; let it not after words of praise shoot forth a serpent's poisons against the brethren and priests of God. But if he later become blameworthy and abominable, if he dissipates his confession by evil conversation, if he pollutes his life with unseemly foulness, if, finally, abandoning the Church where he became a confessor and breaking the concord of its unity, he change his first faith for a later faithlessness, he cannot flatter himself by reason of his confession as if elected to the reward of glory, when by this very fact the merits of punishment have grown the more.

Chapter 22

For the Lord chose even Judas among the Apostles, and yet later Judas betrayed the Lord. Nevertheless, the firmness and faith of the Apostles did not on this account fall, because the traitor Judas defected from their fellowship. So also in this case the sanctity and dignity of the confessors was not immediately diminished, because the faith of some of them was broken. The blessed Apostle speaks in his letter saying: 'For what if some of them have fallen away from the faith? Has their infidelity made of no effect the faith of God? God forbid. For God is true, but every man a liar.'[1] The greater and better part of the confessors stand firm in the strength of their faith and in the truth of the Lord's law and teaching, neither do they depart from the peace of the Church, who remember that they have obtained grace in the Church from God's esteem, and by this very fact do they obtain greater praise for their faith, that they separated themselves from the perfidy of those who had been joined with them in the fellowship of confession, and withdrew from the contagion of their crime. Moreover, illumined by

---

1 Cf. Rom. 3.3,4.

the light of the Gospel, shining with the pure white light of the Lord, they are as praiseworthy in preserving the peace of Christ as they were victorious in their encounter with the devil.

Chapter 23

Indeed, I desire, most beloved brethren, and I likewise advise and entreat, that, if it can be done, no one of the brethren perish, and that our rejoicing Mother enclose in her bosom one body of people in agreement. If, however, saving counsel cannot recall certain leaders of schisms and authors of dissensions who persist in their blind and obstinate madness to the way of salvation, yet the rest of you either taken by your simplicity, or induced by error, or deceived by some craftiness of misleading cunning, free yourselves from the snare of deceit, liberate your wandering steps from errors, recognize the right way of the heavenly road. The words of the Apostle giving testimony are: 'We charge you in the name of the Lord Jesus Christ that you withdraw from all brethren who walk disorderly and not according to the tradition which they received from us.'[1] And again he says: 'Let no one deceive you with vain words; for because of these things comes the wrath of God upon the children of disobedience. Be ye not, therefore, partakers with them.'[2] We must withdraw, rather flee from those who fall away, lest, while one is joined with them as they walk wickedly, and passes over the paths of error and crime, wandering apart from the way of the true road, he himself also be caught in a like crime. God is one and Christ one and His Church one and the faith one and the people one joined together by the tie of concord into a solid unity of

1 2 Thess. 3.6.
2 Eph. 5.6,7.

body. The unity cannot be torn asunder, nor can the one body be separated by a division of its structure, nor torn into bits by the wrenching asunder of its entrails by laceration. Whatever departs from the parent-stem will not be able to breathe and live apart; it loses the substance of health.

Chapter 24

The Holy Spirit warns us, saying: 'Who is the man that desireth life; who loveth to see the best days? Keep thy tongue from evil, and thy lips from speaking guile. Turn away from evil and do good; seek after peace, and pursue it.'[1] The son of peace ought to seek and follow peace; he who knows and loves the bond of charity ought to restrain his tongue from the evil of dissension. Among his divine commands and salutary instructions the Lord now very near His passion added the following: 'Peace I leave you, my peace I give you.'[2] This inheritance He gave us, all the gifts and rewards of His promise He assured us in the conservation of peace. If we are heirs of Christ, let us remain in the peace of Christ; if we are sons of God, we ought to be peace-makers. 'Blessed,' He said, 'are the peace-makers, for they shall be called the sons of God.'[3] The sons of God should be peace-makers, gentle in heart, simple in speech, harmonious in affection, clinging to one another faithfully in the bonds of unanimity.

---

1 Cf. Ps. 33.13-15.
2 John 14.27.
3 Matt. 5.9.

Chapter 25

This unanimity existed of old among the Apostles; thus the new assembly of believers, guarding the commandments of the Lord, maintained their charity. Scripture proves this in the following words: 'But the multitude of those who believed acted with one soul and one mind.'[1] And again, 'And all were persevering with one mind in prayer with the women and Mary the mother of Jesus and His brethren.'[2] Thus they prayed with efficacious prayers; thus they were able with confidence to obtain whatever they asked of God's mercy.

Chapter 26

But with us unanimity has been so diminished that even the liberality of our good works has been lessened. Then they sold their homes and estates, and, laying up treasures for themselves in heaven, they offered to the Apostles the proceeds to be distributed for use among the poor. But now we do not even give a tenth of our patrimony, and, although the Lord orders us to sell, we rather buy and increase. So has the vigor of faith withered in us; so has the strength of believers languished. And therefore the Lord, looking upon our times, says in His Gospel: 'When the Son of man comes, do you think that He will find faith on the earth?'[1] We see that what he foretold is coming to pass. There is no faith in the fear of God, in the law of justice, in love, in works. No one considers fear of the future; no one thinks of the day of the Lord and the anger of God and the punishments

1 Acts 4.32.
2 Acts 1.14.

1 Luke 18.8.

to come upon unbelievers and the eternal torments decreed for the faithless. Whatever our conscience would fear, if it believed, because it does not believe, it does not fear at all. But if it did believe, it would also be on guard; if it were on guard, it would also escape.

Chapter 27

Let us rouse ourselves in so far as we can, most beloved brethren, and, breaking the sleep of old inertia let us awake to the observing and keeping of the Lord's precepts. Let us be such as He Himself ordered us to be when He said: 'Let your loins be girt, and your lamps brightly burning, and you yourself like to men waiting for their Lord, when He shall come from the wedding, that when He comes and knocks, they may open to Him. Blessed are those servants whom the Lord, when He comes, shall find watching.'[1] We ought to be girt, lest, when the day of departure come, it finds us burdened and entangled. Let our light shine forth in good works and glow, so that it may lead us from the night of this world to the light of eternal brightness. Let us always with solicitude and caution await the sudden coming of the Lord, so that, when He knocks, our faith may be vigilant, ready to receive from the Lord the reward of its vigilance. If these mandates are kept, if these warnings and precepts are maintained, we cannot be overtaken while sleeping by the deceit of the devil; we will reign as vigilant servants with Christ as our Lord.

---

1 Luke 12.35-37.

THE LORD'S PRAYER

Translated by

ROY J. DEFERRARI, Ph.D.
The Catholic University of America

THE LORD'S PRAYER

THE TREATISE on the Lord's Prayer was composed early in 252. It is similar in its content to Tertullian's work on prayer, which was written for catechumens and was devoted chiefly to an explanation of the Lord's Prayer, but included also an explanation of the ceremonies for baptism. Cyprian's work, however, is much more lengthy, and is concerned entirely with the prayer itself and is intended solely for the edification of the people. Moreover, Tertullian alone cannot be regarded as the inspiration of the treatise. It grew out of the needs of the time.

This treatise immediately followed that on the unity of the Church, and Cyprian is evidently still quite preoccupied with that problem. From the beginning he re-echoes the thoughts which he has already expressed on the subject. He exhorts his readers in several places to unity and concord. *The Lord's Prayer* is considered as an outstanding monument to Cyprian's genius, and also the best work on the subject in the long history of Christianity. Even after Cyprian himself and his other works were largely forgotten, it had wide circulation. When Hilary of Poitiers (middle of the fourth century) was writing his commentary on the Gospel of St. Matthew, he passed over the portion which contains the Lord's Prayer, on the ground that Cyprian had said all that was to be said about it. St. Augustine shows his great appreciation of it in his letter to Valerian. He notes that Cyprian anticipated the arguments of the Pelagians by 200 years.

Cyprian's treatise may be easily divided into three parts, but there are actually thirty-six separate headings. In the first part, Cyprian points out that the Lord's Prayer was given us by Christ Himself, and so is the most excellent of all prayers, deeply spiritual, and the most effectual of all prayers for obtaining our petitions. The second portion is a thorough explanation of the prayer, treating each of its seven chief clauses. In the third part, Cyprian outlines the conditions for effective prayer, and what prayer really ought to be.

THE LORD'S PRAYER

Chapter 1

THE PRECEPTS of the Gospel, most beloved brethren, are other than divine teachings, foundations for building hope, supports for strengthening faith, nourishments for encouraging the heart, rudders for directing our course, helps for gaining salvation, which, as they instruct the docile minds of believers on earth, conduct them to the heavenly kingdom. God wished many things also to be said and heard through the prophets, His servants; but how much greater are the things which the Son speaks, which the Word of God, who was in the prophets, testifies with His own voice, no longer commanding that the way be prepared for His coming, He Himself coming and opening and showing the way to us, that we who thus far have been wandering in the shadows of death, improvident and blind, illumined by the light of grace, may hold to the way of life with the Lord as our leader and guide.

Chapter 2

He who, among His other salutary admonitions and divine precepts by which He counsels His people unto salvation,

Himself also gave the form of praying, Himself advised and instructed us what to pray for. He who made us to live taught us also to pray, with the same benignity, namely by which He has deigned to give and bestow the other things, so that, while we speak to the Father with that prayer and supplication which the Son taught, we may more easily be heard. Already He had foretold that the hour was coming when 'the true adorers would adore the Father in spirit and in truth';[1] and He fulfilled what He promised before, so that we, who by His sanctification have received the Spirit and truth, may also by His teaching adore truly and spiritually. For what prayer can be more spiritual than that which was given us by Christ, by whom the Holy Spirit was sent to us, what prayer to the Father can be more true than that which was sent forth from the Son, who is truth, out of His mouth? So to pray otherwise than He taught is not ignorance alone but even a sin, since He Himself has established and said: 'You reject the command of God, that you may establish your own tradition.'[2]

Chapter 3

So let us pray, most beloved brethren, as God the Teacher has taught. It is a friendly and intimate prayer to beseech God with his own words, for the prayer of Christ to ascend to His ears. Let the Father acknowledge the words of His Son, when we make prayer. Let Him who dwells within our breast Himself be also in our voice, and since we have Him as the advocate for our sins before the Father, let us put for-

---

1 Cf. John 4.23.
2 Cf. Matt. 15.6; Mark 7.8.

ward the words of our Advocate. For since He says: 'Whatsoever we shall ask the Father in His name, He will give us,'[1] how much more effectively do we obtain what we seek in the name of Christ, if we ask with His own prayer?[2]

Chapter 4

But let those who pray have words and petitions governed by restraint and possessing a quiet modesty. Let us bear in mind that we stand in the sight of God. We must be pleasing in the sight of God both with the habit of body and the measure of voice. For as it is characteristic of the impudent to be noisy with clamors, so on the other hand does it benefit the modest to pray with moderate petitions. Finally, in His teaching the Lord bade us to pray in secret, in hidden and remote places, in our very bed-chambers, because it is more befitting our faith to realize that God is everywhere present, that He hears and sees all, and by the plenitude of His majesty penetrates also hidden and secret places, as it is written: 'I am a God at hand and not a God afar off. If a man hide himself in hidden places, shall I not see him? Do not I fill heaven and earth?'[1] And again, 'In every place the eyes of the Lord behold the good and the evil.'[2] And when we are gathered together with the brethren in one place and celebrate divine sacrifices with a priest of God, we ought to be mindful of modesty and discipline, and not toss our

---

1 Cf. John 16.23.
2 Cf. John 14.6.

---

1 Cf Jer. 23.23.
2 Prov. 15.3.

prayers about at random with uncouth voices and not cast forth with turbulent loquaciousness our petition, which should be commended to God in modesty, because the hearer is not of the voice but of the heart, and is not to be admonished by shouts, who sees our thoughts, as the Lord proves when He says: 'Why do you think vainly in your hearts?'[3] And in another place: 'And all the churches shall know that I am a searcher of the desires and the heart.'[4]

Chapter 5

This does Anna in the first Book of Kings, portraying a type of the Church, maintain and observe, who prays to God not with a noisy petition but silently and modestly within the very recesses of her heart. She spoke with a hidden prayer but with manifest faith; she spoke not with the voice but with the heart, because she knew that so the Lord hears, and she effectually obtained what she sought, because she asked with faith. Divine Scripture declares this saying: 'She spoke in her heart and her lips moved, but her voice was not heard, and the Lord heard her.'[1] Likewise we read in the psalms: 'Speak in your hearts and in your beds be ye sorrowful.'[2] Through Jeremias also the Holy Spirit suggests and teaches these same things, saying: 'In the heart, moreover, O Lord, you ought to be adored.'[3]

---

3 Cf. Matt. 9.4.
4 Cf. Apoc. 2.23.

1 1 Kings 1.13.
2 Cf. Ps. 4.5.
3 Bar. 6.5.

Chapter 6

Moreover, most beloved brethren, let him who adores not ignore this, how the publican prayed with the Pharisee in the temple. Not by impudently lifting his eyes to heaven nor by insolently raising his hands, but striking his breast and testifying to the sins inclosed within did he implore the help of divine mercy, and, although the Pharisee was pleased with himself, this man rather deserved to be sanctified who thus asked, who placed the hope of salvation not in confidence in his innocence, for no one is innocent, but confessed his sins and prayed humbly, and He who forgives the humble heard him as he prayed. This the Lord lays down in his Gospel saying: 'Two men went up to the temple to pray, the one a Pharisee, the other a publican, the Pharisee stood and began to pray thus within himself: "O God, I thank thee that I am not like the rest of men, dishonest, robbers, adulterers, or even like this publican. I fast twice a week; I pay tithes of all that I possess." But the publican standing afar off would not so much as lift up his eyes to heaven, but kept striking his breast, saying: "O God be merciful to me a sinner!" I tell you, this man went down to his home justified rather than the Pharisee; for everyone who exalts himself shall be humbled and he who humbles himself shall be exalted.'[1]

Chapter 7

Learning these things most beloved brethren, from the sacred reading, after we have learned how we should

---

1 Luke 18.10-14.

approach prayer, let us learn also, with the Lord as our teacher, what to pray. 'In this manner', He says, 'Pray ye: Our Father who art in heaven, hallowed be thy name. Thy kingdom come, thy will be done on earth, as it is in heaven. Give us this day our daily bread, and forgive us our debts, as we also forgive our debtors. And suffer us not to be led into temptation, but deliver us from evil.'[1]

Chapter 8

Before all things, the Teacher of peace and Master of unity did not wish prayer to be offered individually and privately as one would pray only for himself when he prays. We do not say: 'My Father, who art in heaven,' nor 'Give me this day my bread,' nor does each one ask that only his debt be forgiven him and that he be led not into temptation and that he be delivered from evil for himself alone. Our prayer is public and common, and when we pray, we pray not for one but for the whole people, because we, the whole people, are one. God, the Teacher of prayer and concord, who taught unity, thus wished one to pray for all, just as He Himself bore all in one. This law of prayer the three children inclosed in the fiery furnace observed, united in prayer and harmonious in the agreement of the spirit. The faith of the divine Scripture so declares, and, when it tells how such did pray, gives an example which we should imitate in our prayers, that we may be able to be such as they. It says: 'Then those three as from one mouth were singing a hymn and blessing God.'[1] They were speaking as from one mouth, but not yet

---

1 Matt. 6.9-13. Instead of *et ne nos induces*, Cyprian has *et ne patiaris nos induci*.

---

1 Cf. Dan. 3.51.

had Christ taught them to pray. And so their words were availing and efficacious as they prayed, because a peaceful and simple and spiritual prayer deserved well of the Lord. Thus also do we find that the Apostles with the disciples prayed after the ascension of the Lord. Scripture says: 'They were all with one mind continuing steadfastly in prayer with the women and Mary, who was the mother of Jesus, and with His brethren.'[2] They were with one mind continuing steadfastly in prayer, declaring alike by their constancy and unity in prayer that God, who makes men of one mind to dwell in a home,[3] does not admit into the divine and eternal home any except those who are of one mind in prayer.

Chapter 9

Moreover, of what nature, most beloved brethren, are the sacraments of the Lord's prayer, how many, how great, collected briefly in words but abounding spiritually in virtue, so that nothing at all is omitted which is not included in our petitions and in our prayers in a compendium of heavenly doctrine! Scripture says: 'Thus pray ye: Our Father who art in heaven.' A new man, reborn and restored to his God by his grace says in the first place 'Father,' because he has now begun to be a son. 'He came,' He says, 'unto his own and his own received him not. But as many as received Him, He gave to them the power to become the sons of God, to those who believe in His name.'[1] He, therefore, who has believed in His name and has become the son of God, there-

---

2 Cf. Acts 1.14.
3 Cf. Ps. 68.6.

---

1 John 1.11,12.

after should begin to give thanks and to profess himself the son of God, when he declares that his father is God in heaven, also to testify in the very first words of his new birth that he reverences his earthly and carnal father and that he has begun to know and to have as father Him only who is in heaven, as it is written: 'Those who say to their father and mother: I do not know you, and who do not recognize their children, these have kept thy words, and observed thy covenant.'[2] Likewise the Lord in His Gospel has bidden us to call not our father upon earth, because one is our Father, who is in heaven.[3] And to the disciple who had made mention of his dead father, He replied: 'Let the dead bury their own dead.'[4] For he had said that his father was dead, when the father of believers is living.

Chapter 10

And, most beloved brethren, we ought not to observe and understand this alone, that we call Him Father who is in heaven, but we join in saying 'Our Father,' that is, of those who believe, of those who sanctified through Him and restored by the birth of spiritual grace have begun to be sons of God. And this voice also reproaches and condemns the Jews, because they not only faithlessly spurned Christ who had been announced to them through the Prophets and had been first sent to them, but also cruelly slew Him; who now cannot call the Lord father, since the Lord confounds and refutes them, saying: 'You are born of the devil as father,

---

2 Cf. Deut. 33.9.
3 Cf. Matt. 23.9.
4 Cf. Matt. 8.22.

and you wish to do the desires of your Father. He was a murderer from the beginning and has not stood in the truth, because the truth is not in him.'[1] And through Isaias the prophet God exclaims with indignation: 'I have begotten and brought up sons, but they have despised me. The ox knows his owner, and the ass the crib of his master, but Israel has not known me, and my people has not understood. Woe to the sinful nation, to a people laden with iniquity, a wicked seed, ungracious children. They have forsaken the Lord and have blasphemed the Holy One of Israel.'[2] And in condemnation of these we Christians say, when we pray, 'Our Father,' because He now has begun to be ours and has ceased to be of the Jews, who have forsaken Him. Nor can a sinning people be a son, but to those to whom the remission of sins is granted is the name of sons ascribed, to these also is eternity promised when the Lord himself says: 'Everyone who commits sin is the servant of sin. But the slave does not abide in the house forever; the son abides there forever.'[3]

Chapter 11

Moreover, how great is the indulgence of the Lord, how great the abundance of His regard for us and His goodness, that He has thus wished us to celebrate prayer in the sight of God, so as to call the Lord 'Father' and, as Christ is the son of God, ourselves also so to be pronounced the sons of God, which name no one of us would dare to take in

1 Cf. John 8.44.
2 Isa. 1.2-4.
3 John 8.34,35.

prayer, had not He Himself permitted us so to pray. So, most beloved brethren, we ought to remember and to know that, when we speak of God, we ought to act as sons of God, so that, just as we are pleased with God as Father, so too He may be pleased with us. Let us live as if temples of God, that it may be clear that the Lord dwells in us. Let not our acts depart from the Spirit, that we who have begun to be spiritual and heavenly may ponder and do nothing except the spiritual and the heavenly, since the Lord God Himself has said: 'Those who glorify me, I shall glorify; but they that despise me, shall be despised.'[1] The blessed Apostle also in his Epistle has laid down: 'You are not your own, for you have been bought at a great price. Glorify God and bear him in your body.'[2]

Chapter 12

After this we say: 'Hallowed be thy name,' not because we wish for God that He be hallowed by our prayers, but because we seek from the Lord that His name be hallowed in us. Moreover, by whom is God hallowed who himself hallows? But because He Himself said: 'Be ye holy, for I am holy,'[1] we petition and ask for this, that we who have been sanctified in baptism may persevere in what we have begun. And for this daily do we pray. For we have need of daily sanctification, that we who sin daily may cleanse our sins by continual sanctification. Moreover, what that sanctification is which is conferred upon us out of God's esteem the

---

1 Cf. 1 Kings 2.30.
2 1 Cor. 6.19,20.

---

1 Cf. Lev. 20.7.

Apostle proclaims when he says: 'Neither fornicators nor idolaters nor adulterers nor the effeminate nor sodomites nor thieves nor the covetous nor drunkards nor the evil-tongued nor the greedy will possess the kingdom of God. And such were some of you, but you have been washed, you have sanctified, you have been justified in the name of our Lord Jesus Christ and in the Spirit of our God.'[2] He says that we have been sanctified in the name of the Lord Jesus Christ and in the Spirit of our God. We pray that this sanctification abide in us, and because our Lord and Judge warned the man who had been healed and quickened by Him to sin no more, lest something worse befall him, we make this petition with constant prayers, we ask this night and day, that the sanctification and quickening which is assumed from the grace of God be preserved by His protection.

Chapter 13

There follows in the prayer: 'Thy kingdom come.' We seek also that God's kingdom be manifested to us, just as we ask that His name be sanctified in us. For when does God not reign, or when does that begin in Him which both always was and does not cease to be? We petition that our kingdom come which was promised us by God, which was acquired by Christ's blood and passion, so that we who formerly served in the world may afterwards reign with Christ as Lord, as He Himself promises and says: 'Come, blessed of my Father, take possession of the kingdom prepared for you from the foundation of the world.'[1] Indeed, most beloved

---

2 1 Cor. 6.9-11.

---

1 Matt. 25.34.

brethren, even Christ Himself can be the kingdom of God whom we daily desire to come, whose coming we wish to be quickly presented to us. For since He Himself is the resurrection, because in Him we rise again, so too the kingdom of God can be understood as Himself, because in Him we are to reign. Moreover, well do we seek the kingdom of God, that is the heavenly kingdom, because there is also an earthly kingdom. But he who has already renounced the world is greater than both its honors and kingdom. And so he who dedicates himself to God and to Christ desires not earthly but heavenly kingdom. Moreover, there is need of continual prayer and supplication, lest we fall away from the heavenly kingdom, just as the Jews to whom this had first been promised fell away, as the Lord makes clear and proves. He says: 'Many shall come from the East and from the West and shall feast with Abraham and Isaac and Jacob in the kingdom of heaven. But the children of the kingdom will be put forth into the darkness outside; and there shall be weeping and gnashing of teeth.'[2] He shows that formerly the Jews were sons of the kingdom, when they persevered in being also the sons of God; after the name of the Father had ceased among them, the kingdom also ceased. And so we Christians who in our prayers have begun to call God 'Father,' pray also that the kingdom of God come to us.

Chapter 14

We also say in addition: 'Thy will be done in heaven as it is on earth,' not that God may do what He wishes, but that we may be able to do what God wishes. For who stands

---

2 Matt. 8.11,12.

in the way of God's doing what He wishes? But since the devil stands in the way of our mind and action obeying God in all things, we pray and petition that God's will be done in us. That it may be done in us, there is need of God's will, that is, of His help and protection, because no one is strong in his own strength, but is safe by the indulgence and mercy of God. Finally also the Lord, showing the infirmity of man which He was bearing, says: 'Father, if it be possible, let this cup pass from me,' and giving forth to His disciples an example not to do their own will but God's, He added: 'Yet not as I will, but as thou willest.'[1] And in another place He says: 'For I have come down from heaven not to do my own will, but the will of Him who sent me.'[2] But if the Son obeyed to do His Father's will, how much more should the servant obey to do his Lord's will, just as John also in his epistle urges and instructs us to do the will of God, saying: 'Do not love the world, nor the things that are in the world. If anyone loves the world, the love of the Father is not in Him, because all that is in the world is the lust of the flesh, and the lust of the eyes, and the pride of life which is not from the Father, but from the lust of the world. And the world with its lust will pass away, but he who does the will of God abides forever, as God also abides forever.'[3] We who wish to abide forever should do the will of God who is eternal.

---

1 Matt. 26.39.
2 John 6.38.
3 Cf. 1 John 2.15-17.

Chapter 15

Moreover, the will of God is what Christ both did and taught. Humility in conversation, steadfastness in faith, modesty in words, justice in deeds, mercy in works, discipline in morals, not to know how to do an injury and to be able to bear one done, to keep peace with the brethren, to love the Lord with a whole heart, to love Him in that He is Father, to fear Him in that He is God, to place nothing at all before Christ, because He placed nothing before us, to cling inseparably to His love, to stand bravely and faithfully at His cross; when there is a struggle over His name and honor to exhibit the constancy in speech with which we confess, under investigation the confidence with which we enter combat, in death the patience for which we are crowned; this is to wish to be co-heir with Christ; this is to do the commandment of God; this is to fulfill the will of the Father.

Chapter 16

Moreover, we ask that the will of God be done on heaven and on earth, each of which pertains to the consummation of our safety and salvation. For since we possess a body from earth and a spirit from heaven, we ourselves are earth and heaven, and in both, that is in both body and spirit we pray that God's will be done. For there is a struggle between flesh and spirit, and as they contend there is daily conflict with each other, so that we do not do the very things which we wish, as the spirit seeks the heavenly and the divine, the flesh desires the earthly and worldly. Accordingly we ask that harmony be effected between these two

by the help and assistance of God, so that, while the will
of God is being done both in the spirit and in the flesh, the
soul which is reborn through Him may be preserved. The
Apostle Paul openly and manifestly declares this in these
words, saying: 'For the flesh lusts against the spirit, and
the spirit against the flesh; for these are opposed to each
other, so that you do not do what you would. Now the
works of the flesh are manifest which are adultery, fornication, uncleanness, licentiousness, idolatry, witchcrafts, murders, enmities, contentions, jealousies, anger, quarrels, dissensions, sects, heresies, envies, drunkenness, carousings, and
such alike. They who do such things will not inherit the
kingdom of God. But the fruit of the Spirit is charity, joy,
peace, magnanimity, goodness, faith, clemency, continence,
chastity.'[1] And so by daily, yes, by unceasing petitions we
pray for this, that both in heaven and on earth the will
of God concerning us be done, because this is the will of
God, that the earthly give way to the heavenly, that the
spiritual and divine prevail.

Chapter 17

And it may thus be understood, most beloved brethren,
that, since the Lord orders and admonishes to love even
our enemies and also to pray for those who persecute us, let
us ask for those who are still on earth and have not yet
begun to be heavenly, so that the will of God, which Christ
accomplished by preserving and renewing humanity, may
be done also with respect to those. For since the disciples
are no longer called by Him 'earth' but the 'salt of the

---

1 Gal. 5.17-22.

earth,' and the Apostle declares that the first man is from
the slime of the earth but the second from heaven, we too,
who should be like God the Father, who makes His sun
to rise on the good and the evil and sends rain upon the
just and unjust, worthy pray and seek, as Christ so admonishes, so that we offer prayer for the salvation of all, so that
just as the will of God has been done, that is, in us through
our faith, that we might be of heaven, so too on earth,
that is among those unwilling to believe, the will of God
may be done, that those who are still earthly by their
first birth may begin to be heavenly, born of water and
of the Spirit.

Chapter 18

As the prayer proceeds, we ask and say: 'Give us this
day our daily bread.' This can be understood both spiritually
and simply, because either understanding is of profit in
divine usefulness for salvation. For Christ is the bread of
life and the bread here is of all, but is ours. And as we say
'Our Father,' because He is the Father of those who understand and believe, so too we say 'our Bread,' because Christ
is the bread of those of us who attain to His body. Moreover, we ask that this bread be given daily, lest we, who
are in Christ and receive the Eucharist daily as food of salvation, with the intervention of some more grievous sin, while
we are shut off and as non-communicants are kept from
the heavenly bread, be separated from the body of Christ
as He Himself declares, saying: 'I am the bread of life
which came down from heaven. If any man eat of my bread
he shall live forever. Moreover, the bread that I shall give
is my flesh for the life of the world.'[1] Since then He says

---

1 Cf. John 6.51,52,58.

that, if anyone eats of His bread, he lives forever, as it is manifest that they live who attain to His body and receive the Eucharist by right of communion, so on the other hand we must fear and pray lest anyone, while he is cut off and separated from the body of Christ, remain apart from salvation, as He Himself threatens, saying: 'Unless you eat the flesh of the Son of man and drink His blood, you shall not have life in you.'[2] And so we petition that our bread, that is Christ, be given us daily, so that we, who abide and live in Christ, may not withdraw from His sanctification and body.

Chapter 19

But it can also be understood that we who have renounced the world and have cast aside its riches and pomps in the faith of spiritual grace seek only food and sustenance for ourselves, as the Lord instructs us saying: 'He who does not renounce all things which are his cannot be my disciple.'[1] Moreover, he who has begun to be a disciple of Christ according to the word of his Master renouncing all things should ask for daily bread, and not put off for long the desires of their petition, as the Lord Himself again prescribes in these words: 'Be not anxious for tomorrow, for tomorrow will have anxieties of its own. Sufficient for the day is its own trouble.'[2] Worthily then does the disciple of Christ ask for his sustenance unto the day, who is forbidden to think of the tomorrow, because it becomes contrary and repugnant to Him that we seek to live long in the world who seek

---

2 John 6.54.

---

1 Cf. Luke 14.23.
2 Matt. 6.34.

that the kingdom of God come quickly. Thus also the blessed Apostle advises, establishing and sustaining the firmness of our hope and faith. He says: 'For we brought nothing into this world, and certainly we can take nothing out. But having sustenance and clothing we are content with these. But those who seek to become rich fall into temptation and snares and into many harmful desires which plunge a man into destruction and damnation. For covetousness is the root of all evils and some in their eagerness to get rich have strayed from the faith and have involved themselves in many troubles.'[3]

Chapter 20

He teaches that not only are riches to be contemned but are also dangerous, that in them is the root of enticing evils, that device the blindness of the human mind with hidden deception. So God rebukes the foolish rich man who ponders on his worldly wealth and boasts of the abundance of his overflowing harvests, saying: 'Thou fool, this night do they demand thy soul of thee; and the things thou hast provided, whose will they be?'[1] The fool was rejoicing in his stores in the night when he was about to die and he whose life was now ebbing pondered on the abundance of his sustenance. However, on the other hand, the Lord teaches that he becomes perfect and complete who by selling all his possessions and distributing them for the use of the poor lays up for himself a treasure in heaven. He says that that man can fol-

---

3 1 Tim. 6.7-10.

1 Luke 12.20.

low Him and imitate the glory of the Lord's passion, who un-encumbered and with his loins girded is not involved in the entanglements of personal property, but unentangled and free he himself also accompanies his possessions sent on before to the Lord. That each one of us may be able to prepare himself for this, thus he learns to pray and from the principle of prayer to know what sort of man he ought to be.

Chapter 21

For daily bread cannot be lacking the just man, since it is written: 'The Lord will not afflict the just soul with famine';[1] and again, 'I have been young, and am old and I have not seen the just man forsaken, nor his seed begging bread';[2] likewise, since the Lord promises, saying: 'What shall we eat or what shall we drink or what are we to put on? For after these things the gentiles seek; for your Father knows that you need all these things. But seek first the king-dom of God and His justice, and all these things shall be given you besides.'[3] To those who seek the kingdom and the justice of God, He promises that all things are added.[4] For since all things are of God, nothing will be lacking to him who has God, if he himself be not lacking to God. Thus a meal is divinely prepared for Daniel who was inclosed in a lions' den by order of the king and the man of God is fed in the midst of the wild beasts who are angry and spare

---

1 Prov. 10.3.
2 Ps. 56.25.
3 Matt. 6.31-33.
4 The petition accordingly covers our spiritual food (John 6.27) and our bodily nourishment (Matt. 6.8).

him. Thus Elias is sustained in his flight and solitude by ministering ravens, and is nourished in persecution by birds bringing food to him. And oh detestable cruelty of human malice, the wild beasts spare, the birds feed, and men lay plots and go mad!

Chapter 22

After this also we pray for our sins, saying: 'And forgive us our debts, as we also forgive our debtors.' After the subsistence of food the pardon of sin is also asked so that he who is fed by God may live in God, and so that not only the present and temporal life may be provided for but also the eternal, to which we may come if our sins are forgiven, which the Lord calls debts, as He says in His Gospel: 'I forgave thee all the debt because thou didst entreat me.'[1] Moreover, how necessarily, how providently and salutarily, are we admonished that we are sinners, who are compelled to plead for our sins, so that, while indulgence is sought from God, the soul is recalled to a consciousness of its guilt! Lest anyone be pleased with himself, as if innocent, and by exalting himself perish the more, he is instructed and taught that he sins daily, since he is ordered to pray daily for his sins. Thus finally John also in his epistle admonishes in these words: 'If we say that we have no sin, we deceive ourselves, and the truth is not in us. But if we acknowledge our sins, the Lord is faithful and just to forgive us our sins.'[2] In his epistle he has combined both, that we should both entreat for our sins and that we should obtain indulgence when we entreat. Therefore, he said that the Lord was faithful to

1 Matt. 18.32.
2 1 John 1.8,9.

forgive sins, preserving the faith of His promise, because He who taught us to pray for our debts and our sins promised that mercy and forgiveness would follow.

Chapter 23

He clearly appended and added the law, binding us by a condition and engagement, that accordingly we ask that our debts be forgiven us according as we ourselves also forgive our debtors, knowing that what we seek for our sins cannot be obtained, unless we ourselves shall have acted likewise toward those sinning against us. Therefore, in another place he says: 'With what measure you measure, it shall be measured to you.'[1] The servant who after all his debt was forgiven him by the Lord was himself unwilling to forgive his fellow servant is confined to prison. Because he was unwilling to forgive his fellow servant, he lost the forgiveness which had been granted him by the Lord. And these things Christ sets forth still more strongly in His precepts by the greater force of His censure. He says: 'When you stand to pray, forgive whatever you have against anyone, that your Father who is in heaven, may forgive you your sins. But if you do not forgive, neither will your Father who is in heaven forgive you your sins.'[2] There remains no excuse for you on the day of judgment, when you are judged according to your sentence, and what you have done, this also you yourself suffer. For God has ordered us to be peace-makers and of one heart and of one mind in His house,[3] and as He has made us, so reborn

---

1 Matt. 7.2.
2 Mark 11.25.
3 Cf. Ps. 67.6.

by a second birth He wishes to preserve us, that we who are the sons of God may remain in the peace of God, and 'that we who have one spirit may have one heart and mind. Thus neither does God receive the sacrifice of the dissident, and He orders him to turn back from the altar and first be reconciled with his brother, so that by pacifying prayers God also can be pacified. The greater sacrifice to God is our peace and fraternal concord and a people united in the unity of the Father and of the Son and of the Holy Spirit.

Chapter 24

For even in the sacrifices which Abel and Cain first offered God did not look upon their gifts but upon their hearts, so that he who pleased Him in his heart pleased Him in his gift. Abel, peacable and just, while he was sacrificing to God innocently, taught others also, when they offer a gift at the altar, to come with fear of God, with simple heart, with the law of justice, with the peace of concord. Worthily did he, since he was such in God's sacrifice, himself later become a sacrifice to God, so that being the first to manifest martyrdom he initiated the Lord's passion by his blood, who had both the justice and peace of the Lord. Finally, such are crowned by the Lord; such on the day of judgment will be vindicated with the Lord. But the discordant and the dissident and he who has not peace with his brethren, according as the blessed Apostle and the Holy Scripture testify, not even if he be slain for His name, shall be able to escape the crime of fraternal dissension, because, as it is written: 'Whoever hates his brother is a murderer,'[1] and a murderer does not arrive

---

1 1 John 3.15.

at the kingdom of heaven nor does he live with God. He cannot be with Christ, who preferred to be an imitator of of Judas rather than of Christ. What a sin that is which cannot be washed away by the baptism of blood; what a crime that is which cannot be expiated by martyrdom!

Chapter 25

Necessarily too the Lord gives us this admonition, to say in our prayer: 'And lead us not into temptation.' In this part it is shown that the adversary has no power against us, unless God has previously permitted it, in order that all our fear and devotion and obedience may be turned to God, since in temptations nothing is permitted evil, unless the power is granted by Him. Scripture proves this when it says: 'Nebuchodonosor, king of Babylon, came against Jerusalem and assaulted it, and the Lord gave it into his hand.'[1] Moreover, power is given to evil against us according to our sins; as it is written: 'Who hath given Jacob for a spoil and Israel to those who despoiled him? Hath not God, against whom they have sinned and were unwilling to walk in His ways and to hear His law, even poured out upon them the indignation of His fury?[2] And again when Solomon sinned and departed from the precepts and the ways of the Lord, it is set down: 'And the Lord stirred up Satan against Solomon himself.'[3]

---

1 Cf. 4 Kings 24; Dan. 1.1.
2 Isa. 42.24,25.
3 Cf. 3 Kings 11.14.

Chapter 26

Power indeed is granted against us in two ways: either for punishment when we sin or for glory when we are approved, as we see was done with respect to Job when God made this clear with the following words: 'Behold all that he hath is in thy hand; only put not forth thy hand upon his person.'[1] And the Lord in His Gospel says at the time of His passion: 'Thou wouldst have no power at all over me, were it not given thee from above.'[2] When, moreover, we ask that we come not into temptation, we are reminded of our infirmity and weakness, lest someone extol himself insolently, lest someone proudly and arrogantly assume something to himself, lest someone think the glory of confession or passion to be his own, although the Lord himself, teaching humility, has said: 'Watch and pray that you may not enter into temptation. The spirit indeed is willing, but the flesh is weak,'[3] so that when humble and submissive confession precedes and all is ascribed to God, whatever is sought suppliantly with fear and honor of God, by reason of His loving kindness it may be granted.

Chapter 27

After all those things, in summation of the prayer there comes a little clause concluding all our petitions and prayer in compact brevity. For at the very last we state: 'But deliver us from evil,' comprehending all adversities which the enemy undertakes against us in this world, from which there can

---

1 Job 1.12.
2 John 19.11.
3 Matt. 26.41.

be strong and faithful protection, if God delivers us, if, as we pray and implore, He furnish us His aid. Moreover, when we say: 'Deliver us from evil,' nothing remains for which we should ask still further; when once we seek God's protection against evil, having obtained this, we stand secure and safe against all the works of the devil and of the world. For what fear indeed is there with regard to the world for him who has God as his protector in the world?

Chapter 28

What wonder, most beloved brethren, if such is the prayer that God has taught, who by His instruction has abbreviated our every prayer in a saving word? This had already been foretold by Isaias the prophet, when, filled with the Holy Spirit, he spoke of the majesty and loving kindness of God. He said: 'Completing and abbreviating His word in justice, since God will make a short word in the whole earth.'[1] For when the Word of God, our Lord Jesus Christ, came to all, and gathering together the learned and unlearned alike He gave forth the precepts of salvation to every sex and age, He made a great compendium of His precepts, so that the memory of the learners might not be burdened in heavenly discipline, but might learn quickly what was necessary to a simple faith. Thus when He taught what eternal life is, He embraced the sacrament of life with great and divine brevity, saying: 'Now this is life eternal, that they may know Thee, the only true God, and Him whom Thou sent, Jesus Christ.'[2] Likewise, when He gathered from the law and prophets the first and greatest commandments, He said: 'Hear, O Israel,

---

1 Cf. Isa. 10.22,23.
2 John 17.3.

the Lord your God is one Lord.'[3] And, 'Thou shalt love the Lord thy God with thy whole heart, and with thy whole strength. This is the first commandment. And the second is like it, Thou shalt love thy neighbor as thyself. On these two commandments depend the whole law and the prophets.'[4] And again, 'Whatever good things you wish men to do to you, even so do you also to them; for this is the law and the prophets.'[5]

Chapter 29

Not by words alone, but also by deeds has God taught us to pray, Himself praying frequently and entreating and demonstrating what we ought to do by the testimony of His own example, as it is written: 'But He Himself was in retirement in the desert, and in prayer,' and again, 'He went out into the mountain to pray and continued all night in prayer to God.'[1] But if He who was without sin prayed, how much more ought sinners to pray, and if He prayed continually, watching through the whole night with uninterrupted petitions, how much more ought we to lie awake at night in continuing prayer!

3 Mark 12.29.
4 Matt. 22.37-40.
5 Cf. Matt. 7.12.

1 Luke 5.16;6.12.

Chapter 30

Moreover, the Lord prayed and asked not for Himself, (for what would an innocent person petition for himself?), but for our sins, just as He Himself declares when He says to Peter: 'Behold, Satan was asking to have you, that he might sift you as wheat. But I have prayed for thee, that thy faith may not fail.'[1] And later He entreats the Father for all, saying: 'Yet not for these only do I pray, but for those also who through their word are to believe in me, that all may be one, even as thou, Father, in me and I in thee; that they also may be in us.'[2] Great alike is God's kindness and compassion for our salvation, so that, not content with having redeemed us with His blood, He in addition also prayed for us. Moreover, behold what the desire was of Him who prayed, that, just as the Father and Son are one, so too we remain in that very unity; that from this it can be understood how much he sins who shatters unity and peace, since the Lord also prayed for this, namely, that His people live, for He knew that discord does not come to the kingdom of God.

Chapter 31

Moreover, when we stand for prayer, most beloved brethren, we should be alert and intent on our petitions with a whole heart. Let every carnal and worldly thought depart, and let the mind dwell on nothing other than that alone for which it prays. Therefore, the priest also before his prayer prepares the minds of the brethren by first uttering

1 Luke 22.31.
2 Cf. John 17.20,21.

a preface, saying: 'Lift up your hearts,' so that when the people respond: 'We lift them up to the Lord,' they may be admonished that they should ponder on nothing other than the Lord. Let the breast be closed against the adversary and be open to God alone, and let it not suffer the enemy of God to approach it at the time of prayer. For he frequently creeps up and penetrates and with subtle deceit calls our prayers away from God, so that we have one thing in the heart, another in the voice, when not the sound of the voice but the mind and the thought should be praying to the Lord with sincere intention. But what slothfulness it is to be drawn away and to be captured by foolish and profane thoughts, when you are praying to the Lord, as if there were anything that you should ponder more than what you speak with God. How do you ask that you be heard by God, when you do not hear your very self? Do you wish the Lord to be mindful of you when you pray, when you yourself are not mindful of yourself? This is to be entirely off-guard against the enemy; this is, when you pray to God, to offend the majesty of God by the negligence of prayer; this is to be alert with the eyes and to be asleep with the heart, although a Christian, even when he is sleeping, should be alert with the heart, as it is written in the person of the Church speaking in the Canticle of Canticles? 'I sleep and my heart watcheth.'[1] Therefore, the Apostle solicitously and cautiously admonishes, saying: 'Be assiduous in prayer, being wakeful therein,'[2] that is, teaching and showing that they can obtain what they ask of God, who God sees are alert in prayer.

---

1 Cant. 5.2.
2 Col. 4.2.

Chapter 32

Moreover, let those who pray not come to God with fruitless and destitute prayers. The petition is ineffective when a sterile prayer is offered to God. For, since every tree that does not bear fruit is cut down and cast into the fire,[1] likewise words without fruits cannot merit God's favor, since they are fruitful in no deed. And so divine Scripture instructs us with these words: 'Prayer is good with fasting and alms.'[2] For He who on the day of judgment is to render a reward for deeds and alms, today also is a kindly listener to prayer which comes with works. Thus finally did Cornelius, the centurion, merit to be heard, when he prayed. He was one who performed many alms-deeds among the people and who always prayed to God. Before him as he prayed at the ninth hour an angel stood giving testimony to his work in these words: 'Cornelius, thy prayers and thy alms have gone up for a memorial before God.'[3]

Chapter 33

Quickly do those prayers ascend to God, which the merits of our works impose upon God. Thus did the angel Raphael stand before Tobias, as he always prayed and always worked, saying: 'It is honorable to reveal and confess the works of God. For when thou didst pray with Sara, I offered the memory of your prayer in the sight of the glory of God, and when thou didst bury the dead directly, and because thou

---

1 Cf. Matt. 7.19.
2 Tob. 12.8.
3 Cf. Acts 10.4.

didst not delay to rise and to leave thy dinner, but didst go out and hide the dead, I was sent to tempt thee; and again God sent me to heal thee and Sara thy son's wife. For I am Raphael, one of the seven just angels who go in and out before the glory of God.'[1] Through Isaias also the Lord admonishes and teaches like things, testifying with these words: 'Loose every bond of wickedness, undo the bundles of the unbridled traders, release the broken for rest, and break asunder every unjust burden. Break thy bread to the hungry and bring the needy and the harborless into thy house. If thou shalt see one naked, cover him, and despise not the children of thy own seed. Then shall thy light break forth as the morning and thy garments shall speedily arise and thy justice shall go before thee and the glory of God shall surround thee. Then shalt thou call and the Lord shall hear thee, when thou shalt cry and He will say: 'Here I am.'[2] He promises that He is present and hears, and He says that He protects those who loosening the knots of injustice from the heart, and performing alms-deeds around the members of God's household according to His precepts, as they hear what God orders to be done, themselves also deserve to be heard by God. The blessed Apostle Paul, when aided in the necessity of affliction, by the brethren said that the words which were done were sacrifices to God. He said: 'I am fully supplied now that I have received from Epaphroditus what you have sent, a sweet odor, an acceptable sacrifice, well pleasing to God.'[3] For when one has pity on the poor, he lends to God; and he who gives to the least, gives to God; in a spiritual sense he sacrifices to God the odors of sweetness.

1 Cf. Tob. 12.7.12-15.
2 Cf. Isa. 58.6-9.
3 Phil. 4.18.

Chapter 34

Now in celebrating prayer we find that the three boys with Daniel strong in the faith and victorious in captivity observed the third, the sixth, and the ninth hours, namely for a sacrament of the Trinity, which in the latest times had to be manifested. For the first hour going into the third shows the number of the Trinity consummated, and likewise the fourth proceding to the sixth proclaims a second Trinity, and when the ninth is completed from the seventh, the perfect Trinity is numbered every three hours. Having determined upon these spaces of hours in a spiritual sense a long time ago, the worshippers of God were subject to them as the established and lawful times for prayer. Later the fact was made manifest that formerly the sacraments existed, because the just of old so prayed. For upon the disciples at the third hour did the Holy Spirit descend, which fulfilled the grace of the Lord's promise. Likewise Peter at the sixth hour going upward upon the house-top was instructed alike by a sign and the voice of God admonishing him, to admit all to the grace of salvation, although before He was hesitant about baptizing the Gentiles. The Lord also, having been crucified from the sixth to the ninth, washed away our sins by His blood, and, that he might be able to redeem and quicken us, He then completed the victory by His passion.

Chapter 35

But for us, most beloved brethren, besides the hours of praying observed of old, both the times and the sacraments have increased. For we must also pray in the morning, that the resurrection of the Lord may be celebrated by morning prayer. The Holy Spirit set this forth of old, when He said in the psalms: 'O my king and my God. For to thee will I pray: O Lord, in the morning thou shalt hear my voice. In the morning I will stand before thee, and will see thee.'[1] And again through the prophet the Lord says: 'At dawn they will be on watch for me, saying: let us go and return to the Lord our God.'[2] Likewise at the setting of the sun and at the end of the day necessarily there must again be prayer. For since Christ is the true Sun and the true Day, as the sun and the day of the world recede, when we pray and petition that the light come upon us again, we pray for the coming of Christ to provide us with the grace of eternal light. Moreover, the Holy Spirit in the psalms declares that Christ is called the Day. He says: 'The stone which the builders rejected has become the cornerstone. This is the Lord's doing; it is wonderful in our eyes. This is the day which the Lord has made; let us exalt and rejoice therein.'[3] Likewise Malachias the prophet testifies that He is called the Sun when he says: 'But unto you that fear my name, the Sun of justice shall arise, and healing is in His wings.'[4] But if in holy Scripture Christ is the true Sun and the true Day, no hour is excepted for Christians, in which God should be adored frequently and always, so that we who are in Christ, that is, in the true Sun and in the true Day, should be insistent throughout the whole day in our petitions and should pray; and when, by the law of the world, the revolving night, recurring in its alternate changes, succeeds, there can be no harm from the nocturnal

---

1 Cf. Ps. 5.3,4.
2 Cf. Osee 6.1.
3 Ps. 117.22-24.
4 Mal. 4.2.

shades for those who pray, because to the sons of light even in the night there is day. For when is he without light who has light in his heart? Or when does he not have sun and day, to whom Christ is Sun and Day?

Chapter 36

Moreover, let us who are always in Christ, that is, in the light not cease praying even in the night. Thus the widow Anna without intermission always petitioning and watching, persevered in deserving well of God, as it is written in the Gospel: 'She did not leave the temple, serving with fastings and prayers night and day.'[1] Either the Gentiles who have not yet been enlightened or the Jews who deserted the light and remained in darkness should have seen; let us, most beloved brethren, who are always in the light of the Lord, who remember and retain what we have begun to be after receiving grace compute the night as day. Let us believe that we walk always in the light;[2] let us not be hindered by the darkness which we have escaped; let there be no loss of prayers in the hours of the night, no slothful or neglectful waste of opportunities for prayer. Let us who by the indulgence of God have been recreated spiritually and reborn imitate what we are destined to be; let us who in the kingdom will have day alone without the intervention of night be just as alert at night as in the day; let us who are destined to pray always and to give thanks to God, not cease here also to pray and to give thanks.

---

1 Luke 2.37.
2 Cf. 1 John 1.7.

TO DEMETRIAN

Translated by

ROY J. DEFERRARI, Ph.D.
The Catholic University of America

TO DEMETRIAN

EMETRIAN, to whom this treatise is addressed, was in all probability a magistrate, possibly a rhetorician, in any case a very bitter enemy of the Christians. The theory had already been developed, even before Cyprian's time, that the calamities of the Roman Empire, whatever they might be at the moment—war, pestilence, famine, drought—were to be attributed to the Christian contempt for the pagan gods. Demetrian had revived this rumor. The answer which the Christian apologists gave to the charge was that these misfortunes were really divine punishments inflicted on the Romans because of their obstinacy and wickedness, and in particular for their persecution of the Christians.

Before Cyprian, Tertullian[1] had denounced the same charges. After Cyprian, Arnobius[2] and Lactantius[3] were obliged to refute this slander. Later, St. Augustine felt that he should take up the matter again, which he treats in great detail in the early books of the *City of God*.

Cyprian begins by referring to the growing decrepitude

---

1 *Apol.* 40; *Ad. nat.* 1.9; *Ad Scep.* 3.
2 *Adv. nat* 1.
3 *Div. inst.* 5.4.3.

of the universe and by reason of this deterioration and decay
its inability to produce as it used to do in the spring of
creation. In Chapter 8 we find a curious passage on slavery,
slightly reminiscent of Stoicism: 'You yourself exact servitude
from your slave and you, a man, compel a man to submit
and obey you, and, although you both have the same lot
as to being born, one condition as to dying, identical material
of bodies, a common order of souls, although your coming
into this world and later your departure from the world
is with equal right and by the same law, nevertheless, unless
you are served according to your decision, unless you are
obeyed according to the obedience of your will, you, as an
imperious and excessive exactor of servitude, flog, whip,
afflict, and torture with hunger, thirst, nakedness, and frequently with the sword and imprisonment.'[4] But Cyprian
soon settles down to give us a pamphlet of a fine, passionate
vigor.

Some have objected to the tone of *Ad Demetrianum* as
lacking due respect. Lactantius[5] criticizes Cyprian for making
too extensive a use of proofs from Scripture. Such arguments
will make no impression on the pagan Demetrian; arguments
based on reason will alone convince him, he proclaims. But
Cyprian is not thinking of Demetrian alone. He is chiefly
concerned with treating the question to the complete satisfaction of all Christians, especially those who are in danger
of losing their faith because of these accusations. The work
has much in common with the Apology and *To Scapula*
of Tertullian, but its satire is regarded as even more effective
than that of Tertullian. All in all it is one of the most powerful
and original of Cyprian's works.

---

4 Seneca, *Ep.* 47.6.
5 *Div. inst.* 5.4.

The date of *To Demetrian* is uncertain. The reference to the death of Decius and his children in Chapter 17 would establish a rather definite date, but this passage is of doubtful authenticity. Because Cyprian's biographer, Pontius, lists it after the treatise on the Lord's Prayer, it is usually dated 252. A later date is sometimes suggested.

TO DEMETRIAN

Chapter 1

I HAD TREATED YOU with contempt, Demetrian, as you railed with sacrilegious mouth against God, who is one and true, and frequently cried out with impious words, thinking it more fitting and better to ignore with silence the ignorance of a man in error than to provoke with speech the fury of a man in madness. And I did not do this without the authority of the divine teaching, since it is written: 'Do not say anything in the ears of the foolish, lest when he hears he may mock your wise words,'[1] and again: 'Do not answer the foolish according to his folly, lest you become like him,'[2] and let us be admonished to keep within our own conscience what is holy, and not to expose it to be trampled upon by swine and dogs, for the Lord speaks saying: 'Do not give that which is holy to the dogs, and do not cast your pearls before swine, lest they trample them under their feet.'[3] For when you came to me often rather with an eagerness to contradict than with a wish

1 Prov. 23.9.
2 Prov. 26.4.
3 Matt. 7.6.

167

to learn, and you preferred impudently to insist on your own views, shouting with noisy words, rather than to listen patiently to our own, it seemed foolish to contend with you, since it would be an easier and lighter task to restrain the angry waves of a turbulent sea by shouting than to check your madness by arguments. Surely it is a futile labor and of no effect to offer light to someone blind, words to a deaf person, and wisdom to a brute, since a brute cannot understand, and a blind person cannot admit light, and one deaf cannot hear.

Chapter 2

Bearing this in mind, I often kept silence and overcame impatience by patience, since I could neither teach the unteachable nor check the impious with religion, nor repress him who raves with kindliness. But yet, when you say that very many are complaining and are blaming us because wars are arising more frequently, because the plague, famine are raging, and because long droughts are suspending rains and showers, I should be silent no longer, lest presently our silence begin to be a matter not of modesty, but of diffidence, and if we scorn to refute false charges, we seem to acknowledge the crime. Therefore, I reply to you, Demetrian, as well as to the others whom you by chance have stirred up, and whom, by sowing hatreds against us by your malicious words, you have made companions of yours in great numbers by the increase of your root and origin, yet who, I believe, admit the reasonableness of our speech. For he who has been moved to evil by deceiving falsehood will be moved to good much more by truth.

Chapter 3

You have said that all those things by which the world is now being shaken and oppressed have occurred through us, and that they ought to be imputed to us, because your gods are not worshipped by us. You who in this respect are ignorant of divine knowledge and are a stranger to the truth, in the first place ought to know this, that the world has grown old, does not enjoy that strength which it had formerly enjoyed, and does not flourish with the same vigor and strength with which it formerly prevailed. The world itself is now saying this, even as we are silent and offer no citations from holy Scriptures and divine prophecies, and it testifies to its decline by the proof of its failing estate. In the winter the supply of rain is not so plentiful for the nourishment of seeds; there is not the accustomed heat in the summer for ripening the harvest; neither are the corn fields so joyous in the spring nor are the autumn seasons so fecund in their leafy products. To a less extent are slabs of marble dug out of the disembowelled and wearied mountains; to a less extent do the mines already exhausted produce quantities of silver and gold, and the impoverished veins are lessened day by day. The farmer is vanishing and disappearing in the fields, the sailor on the sea, the soldier in the camp, innocence in the market, justice in the courts, harmony among friendships, skill among the arts, discipline in morals. Do you think that there can be as much substance in an aging thing, as there would have flourished formerly, when it was still young and vigorous with youth? Whatever at its very last is sinking to its setting and end must be diminishing. Thus the sun at its setting casts forth rays of less bright and fiery splendor; thus the moon, as its course declines, diminishes with exhausted horns; and the tree, which had once been green and fertile, afterwards, as its branches dry up, becomes sterile, deformed by old age; and the fountain, which before flowed forth profusely from its overflowing veins, in failing old age scarcely trickles with moderate moisture. This sentence has been passed upon the world; this is the law of God; that all things which have come into existence die; and that those which have increased grow old; and that the strong be weakened; and that the large be diminished; and that when they have been weakened and diminished they come to an end.

Chapter 4

You impute to the Christians that everything is diminished as the world grows old. What if old men also impute to Christians that they have less strength in old age, that no longer as before are they vigorous in the sense of hearing, in the swiftness of their feet, in the sharpness of their eyes, in the force of their strength, in the freshness of their vitals, in the fulness of their limbs, and that, whereas before the old age of man extended eight hundred and nine hundred years, now it can scarcely arrive at the number of one hundred. We see grey hair among boys; hair falls out before it grows; and age does not cease in old age but begins with old age. Thus, still at its beginning birth rushes to its end;[1] thus whatever is born degenerates with the old age of the world, itself, so that no one should marvel that everything in the world has begun to fail, when the entire world itself is already in a decline and at its end.

---

1 Cf. Wisd. 5.13.

Chapter 5

Moreover, that wars continue with greater frequency, that barrenness and famine accumulate anxiety, that health is broken by raging diseases, that the human race is laid waste by ravages of pestilence, this too you should know was predicted, that in the last days evils are multiplied and adversities are diversified and presently with the approach of the day of judgment more and more is the censure of an indignant God roused to the scourging of the human race. For these things do not occur, as your false complaints and inexperience ignorant of the truth boast and cry out, because your gods are not worshipped by us, but because God is not worshipped by you. For since He himself is the Lord and the Director of the universe, and since all things are done at His decision and nod and nothing can be done except what He Himself has done or has permitted to be done, surely when those things are done which show the anger of an offended God, these are done not on account of us by whom God is worshipped, but are inflicted because of your sins and merits, by whom God is neither sought nor feared, nor are empty superstitions abandoned and true religion recognized, so that He who is the one God for all is alone worshipped and sought by all.

Chapter 6

Finally, hear Him as He speaks, as he instructs and advises us with His divine words: 'Thou shalt worship the Lord thy God, and Him only shalt thou serve,'[1] and again: 'Thou

---

1 Deut. 6.13..

shalt not have strange gods before me,'[2] and again: 'And
go not after strange gods to serve them, and adore them;
nor provoke me to wrath by the works of your hands to scatter
you.'[3] The prophet likewise, filled with the Holy Spirit, attests
and proclaims the wrath of God in these words: 'Thus saith
the Lord omnipotent: "Because my house is desolate, and
you make haste every man to his own house, therefore the
heaven will abstain from dew, and the earth will withdraw
her fruits, and I shall bring a sword upon the earth and
upon the corn and upon the vine, and upon the oil, and
upon man and upon beasts and upon all the labors of their
hands." '[4] Likewise, another prophet repeats and says: 'I shall
cause it to rain upon one city, and I shall not cause it to rain
upon another city. One piece shall be rained upon, and the
piece upon which I shall not rain, shall wither. Two and
three cities shall gather in one city to drink water, but shall
not be filled. Yet you returned not to me, saith the Lord.'[5]

Chapter 7

Behold, the Lord is indignant and wrathful and, because
you do not turn to Him, threatens. And you wonder or complain in this your obstinacy and contempt, if the rain descends
rarely from above, if the earth lies neglected because of the
accumulation of dust, if the barren globe with difficulty produces feeble and pallid blades of grass, if the destructive hail

2 Exod. 20.3.
3 Jer. 25.6.
4 Ag. 1.9-11.
5 Amos. 4.7,8.

weakens the vines; if the overwhelming whirlwind uproots the olive, if drought stanches the spring, if a breeze spreading pestilence befouls the air, if deadly disease consumes mankind, although all these things come because of the sins that provoke them, and God is exasperated the more when such great evils avail nothing. For the same God declares in holy Scriptures in these words that these things occur either for discipline of the obstinate or for the punishment of the devil: 'In vain have I struck your children; they have not received correction.'[1] And the prophet devoted and dedicated to God replies to these same words and says: 'Thou has struck them and they have not grieved; thou hast bruised them and they have refused to receive correction.'[2] Behold, blows are inflicted by God and there is no fear of God. Behold stripes and scourgings from above are not lacking, and there is no trembling, no alarm. What if even such censure did not interfere with human affairs? How much greater still would the audacity of men be, if it were secure in the impunity of its crimes?

Chapter 8

You complain because now the rich springs and the salubrious breezes and the frequent rains and the fertile earth furnish you less support, because the elements do not serve interests and pleasures so much. But do you serve God through whom all things serve you; do you wait upon Him, at whose nod all things wait upon you? You yourself exact servitude from your slave and you, a man, compel a man

1 Jer. 2.30.
2 Jer. 5.3.

to submit and obey you, and although you both have the same lot as to being born, one condition as to dying, identical material of bodies, a common order of souls, although your coming into this world and later your departure from the world is with equal right and by the same law, nevertheless, unless you are served according to your decision, unless you are obeyed according to the obedience of your will, you as an imperious and excessive exactor of servitude, flog, whip, afflict, and torture with hunger, thirst, nakedness, and frequently with the sword and imprisonment. Do you acknowledge the Lord, your God, when you yourself thus exercise Lordship?

Chapter 9

Therefore, deservedly are the stripes and lashes of God not lacking in these attacking plagues. Since these avail nothing here and do not turn you one by one to God by such terror of destruction, there awaits you later the eternal prison and everlasting flame and perpetual punishment, nor will the groaning of the suppliants be heard there, because the terror of the indignant God was not heard here, who cried out through the prophet, saying: 'Hear the word of the Lord, ye children of Israel, for the Lord shall enter into judgment with the inhabitants of the land, for there is no mercy, and there is no truth, and there is no knowledge of God in the land. Cursing, and lying, and killing, and theft, and adultery have overflowed upon the land, and blood has touched blood. Therefore shall the land mourn with all its inhabitants, and with the beasts of the field, with the creeping things of the earth, with the fowls of the air, and the fishes of the sea shall fail, so that no one passes judgment, no one convicts another.'[1] God says that He is indignant because there is no knowledge of God on earth, and God is not known, neither is he feared. God rebukes and accuses the sins of lying, of lust, of fraud, of cruelty, of impiety, and of madness, but no one is converted to innocence. Behold, the events that were formerly foretold by the words of God are coming to pass, and no one by faith in the present is warned to take counsel for the future. Among these adversities, bound and hemmed in by which the soul breathes with difficulty, there is time for men to be evil and in so great perils to pass judgment not so much on themselves as on others. You are indignant that God is indignant, as if you deserved anything good by living evilly, as if all those things that happen were still not less and lighter than your own sins.

Chapter 10

You who judge others, at some time be also a judge of yourself, look into the recesses of your own conscience; rather, because there is no shame, indeed, in doing wrong, and sin is so committed as if pleasure came rather through sins themselves, do you who are seen clearly and nakedly by all yourself also look upon yourself. For you are either swollen with pride, or greedy with avarice, or cruel with anger, or prodigal with gambling, or drunk with wine-bibbing, or envious with jealousy, or incestuous with lust, or violent with cruelty; and do you wonder that the wrath of God increases for the punishment of the human race, when what is worthy to be punished increases daily? You complain that an enemy rises up, as if, though an enemy were waiting, there could

---

1 Osee 4.1-4.

be peace among the very togas of peace, as if, though external
arms and dangers from barbarians were repressed, the weapons of domestic attack from the calumnies and injuries of
powerful citizens were not ranging more fiercely and more
seriously from within; you complain about barrenness and
famine, as if drought causes more famine than rapacity, as
if the fierceness of want did not increase more flagrantly
from the striving after the yearly crops and the accumulation
of their price; you complain that the heavens are shut off
from showers, although the granaries on earth are so shut
off; you complain that less is being produced, as if what has
been produced were offered to the needy; you accuse of the
crime of plague and disease, although by plague itself and
disease the crimes of individuals are either detected or increased, while mercy is not shown the weak and avarice and
rapine await open-mouthed for the dead. The same men
are timid in the observance of piety, rash for impious gains,
avoiding the deaths of the dying, but seeking the spoils of
the dead, so that it appears that the wretched in their sickness have even been abandoned perhaps for this, that they
may not be able to escape when they are being treated,
for he who enters upon the property of the dying wished
the sick man to die.

Chapter 11

So great a terror of destruction cannot give the teaching
of innocency, and in the midst of a people dying with recurring slaughter no one considers that he too is mortal.
There is running about everywhere, there is seizure, there
is taking possession, there is no concealment of plundering,

no delay; as if it were lawful, as if it were right, as if he who does not seize were experiencing damage and a proper loss; thus every one hastens to seize. Among thieves there is at least some shame for their crimes; they love pathless ravines and deserted solitudes, and wrongs are so committed there that nevertheless the crime of the wrong-doers is veiled by shadows and night. Avarice rages openly and safe by its very boldness thrusts forth in the light of the market-place the arms of unrestrained lust. Thus they are cheats, thus poisoners, thus in the middle of the city murderers are eager for sinning as they sin with impunity. The crime is confessed by the guilty, but the innocent is not found to press the charge. There is no fear of the accuser or the judge; the wicked obtain impunity, while the modest are silent, accomplices are afraid, and those who are to judge have a price. And so through the prophet the truth of the matter is set forth with the divine spirit and inspiration; a certain and manifest method is shown: that the Lord can prohibit adversities, but the merits of sinners cause Him to give no aid. 'Behold,' he says 'does not the hand of the Lord prevail to save [men], or will His ear be heavy that it cannot hear? But your iniquities divide between you and your God, and on account of your sins He turns his face away from you lest He have mercy.'[1] Therefore, let your sins and offences be computed; let the wounds of your conscience be considered; and let each one cease to complain about God and about us, if he understands that he deserves what he suffers.

---

1 Isa. 59.1,2.

Chapter 12

Behold of what nature is the subject of our discourse chiefly about—that you molest us who are innocent, that you in contempt of God attack and oppress the servants of God? It is of little importance that your life is stained by a variety of mad vices, with the iniquity of deadly crimes, with a collection of bloody rapines, that the true religion is overturned by false superstitions, that God is in no way ever sought or feared. Still more you provoke with unjust persecutions the servants of God and those dedicated to His majesty and will. It is not enough that you yourself do not worship God. Still more with a sacrilegious attack do you persecute those who do worship. Neither do you worship God, nor do you permit Him to be worshipped at all, although others who not only venerate those empty idols and images fashioned by the hand of man but also certain portents and monsters please you, the worshipper of God alone displeases. Everywhere in your temples the funeral pyres and piles of cattle smoke, but the altars of God do not exist or are concealed. Crocodiles and bees and stones and serpents are worshipped, and God alone on earth either is not worshipped or His worship does not exist with impunity. The innocent, the just, the dear to God you deprive of a home, you despoil of their inheritance, you load down with chains, you shut up in prison, you punish by beasts, by the sword, by fire. And you are not content with the collection of our pains and with the simple and swift brevity of the punishments; you apply long torments by lacerating our bodies, you multiply the numerous punishments by tearing our vitals; nor can your savagery and inhumanity be content with customary torments; your ingenious cruelty devises new inflictions.

Chapter 13

What is this insatiable madness for torture, what this interminable lust for cruelty? Why not rather choose one of two alternatives: to be a Christian either is a crime or it is not. If it is a crime, why do you not kill him who confesses it? If it is not a crime, why do you persecute the innocent? For I ought to have been tortured, if I had denied it. If out of fear of your punishment I concealed with lying deceit that which I had been before and that I had not worshipped your gods, then I ought to have been tortured, I ought to have been forced to a confession of the crime with force of pain, just as in other trials defendants who deny that they are guilty of the crime of which they are accused, so that the truth of the misdeed, which is not forthcoming by the testimony of the word, is extracted by pain of body. But now when of my free will I confess and cry out and with words frequent and repeated again and again I attest that I am a Christian, why do you apply tortures to me as I confess and destroy your gods not in hidden and secret places but openly and publicly in the very forum within the hearing of the magistrates and officers, so that, even if that with which you charged me before had been a little thing, it has increased to something which you ought both to hate and punish the more? Why, when I pronounce myself a Christian in a crowded place with people standing all around, and confound you and your gods by a clear and public pronouncement, why do you concern yourself with the weakness of the body, why do you contend with the feebleness of earthly flesh? Attack the vigor of the mind, break the strength of the mind, destroy faith, conquer, if you can, by discussion, conquer by reason.

Chapter 14

Indeed, if your gods have any divinity and power, let them themselves rise to their vindication, let them themselves defend themselves by their own majesty. But of what advantage can they be to their worshippers, who cannot avenge themselves on those who do not worship them. For if he who avenges is of greater power than he who is avenged, you are greater than your gods. Therefore, if you are greater than those whom you worship, you should not worship them, but you should be worshipped by them. Thus your vengeance defends them when afflicted, just as also your protection guards them, when enclosed, from perishing. You should be ashamed to worship those whom you yourself defend; you should be ashamed to hope for protection from those whom you protect.

Chapter 15

Oh, if you would hear and see them, when they are adjured by us, when they are tortured by spiritual scourges and are ejected by torments of words from the bodies of the possessed, when howling and groaning at a human voice and feeling the lashes and scourges of divine power they confess the judgment which is to come. Come and learn that what we say is true, and since you say that you thus worship the gods, then believe them whom you worship. Or if you should wish to believe yourself also, within your hearing he [the demon] will speak of you yourself, who now has possessed your breast, who now has blinded your mind with the night of ignorance. You will see that we are entreated by those whom you entreat, that we are feared by those whom you adore. You will see that they stand bound under our hand and tremble as captives whom you look up to and venerate as lords. Surely even so you can be confounded in those errors of yours, when you see and hear that your gods on our questioning immediately betray what they are, and that even in your presence cannot conceal those deceptions and trickeries.

Chapter 16

So what cowardice of mind is this, rather, what blind and stupid madness of fools not to come from darkness to the light, and when bound by the bonds of eternal death to be unwilling to receive the hope of immortality, not to fear God as He threatens saying: 'He that sacrificeth to gods shall be put to death, save only to the Lord';[1] and again: 'They have adored them whom their fingers have made, and man hath bowed himself down, and man hath been debased, and I shall not forgive them'?[2] Why do you humble and bend yourself to false gods? Why do you bow your captive body before foolish images and creations of earth? God made you erect, and, although the other animals are prone and are depressed with posture bent toward earth, you have an exalted stature and a countenance raised upward toward heaven and the Lord. Look there, direct your eyes there, seek God on high. That you may be able to be free of things here below, hold up and raise your heart to the heavenly things on high. Why do you prostrate yourself into the ruin of death with the serpent whom you worship?

1 Exod. 22.20.
2 Isa. 2.8,9.

Why do you fall into the destruction of the devil through him and with him? Preserve the sublime nature with which you were born. Persevere just as you were made by God. Establish your soul with the state of your face and body. That you may be able to know God, know yourself first. Abandon the idols which human error invented. Turn to God, and if you implore Him, He comes to your aid. Believe in Christ whom the Father sent to quicken and restore us. Cease to injure the servants of God and of Christ with your persecutions for when they are injured divine vengeance defends them.

Chapter 17

For this reason it is that no one of us fights back when he is apprehended, nor do our people avenge themselves against your unjust violence though numerous and plentiful. Our certainty of the vengeance which is to come makes us patient. The harmless give way to the harmful; the innocent acquiesce in the punishments and tortures certain and confident that whatever we suffer will not remain unavenged, and that the greater is the injury of the persecution, the more just and serious will be the vengeance for the persecution. Never is there any uprising from the wickedness of impious man against our name, that is not immediately accompanied by divine vengeance. To be silent on the old memories of the past and not to reflect upon the oft-repeated vengeances in behalf of the worshippers of God with clarion voice, the testimony of a recent event is enough to prove that our defense recently followed so swiftly and in such great swiftness, so mightily in the ruin of affairs, in the loss of wealth, in the waste of soldiers, and in a decrease of forts. And let no one think that this happened by chance or consider that it was fortuitous, since long ago divine Scripture laid down and said: 'Vengeance is mine, I shall repay, says the Lord,'[1] and let the Holy Spirit again warn us saying: 'Say not: I will avenge myself on my enemy, but wait in the Lord so that He may aid thee.'[2] Thus it is clear and manifest that not through us but for us do all these things happen which come down from the anger of God.

Chapter 18

Nor let anyone, therefore, think that Christians are not avenged by these things that happen, because they also seem to be affected by the onrush of events; that man feels the punishment of the adversities of the world whose every joy and glory is in the world; that man grieves and mourns if it is ill with him in this life, with whom it cannot be well after this life, the fruit of whose living is taken entirely here, whose solace is all ended here, whose fleeting and short life reckons some sweetness and pleasure here, but, when he has passed from here, only punishment unto grief remains. But there is no grief from the attack of present evils for those who have confidence in future blessings. Finally we are not prostrated by adversities, nor are we broken down, nor do we grieve, nor do we murmur in any catastrophe of events or in sickness of body. Living by the spirit rather than by the flesh we overcome the weakness of the body by the strength of the soul. By those very things that torture and weary us we know and are confident that we are proved and strengthened.

---

1 Rom. 12.19.
2 Cf. Prov. 20.22.

Chapter 19

Do you think that we endure adversities equally with you, when you see that the same adversities are not sustained equally by us and by you? With you there is always a clamorous and querulous impatience; with us there is a strong and religious patience always quiet and always grateful to God, and it does not claim anything here for itself, either pleasant or prosperous, but gentle and kind and firm against all the disturbances of a changing world it awaits the time of the divine promise. For as long as this body remains common with the rest, its corporal condition must also be common, and it is not granted the members of the human race to be separated from one another, unless there is withdrawal from this life. Meanwhile, we, good and evil, are contained within our house. Whatever comes within the house we endure with equal fate, until, when our temporal earthly period has been fulfilled, we are distributed among the homes of eternal death or immortality. So then we are not comparable and equal with you, because, while we are still in this world and in this flesh, we incur equally with you the annoyances of the world and of the flesh. For since all that punishes is in the sense of pain, it is manifest that he is not a participant in your punishment whom you see does not suffer pain with you.

Chapter 20

There flourishes with us the strength of hope and firmness of faith, and in the midst of the very ruins of a collapsing world our mind is lifted up and our courage is unshaken, and never is our patience unhappy, and our soul is always secure in its God, just as the Holy Spirit says and exhorts through the prophet, strengthening the firmness of our hope and faith by His heavenly voice. He says: 'The fig tree shall not bear fruit, and there shall be no spring in the vines. The labor of the olive tree shall deceive and the fields shall yield no food. The sheep shall lack pasture, and there shall be no oxen in the stable. But I will rejoice in the Lord, and I will joy in God my Savior.[1] He says that the man of God and the worshipper of God relying on the truth of hope and established in the stability of faith is not moved by the assaults of this world and life. Although the vine fails and the olive deceives and the field with its grass dying from drought becomes parched and withers, what is this to Christians? What to God's servants whom paradise invites, whom all the graces and abundance of the heavenly kingdom awaits? They always exult in the Lord and rejoice and are happy in their God and bravely endure the evils and adversities of the world, while they look forward to the blessings and prosperity of the future. For we, who after putting off our earthly birth, have been recreated and reborn in the Spirit and no longer live to the world but to God, will not receive God's gifts and promises except when we have come to God. And yet for warding off the enemy and for obtaining rain and for either removing or mitigating adversities we always beseech and pour forth prayers, and, propitiating and placating God, we pray constantly and fervently day and night for your peace and salvation.

---

1 Cf. Hab. 3.17,18.

Chapter 21

Thus let no one flatter himself that meanwhile for us and the profane, the worshippers of God and the adversaries of God by reason of the equality of flesh and body there is a common condition of worldly troubles, so that from this he think that not all the things that happen are imposed upon you, since by the prediction of God Himself and the attestation of the prophets it was predicted before that God's wrath would come upon the unjust, that persecutions which would harm us in a human way would not be lacking, but also that vengeance to defend in a divine way those who were hurt would follow.

Chapter 22

How great the things which meanwhile are being done here for us! Something is given as an example that the wrath of God may be known. But on the other hand there is the day of judgment which holy Scripture announces saying: 'Howl ye, for the day of the Lord is near: it shall come as a destruction from the Lord. For behold the day of the Lord shall come, a cruel day, and full of indignation, and of wrath, to lay the land desolate, and to destroy the sinners out of it.'[1] And again: 'Behold the day of the Lord comes kindled as a furnace, and all the proud and all the wicked shall be as stubble; and the day coming shall set them on fire, says the Lord.'[2] The Lord prophecies that aliens will be burned and consumed, that is, aliens from the divine race, and the profane, those who have not been reborn spiritually

1 Isa. 13.6.
2 Mal. 4.1.

and have not become sons of God. For in another place God says that only those can escape who have been reborn and signed with the sign of Christ; when sending His angels to lay waste the world and to destroy the human race He threatens more seriously than the last time, saying: 'Go ye and slay and do not spare your eyes. Do not have pity on the old or the young, but slay the maidens and the women and the children that they may be blotted out. But everyone on whom the sign has been written you shall not touch.'[3] But what this sign is and in what part of the body it is placed, God makes clear in another place saying: 'Go through the midst of Jerusalem and mark the sign upon the foreheads of the men who mourn and grieve for all the iniquities that are done in the midst of them.'[4] And that this sign pertains to the passion and blood of Christ and that he is kept safe and unharmed whoever is found in this sign, is likewise proved by the testimony of God who says: 'And the blood shall be unto you for a sign upon the houses where you shall be; and I shall see the blood and shall protect you, and the plague of destruction shall not be on you, when I shall strike the hand of Egypt.'[5] What preceded before in a figure in the slaying of a lamb is fulfilled in Christ the truth which followed later. Just as then, when Egypt was smitten, no one could escape except by the blood and sign of the lamb, so too, when the world begins to be laid waste and smitten, he alone escapes who is found in the blood and sign of Christ.[6]

---

3 Ezech. 9.5,6.
4 Ezech. 9.4.
5 Exod. 12.13.
6 Cf. Ezech. 9.4; Apoc. 7.3, 9.4.

Chapter 23

Therefore, while there is time, look to the trees, and eternal salvation, and, since the end of the world is now at hand, out of fear of God turn your minds to God. Let not your powerless and vain dominion in the world over the just and the meek delight you, since also in the fields the tares and the darnel have dominion over the cultivated and fruitful corn, and you should not say that evils happen because your gods are not worshipped by us, but you should realize that this is God's anger, this is God's censure, so that He who is not recognized for His blessings may at least be recognized for His plagues. Seek God at least late, since He has now for a long time been warning and exhorting you through the prophet, saying: 'Seek God, and your soul shall live.'[1] Acknowledge God at least late, because Christ too at His coming advises and teaches this, saying: 'Now this is everlasting life, that they may know Thee the only true God, and him whom Thou hast sent, Jesus Christ.'[2] Believe Him who by no means deceives. Believe Him who has foretold that all these things would come to pass. Believe Him who will give the reward of eternal life to those who believe. Believe Him who by the fires of Gehenna will inflict eternal punishments on the incredulous.

Chapter 24

What glory of the faith will there be then, what punishment for perfidy, when the day of judgment shall come! What joy for believers, what sorrow for unbelievers, that they were unwilling before to believe here and cannot now return

1 Cf. Amos. 5.6.
2 John 17.3.

to believe! An ever burning Gehenna and a devouring punishment of lively flames will consume the condemned, and there will be no means whereby the torments can at any time have respite and end. Souls with their bodies will be reserved in infinite tortures for suffering. There he will be seen always by us, who here saw us for a time, and the brief of cruel eyes in the persecutions that took place will be compensated by a perpetual spectacle according to the faith of holy Scripture which says: "Their worm shall not die and their fire shall not be extinguished, and they shall be for a spectacle for all flesh.'[1] And again: 'Then shall the just stand with great constancy against those that have afflicted them and taken away their labors. These seeing it shall be troubled with great fear, and shall be amazed at the suddenness of their unexpected salvation, saying within themselves, repenting and groaning for anguish of spirit: "These are they whom we had some time in derision, and for a parable of reproach." We fools esteemed their life madness and their end without honor. How are they numbered among the sons of God and their lot is among the saints? Therefore, we have erred from the way of truth, and the light of justice hath not shined unto us, and the sun hath not risen upon us. We wearied ourselves in the way of iniquity and destruction and have walked through hard ways, but the way of the Lord we have not known. What hath pride profited us? Or, what advantage hath the boasting of riches brought us? All those things are passed away like a shadow.'[2] Then there will be the pain of punishment without the fruit of repentance, useless weeping, and ineffectual prayer. Too late do they believe in eternal punishment who were unwilling to believe in eternal life.

---

1 Isa. 66.24.
2 Wisd. 5.1-9.

Chapter 25

Therefore, while you may, provide for security and life. We offer you the salutary aid of our mind and counsel. And since we may not hate, and thus we are more pleasing to God, while we do not return injury for injury, we urge, while the opportunity is at hand, while there still remains something of this life, to make satisfaction to God, and to come forth from the depth of dark superstition into the bright light of true religion. We do not envy your advantages nor do we conceal divine benefits. We repay your hatreds with kindness, and for the torments and punishments which are inflicted upon us we point out the ways of salvation. Believe and live, and do you who persecute us in time rejoice with us for eternity. When there has been a withdrawal hence, then there is no opportunity for repentance, no accomplishment of satisfaction. Here life is either lost or kept; here by the worship of God, and by the fruit of faith provision is made for eternal salvation. Let no one either by sins or by years be retarded from coming to the acquiring of salvation. To him who still remains in this world no repentance is too late. The approach to God's forgiveness is open, and for those who seek and understand the truth the access is easy. Although you entreat for your sins at the very end and sunset of temporal life and you implore God who is one and true by the confession and faith of the acknowledgment of Him, pardon is granted to him who confesses, and to him who believes saving forgiveness is conceded out of God's goodness, and there is a crossing into immortality at the very moment of death.

Chapter 26

This grace does Christ bestow; this gift of His mercy He confers by undergoing death with the victory of the cross, by redeeming the believer at the price of His blood, by reconciling man with God the Father, by quickening mortality by heavenly regeneration. This one, if it can be done, let us follow; under the sacrament and sign of this one let us be counted. This one opens up to us the way of life; this one causes us to be led back to paradise; this one guides us to the kingdom of heaven. With Him we shall always live, having become sons of God through Him; with Him we shall always rejoice, having been restored by His blood. We Christians will be both glorious with Christ and blessed of God the Father, rejoicing in perpetual delight always in the sight of God, and giving thanks to God always. For he cannot be other than ever happy and grateful who, after he has been subject to death, has been made secure in immortality.

MORTALITY

Translated by

ROY J. DEFERRARI, Ph.D.
The Catholic University of America

MORTALITY

CYPRIAN'S TREATISE, *Mortality,* is one of the earliest contributions to the Christian literature of consolation and the most valuable source of information on a plague which spread over the Roman Empire. In assigning a date to this work which appears in the earliest manuscripts and which is enumerated in Pontius' list of Cyprian's writings, one is aided by the words of the author. Undoubtedly, Cyprian wrote this as a sermon to be delivered to the Christians of his diocese who were alarmed over the high death rate (*Mort.* 1) and who at the same time lamented that they were thus being deprived of martyrdom (*Mort.* 17). Eutropius (60.5) and Osorius (7.21) record the fact that this plague was the only noteworthy event in the reign of Gallus and Volusianus (251-253). Furthermore, Cyprian speaks of a new army which, recruited at the time of the plague, will fight without fear of death when the battle comes (*Mort.* 15)—a reference, no doubt, to the prospect of a new persecution which is mentioned again in Epistles 57-58, and which Monceaux assigns to the year 252. Epistle 59.6 states that toward the middle of 252 a decree of Gallus ordered public sacrifices in all parts of the Empire, and that this

occasioned a new persecution of the Christians. Hence, one
is led to believe that *Mortality* was composed in that year.

The morale of the Christians was low. Only the year before,
the Church in Africa had been agitated by the discussion over
the readmission of the *lapsi* and *libellatici* who had renounced
their faith during the Decian persecution. A short time later
the Christians were the objects of verbal attacks on the part
of the pagans who held their unwillingness to participate in
the State religion responsible for the plague raging in Africa.
Conditions in the plague-stricken city were appalling; no one
wanted to care for the sick, relatives even exposed members
of their family lest they themselves suffer from contagion,
bodies lay in the street, greed was rampant.

At this period Cyprian showed himself a real leader of his
people. Pontius relates (*Vita* 7-10) that before an assembly
Cyprian spoke of the blessings of mercy and of the merit
to be gained by helping not only the faithful but also the
pagans. He went further in an effort to relieve the situation;
he assigned duties to individuals in proportion to their wealth
and position. Those who could not give money gave their
services. To comfort the members of his flock, to strengthen
them in the throes of such a calamity, to reconcile them to
the will of God, and to recall to their minds the glories of
paradise impelled Cyprian to write his *Mortality*.

In a work of this sort it is not surprising to find that
Cyprian borrowed, consciously or not, some of the common-
place expressions employed by earlier writers, such as Cicero
and Seneca. They were part of his literary heritage but he
did not cite them as authorities. Not once did he refer formally
to arguments or thoughts other than those derived from the
Scriptures or from reason.

In developing his theme Cyprian follows the method of

presentation of his other treatises, namely, that of going straight to the point by quoting from the Scriptures, by commenting on the text, and by applying it to the present circumstances. The following outline illustrates his procedure.

I. Introduction
   (1) By a discourse drawn from the Scriptures the spiritual weakness of the Christians, displayed in this trial, may be overcome

II. Death is not to be feared but welcomed (2-19)
   (1) The plague is not an unexpected evil, for it was prophesied as a sign of the coming of the kingdom of God with its everlasting happiness (2-3)
   (2) Life is a series of contests with the forces of the devil; death is release from these cares (4-5)
   (3) Reluctance to die shows a love of worldly joys and little confidence in Scripture or the providence of God (6-7)
   (4) By bearing the plague with resignation a Christian will store up merit for himself (8-19)
      (a) The affliction of Christians as well as pagans benefits the former by testing their faith (8-13)
      (b) The pains and results of the disease have a salutary effect on the Christians, for they free the latter from the world or prepare them for glory to come (14-16)
      (c) The loss of martyrdom should not cause concern; obedience and resignation to God's will are requisite for heaven (17-19)

III. There should be no mourning for the dead (20-24)
   (1) Mourning reveals a lack of confidence in the promises of God (20-24)

IV. Conclusion (25-26)
    (1) Death from the plague brings an earlier release
        from the world (25)
    (2) Consider the joys of paradise.

The symptoms and effects of the plague are graphically described by Cyprian, yet it cannot be definitely identified with any of the great pestilences known to modern times. Its demoralizing effects on the populace (cf. Eusebius 7.22) are corroborated by Pontius and Dionysius who were eye-witnesses; they furnish precious information on the practical application of the principles of Christian charity at that time, even though these sources give no details as to the existence of formal Christian organization for this purpose.

Throughout this work Cyprian gives evidence of the warm sympathy and charity which aroused the admiration of St. Augustine (*De doctrina Christiana* 4.31). Vigorous and direct in his approach to practical problems he encouraged and strengthened his flock by his philosophy of Christian Stoicism.

The text used in this translation is that of W. von Hartel in the Vienna *Corpus* (3.1.297-314). In the Scriptural passages the Challoner revision of the Rheims-Douay translation of the Bible is used wherever it corresponds with the text used by Cyprian.

MORTALITY

Chapter 1

Although in most of you, beloved brethren, there is a resolute mind and a firm faith and a devout spirit, which is not
disturbed at the numbers in the present mortality,[1] but like
a strong and unmoving rock breaks rather the turbulent
attacks of the world and the violent waves of the age and
is itself not broken, and is not vanquished but tried by temptations, yet because I observe that among the people, some
either through weakness of spirit, or littleness of faith, or
the charm of life in the world, or weakness of sex, or, what
is worse, because of a wandering from the truth, are standing
less firmly and are not revealing the divine and invincible
strength of their hearts, the matter must not be ignored or
passed over in silence, but, so far as our weak power suffices,
with full strength, and with a discourse drawn from the
Lord's text, the cowardice of a luxury-loving mind must be
checked and one who has already begun to be a man of
God and Christ must be considered worthy of God and
Christ.

---

1 The word *mortalitas* is found only rarely in classical Latin, where it
has the meaning of death (Cicero, *De natura deorum* 1.10.26). In
this treatise Cyprian uses it in a new sense to indicate the plague
(*Mort.* 8.15-17). However, it here denotes the death rate, as in
Chronogr. (Mommsen 648.2).

Chapter 2

For, beloved brethren, he who serves as a soldier of God, who, being stationed in the camp of heaven, already hopes for the divine things, ought to recognize himself, so that we should have no fear, no dread at the storms and whirlwinds of the world, since the Lord predicted that these things would come through the exhortation of His provident voice, instructing and teaching and preparing and strengthening the people of His church to all endurance of things to come. He foretold and prophesied that wars and famine and earthquakes and pestilence would arise in the various places, and, that an unexpected and new fear of destructive agencies might not shake us, He forewarned that adversity would increase more and more in the last times. Behold the things which were spoken of are coming to pass, and since the things which were foretold are coming to pass, there will follow also whatsoever were promised, as the Lord Himself promises, saying: 'When you shall see these things come to pass, know that the kingdom of God is at hand.'[1] The kingdom of God, beloved brethren, has begun to be at hand; the reward of life and the joy of eternal salvation and perpetual happiness and the possession of paradise once lost are now coming with the passing of the world;[2] now the things of heaven are succeeding those of earth, and great things small, and eternal things, transitory. What place is there here for anxiety and worry? Who in the midst of these things is

---

1 Cf. Luke 21.31.
2 From the time of the fall of Jerusalem early Christian writers felt that the end of the world was approaching. Cyprian shared this view and gave frequent expression to it in his writings. (cf. Demetr. 5.23; Fort. 1; Epist. 58.1) .

fearful and sad save he who lacks hope and faith? For it is for him to fear death who is unwilling to go to Christ. It is for him to be unwilling to go to Christ who does not believe 'that he is beginning to reign with Christ.

Chapter 3

It is written that 'the just man liveth by faith.'[1] If you are a just man and live by faith, if you truly believe [in God], why do you, who are destined to be with Christ and secure in the promise of the Lord, not rejoice that you are called to Christ and be glad that you are free from the devil? Finally, Simeon, the just man who was truly just, who with full faith kept the commandments of God, when the answer had been given him from heaven that he would not die before he had seen Christ, and when Christ as an infant had come into the temple with His mother, knew in spirit that Christ was now born, concerning whom it had been foretold to him before, and on seeing Him he knew that he himself would quickly die. Happy, therefore, at the death that was now at hand and untroubled at the approaching summons, he took the child into his hands and blessing God, he cried out and said: 'Now thou dost dismiss thy servant, O Lord, according to thy word in peace, because my eyes have seen thy salvation,'[2] proving surely and bearing witness that then do the servants of God have peace, then do they have a free, then a tranquil repose, when we on being released from the storms of the world have sought the harbor of our abode and eternal security, when on this death being accomplished

1 Rom. 1.17.
2 Luke 2.29.

we have to come to immortality. For that is our peace, that our sure tranquility, that our steadfast and firm and ever-lasting security.

Chapter 4

For the rest, what else is waged daily in the world but a battle against the devil, but a struggle with continual onsets against his darts and weapons? With avarice, with lewdness, with anger, with ambition, we have a conflict; with the vices of the flesh, with the allurements of the world, we have a continual and stubborn fight. The mind of man besieged and surrounded on all sides by the assault of the devil with difficulty opposes these foes one by one, with difficulty resists them. If avarice is cast to the ground, lust springs up; if lust is put down, ambition takes its place; if ambition is disdained, anger provokes, pride puffs up, drunkenness invites, envy destroys harmony, jealousy severs friendships. You are forced to curse, which the divine law prohibits; you are compelled to swear, which is forbidden.

Chapter 5

So many persecutions the mind endures daily, by so many dangers is the heart beset. And does it delight to remain here long, amidst the devil's weapons, when we should rather earnestly desire and wish to hasten to Christ aided by a death coming more speedily, since He Himself instructs us, saying: 'Amen, amen, I say to you, that you shall lament and weep, but the world shall rejoice: you shall be sorrowful but your sorrow shall come into joy?'[1] Who would not long to be free from sorrow? Who would not hurry to come to joy? Now when our sorrow will come to joy, our Lord Himself again tells us, saying: 'I will see you again, and your heart shall rejoice; and your joy no man shall take from you.'[2] Since, then, to see Christ is to rejoice, and since none of us can have joy unless he shall see Christ, what blindness or what madness it is to love the afflictions and punishments and tears of the world and not rather to hurry to the joy which can never be taken from us.

Chapter 6

But this happens, beloved brethren, because faith is lacking, because no one believes those things to be true which God promises, who is truthful and whose word is eternal and steadfast to those who believe. If an influential and reputable man were to promise you something, you would have confidence in his promise and you would not believe that you would be deceived or cheated by the man who you knew stood by his words and actions. God is speaking to you, and do you waver faithless in your unbelieving mind? God promises immortality and eternity to you leaving this world, and do you doubt? This is not to know God at all. This is to offend Christ, the Teacher of believing, by the sin of disbelief. This is, though one is in the Church, not to have faith in the House of Faith.

---

1 John 16.20.
2 John 16.22.

Chapter 7

What an advantage it is to depart from the world Christ Himself the teacher of our salvation and welfare makes manifest, who, when His disciples were sorrowful because He said that He was now about to go away, spoke to them saying: 'If you loved me you would indeed be glad, because I go to the Father,'[1] thus teaching and showing that there should be rejoicing rather than sorrowing when the dear ones whom we love depart from the world. And mindful of this fact, the blessed Apostle Paul sets this down in his Epistle and says: 'For to me to live is Christ; and to die is gain,'[2] counting it the greatest gain to be no longer held by the snares of the world, to be no longer subject to any sins and faults of the flesh, but, released from tormenting afflictions and freed from the poisoned jaws of the devil, to set out, at Christ's summons, for the joy of eternal salvation.

Chapter 8

Now it troubles some that the infirmity of this disease carries off our people equally with the pagans, as if a Christian believes to this end, that, free from contact with evils, he may happily enjoy the world and this life, and, without having endured all adversities here, may be preserved for future happiness. It troubles some that we have this mortality in common with others. But what in this world do we not have in common with others as long as this flesh, in accordance with the law of our original birth, still remains

---

1 John 14.28.
2 Phil. 1.21.

common to us? As long as we are here in the world we are united with the human race in equality of the flesh, we are separated in spirit. And so, until this corruptible element puts on incorruptibility and this mortal element receives immortality and the spirit conducts us to God the Father, the disadvantages of the flesh, whatever they are, we have in common with the human race. Thus when the earth is barren with scanty production famine excepts no one; thus when a city has been taken by a hostile attack, bondage ruins all its inhabitants together; and when clear skies keep back the rain there is the one drought for all; and when craggy rocks destroy a ship the shipwreck is common to all on board without exception; and eye trouble and attacks of fevers and every ailment of the members we have in common with others as long as this common flesh is borne in the world.

Chapter 9

Nay, rather, if the Christian recognizes and understands under what condition, under what law he has believed, he will know that he must labor more in the world than others, as he must carry on a greater struggle against the assault of the devil. Divine Scripture teaches and forewarns, saying: 'Son, when thus comest to the service of God, stand in justice, and in fear, and prepare thyself for temptation,'[1] and again: 'in thy sorrow endure, and in thy humiliation keep patience, for gold and silver are tried in the fire.'[2]

---

1 Eccli. 2.1.
2 Eccli. 2.4,5.

Chapter 10

Thus Job, after the losses of his property, after the deaths of his children, and after being grievously tormented also by ulcers and worms, was not vanquished but was tried, who, showing the patience of his devout mind in the very midst of his afflictions and sufferings says: 'Naked came I out of of my mother's womb, and naked also shall I go under the earth; the Lord gave, and the Lord hath taken away; as it seemeth best to the Lord so is it done: blessed be the name of the Lord.'[1] And when his wife also urged him in impatience at the severity of his suffering to utter something against God in complaining and hateful language, he answered and said: 'Thou hast spoken like one of the foolish women: if we have received good things at the hand of God shall we not endure the evil? In all these things which befell him Job sinned not by his lips in the sight of the Lord.'[2] And, therefore, the Lord God bears witness to him, saying: 'Hast thou noticed my servant Job? there is no one like him in the earth, a man without complaint, truthful and serving God.'[3] And Tobias, after his splendid works, after the many glorious commendations of his mercy, having suffered blindness of the eyes, fearing and blessing God in his adversity, by that very affliction of his body increased in praise. And him also his wife tried to corrupt, saying: 'Where are your acts of clemency? Behold what you are suffering!'[4] But he steadfast and firm in his fear of God and armed for all en-

---

1 Cf. Job. 1.21.
2 Job. 2.10.
3 Job. 1.8. Sabatier notes that this reading occurs also in St. Augustine.
4 Tob. 2.14 (16). Cyprian's quotation of this passage is similar to the Greek.

durance of suffering by the faith of his religion did not yield
in his affliction to the temptations of his weak wife, but deserved more of God through his greater patience. And afterwards the angel Raphael praises him and says: 'It is honorable to reveal and confess the works of God. For when
Sarra and I prayed I offered the memory of your prayer
before the splendor of God: and because you buried the
dead, likewise, and because you did not hesitate to rise and
leave your dinner and you went and buried the dead, I was
sent even to tempt you. And again, God sent me to cure
you and Sarra your daughter-in-law: for I am Raphael one
of the seven holy angels who stand and serve before the
splendor of God.'[5]

Chapter 11

This endurance the just have always had; this discipline
the apostles maintained from the law of the Lord, not to
murmur in adversity, but to accept bravely and patiently
whatever happens in the world, since the Jewish people always offended in this, that they murmured very frequently
against God, as the Lord God testifies in Numbers, saying:
'Let their murmuring cease from me and they shall not die.'[1]
We must not murmur in adversity, beloved brethren, but
must patiently and bravely bear with whatever happens, since
it is written: 'A contrite and humble heart God does not
despise.'[2] In Deuteronomy also the Holy Spirit through Moses
admonishes us, saying: 'The Lord God shall afflict thee and

5 Tob. 12.11-15.

1 Num. 17.25 (10).
2 Ps. 50.19.

cast famine on thee and shall examine in thy heart if thou
hast kept his precepts well or not,'[3] and again: 'The Lord
your God tempts you to know if you love the Lord your
God with your whole heart and with your whole mind.'[4]

Chapter 12

Thus Abraham pleased God because, in order to please
God, he neither feared to lose his son nor refused to commit
parricide. You cannot lose your son by the law and the chance
of mortality, what would you do if you were ordered to kill
your son? The fear of God and faith ought to make you
ready for all things. Though it should be the loss of private
property, though it should be the constant and violent affliction of the members by wasting diseases, though it should be
the mournful and sorrowful tearing away from wife, from
children, from departing dear ones, let not such things be
stumbling blocks for you, but battles; nor let them weaken
or crush the faith of the Christian, but rather let them reveal
his valor in the contest, since every injury arising from present
evils should be made light of through confidence in the blessings to come. Unless a battle has gone before there cannot
be a victory; when a victory has been won in the conflict
of battle, then a crown also is given to the victors. The pilot
is recognized in the storm, in the battle-line the soldier is
tested. Light is the boast when there is no danger; conflict
in adversity is the trial of truth. The tree which is firmly
held by a deep root is not shaken by onrushing winds, and
the ship which has been framed with strong joints is beaten

3 Deut. 8.2.
4 Deut. 13.3.

by the waves but is not staved in; and when the threshing floor treads out the harvest the strong hard grain scorn the winds; the empty straw is whirled and carried away by the breeze.

Chapter 13

Thus also the Apostle Paul, after shipwrecks, after scourgings, after many grievous tortures of the flesh and body, says that he was not harassed but was corrected by adversity, in order that while he was the more heavily afflicted he might the more truly be tried. There was given to me, he says, a sting of my flesh, an angel of Satan, to buffet me lest I be exalted. For which thing thrice I besought the Lord, that it might depart from me. And He said to me: 'My grace is sufficient for thee: for power is made perfect in infirmity.'[1] When, therefore, some infirmity and weakness and desolation attacks us, then is our power made perfect, then our faith is crowned, if though tempted it has stood firm, as it is written: 'The furnace trieth the potter's vessels, and the trial of affliction just men.'[2] This finally is the difference between us and the others who do not know God, that they complain and murmur in adversity, while adversity does not turn us from the truth of virtue and faith, but proves us in suffering.

---

1 2 Cor. 12.7-9.
2 Eccli. 27.5 (6) .

Chapter 14

That now the bowels loosened into a flux exhaust the strength of the body, that a fever contracted in the very marrow of the bones breaks out into ulcers of the throat, that the intestines are shaken by continual vomiting, that the blood-shot eyes burn, that the feet of some or certain parts of their members are cut away by the infection of diseased putrefaction, that, by a weakness developing through the losses and injuries of the body, either the gait is enfeebled, or the hearing impaired, or the sight blinded, all this contributes to the proof of faith.'[1] What greatness of soul it is to fight with the powers of the mind unshaken against so many attacks of devastation and death, what sublimity to stand erect amidst the ruins of the human race and not to lie prostrate with those who have no hope in God, and to rejoice rather and embrace the gift of the occasion, which, while we are firmly expressing our faith, and having endured sufferings, are advancing to Christ by the narrow way of Christ, we should receive as the reward of His way and faith, He himself being our judge! Let him certainly be afraid to die who, not having been reborn of water and the spirit is delivered up to the fires of hell. Let him be afraid to die who is not listed under the cross and passion of Christ. Let him be afraid to die who will pass from this death to a second death. Let him be afraid to die whom, on departing from the world, the eternal flame will torment with everlasting punishments. Let him be afraid to die to whom this is granted by a longer delay, that his tortures and groans meanwhile may be deferred.

---

1 Despite this vivid description of the effects of the plague, the plague itself cannot be definitely identified with any of the great pestilences known to modern times.

Chapter 15

Many of us are dying in this mortality, that is many of us are being freed from the world. This mortality is a bane to the Jews and pagans and enemies of Christ; to the servants of God it is a salutary departure. As to the fact that, without any discrimination in the human race, the just also are dying with the unjust, it is not for you to think that the destruction is a common one for both the evil and the good. The just are called to refreshment, the unjust are carried off to torture; protection is more quickly given to the faithful; punishment to the faithless. We are improvident, beloved brethren, and ungrateful for divine favors and we do not recognize what is being granted us. Behold the virgins are departing in peace, going safely with their glory, not fearing the threats of the antichrist and his corruptions and his brothels. Boys are escaping the danger of their unsettled age; they are coming happily to the reward of their continency and innocence. No longer does the delicate matron dread the racks, having by a speedy death gained escape from the fear of persecution and the hands and tortures of the hangman. Through their panic at the mortality and the occasion the fearful are aroused, the negligent are contrained, the slothful are stimulated, the deserters are compelled to return, the pagans are forced to believe, the old members of the faithful are called to rest, for the battle a fresh and numerous army of greater strength is being gathered, which, entering service in the time of the mortality, will fight without fear of death when the battle comes.

Chapter 16

What a significance, beloved brethren, all this has! How suitable, how necessary it is that this plague and pestilence, which seems horrible and deadly, searches out the justice of each and every one and examines the minds of the human race; whether the well care for the sick, whether relatives dutifully love their kinsmen as they should, whether masters show compassion to their ailing slaves, whether physicians do not desert the afflicted begging their help, whether the violent repress their violence, whether the greedy, even through the fear of death, quench the ever insatiable fire of their raging avarice, whether the proud bend their necks, whether the shameless soften their affrontry, whether the rich, even when their dear ones are perishing and they are about to die without heirs, bestow and give something! Although this mortality has contributed nothing else, it has especially accomplished this for Christians and servants of God, that we have begun gladly to seek martyrdom while we are learning not to fear death. These are trying exercises for us, not deaths; they give to the mind the glory of fortitude; by contempt of death they prepare for the crown.[1]

Chapter 17

But perhaps someone may object and say: 'Now in the present mortality this is a source of sorrow to me that I who had been prepared for confession and had dedicated myself with my whole heart and with all my courage to the endur-

---

2 This picture of conditions in Carthage during the plague is repeated by Cyprian in Demetr. 10, and by Pontius, *Vita* 9.

ance of suffering, am deprived of my martyrdom,[1] since I am being forestalled by death.' In the first place, martyrdom is not in your power but in the giving of God, and you cannot say that you have lost what you do not know whether you deserved to receive. Then, secondly, God is a searcher of the reins and heart and the observer and judge of hidden things; He sees and praises and approves you. And He who perceives that your virtue ready will give a reward for virtue. Had Cain already killed his brother when he was offering his gift to God? And yet God in His foresight condemned beforehand the murder contemplated in his mind. Just as in that instance the evil thought and pernicious design was foreseen by a provident God, so also in the case of the servants of God among whom confession is contemplated and martyrdom is conceived in the mind, the intention dedicated to good is crowned, with God as judge. It is one thing for the intention to be lacking for martyrdom; it is another thing for martyrdom to have been lacking for the intention. Such as the Lord finds you when He summons, such likewise also does He judge you, since He himself bears witness and says: 'and all the churches shall know that I am the searcher of reins and heart.'[2] For God does not ask for our blood but our faith; for neither Abraham nor Isaac nor Jacob was put to death, but, nevertheless, honored for the merits of their faith and righteousness, they have deserved to be first among the patriarchs, and to their feast is gathered whosoever is found faithful and just and praiseworthy.

---

1 Cf. *Epist.* 10.5 and 12.1 for similar expressions of comfort for those who had been denied martyrdom.
2 Apoc. 2.23.

Chapter 18

We should remember that we ought to do not our will but God's will, in accordance with the prayer which the Lord has ordered us to say daily. How absurd it is and how perverse that, while we ask that the will of God be done, when God calls us and summons us from this world, we do not at once obey the command of His will! We struggle in opposition and resist and in the manner of obstinate slaves we are brought with sadness and grief to the sight of God, departing from here under the bond of necessity, not in obedience to our will, and we wish to be honored with the rewards of heaven by Him to whom we are coming unwilling. Why then do we pray and entreat that the kingdom of heaven may come, if earthly captivity delights us? Why in our often repeated prayers do we ask and beseech that the day of His kingdom may come quickly, if there are greater longings and stronger desires to serve the devil here than to reign with Christ?

Chapter 19

Finally, in order that the signs of divine providence might become more clearly manifest that the Lord, foreknowing the future, looks to the true salvation of His own, when one of our colleagues and fellow priests, exhausted by illness and alarmed in the face of approaching death, prayed for a respite for himself, there stood beside him, as he prayed and was now almost dying, a young man venerable in honor and majesty, noble in stature, shining in aspect, and upon whom as he stood before it the human sight could scarcely look with the eyes of the flesh, except that on the point of departing from the world it could already regard such a one. And he, not without a certain indignation of mind and voice, spoke angrily and said: 'You are afraid to suffer, you do not wish to depart, what shall I do with you?'—the voice of one rebuking and warning, who, anxious at the thought of presecution but untroubled at the summons of death, does not yield to the present longing but looks to the future. Our brother and colleague who was about to die heard what he was to say to others. For he who heard this at the point of death heard it to the end that he should say it; he did not hear it for himself, but for us. For what could he learn now as he was about to depart? Nay rather he learned it for us who remain that, through knowing that the priest who prayed for a respite was rebuked, we might know what is of benefit to all.

Chapter 20

How often it has been revealed to us ourself also, the least and the last, how frequently and manifestly have I been commanded, through God's vouchsaving, that I should bear witness constantly, that I should preach publicly that our brethren who have been freed from the world by the summons of the Lord should not be mourned, since we know that they are not lost but sent before; that in departing they lead the way; that as travellers, as voyagers are wont to be, they should be longed for, not lamented; and that dark clothing should not be worn here, inasmuch as they have already assumed white garments there; and that no occasion should be given to the pagans to censure us deservedly and justly, on the ground that we grieve for those who we say are living with God, as if entirely destroyed and lost, and that we do not show by the testimony of the heart and breast the faith which we declare in speech and word! We are prevaricators of our hope and faith, if what we say seems pretended, feigned, falsified. It profits nothing to show forth virtue in words and destroy truth in deeds.

Chapter 21

Finally, the Apostle Paul censures, rebukes, and blames any who are sorrowful at the death of their dear ones. 'We will not,' he says, 'have you ignorant, brethren, concerning them that are asleep, that you be not sorrowful, even as others who have no hope. For if we believe that Jesus died, and rose again; even so them who have slept through Jesus, will God bring with him.'[1] He says that they are sorrowful at the death of their dear ones who have no hope. But we who live in hope and believe in God and have faith that Christ suffered for us and rose again, abiding in Christ and rising again through Him and in Him, why are we ourselves either unwilling to depart hence from this world, or why do we mourn and grieve for our departing ones as if they were lost, since Christ our Lord and our God himself admonishes us and says: 'I am the resurrection: he that believeth in me, although he be dead, shall live: And everyone that liveth and believeth in me, shall not die forever'?[2] If we believe in Christ let us have faith in His words and promises, that we who are not to die forever may come in joyful security to Christ with whom we are to conquer and reign for eternity.

---

1 Thess. 4.13.
2 John 11.25.

Chapter 22

As to the fact that meanwhile we die, we pass by death to immortality, nor can eternal life succeed unless it has befallen us to depart from here. This is not an end, but a passage and, the journey of time being traversed, a crossing over to eternity. We would not hasten to better things? Who would not pray to be more quickly changed and reformed to the image of Christ and to the dignity of heavenly grace, since the Apostle Paul declares: But our conversation, he says, is in heaven: from whence also we look for the Lord Jesus Christ, who will reform the body of our lowness, made like to the body of his glory?[1] Christ the Lord also promises that we shall be such, since He prays to His Father for us that we may be with Him and may rejoice with Him in the eternal abodes and heavenly kingdom saying: Father, I will that where I am, they also to whom thou has given me may be with me and may see my glory which thou hast given me before the world was made. He who is to come to the abode of Christ, to the glory of the heavenly kingdom, ought not to grieve and mourn, but rather, in accordance with the promise of the Lord, in accordance with faith in the truth, to rejoice in this his departure and translation.

Chapter 23

Thus, finally, we find that Enoch also, who pleased God, was transported, as divine Scripture testifies in Genesis and says: 'And Enoch pleased God and was not seen later because

1 Phil. 3.20,21.

218 SAINT CYPRIAN

God took him.'[1] This was to have been pleasing in the sight of God: to have merited being transported from this contagion of the world. But the Holy Spirit teaches also through Solomon that those who please God are taken from here earlier and more quickly set free, lest, while they are tarrying too long in this world, they be defiled by contacts with the world. 'He was taken away lest wickedness should deter his understanding, for his soul pleased God; therefore he hastened to bring him out of the midst of iniquity.'[2] Thus also in the psalms the soul devoted to its God in spiritual faith hastens to God, as it is written: 'How lovely are thy dwellings, O God of hosts. My soul longs for and hastens to the courts of God.'[3]

Chapter 24

It is for him to wish to remain long in the world whom the world delights, whom the world allures by blandishing and deceiving with the enticements of worldly pleasure. Furthermore, since the world hates a Christian, why do you love that which hates you and not rather follow Christ who has redeemed and loves you? John in his Epistle cries out and tells us and exhorts us, lest in our pursuit of carnal pleasures we should love the world. 'Love not the world,' he says, 'nor the things which are in the world. If any man love the world, the charity of the Father is not in him. For all that is in the world is the concupiscence of the flesh and the concupiscence of the eyes and the ambition of the world, which is not of the Father but is of the concupiscence of the world.

1 Gen. 5.24.
2 Wisd. 4.11.
3 John 2.15.

And the world will pass away, and the concupiscence thereof; but he that does the will of God abideth forever even as God also abideth forever.'[1] Rather, beloved brethren, with sound mind, with firm faith, with rugged virtue, let us be ready for every manifestation of God's will; freed from the terror of death, let us think of the immortality which follows. Let us show that this is what we believe, so that we may not mourn the death even of our dear ones and, when the day of our own summons comes, without hesitation but with gladness we may come to the Lord at His call.

Chapter 25

While the servants of God have always had to do this, they ought to do it all the more quickly, now with the world falling and oppressed by the storms of attacking evils, so that we who perceive that grievous things have already begun and know that more grievous things are imminent should count it the greatest gain if we should speedily depart from here. If the walls of your house were tottering from decay, if the roof above were shaking, if the house now worn out, now weary, were threatening imminent ruin with its framework collapsing through age, would you not leave with all speed? If, while you were sailing, a wind and furious storm with waves violently agitated were presaging future shipwreck, would you not more quickly seek port? Behold, the world is tottering and collapsing and is bearing witness to its ruin, not now through age, but through the end of things;[1] and you are not thanking God, you are not congratulating yourself that, rescued by an earlier departure, you are being freed from ruin and shipwrecks and threatening disasters!

---

1 Cf. *Mort.* 2.

Chapter 26

We should consider, beloved brethren, and we should reflect constantly that we have renounced the world and as strangers and foreigners we sojourn here for a time. Let us embrace the day which assigns each of us to his dwelling, which on our being rescued from here and released from the snares of the world, restores us to paradise and the kingdom. What man, after having been abroad, would not hasten to return to his native land? Who, when hurrying to sail to his family, would not more eagerly long for a favorable wind that he might more quickly embrace his dear ones? We account paradise our country, we have already begun to look upon the patriarchs as our parents. Why do we not hasten and run, so that we can see our country, so that we can greet our parents? A great number of our dear ones there await us, parents, brothers, children; a dense and copious throng longs for us, already secure in their safety but still anxious for our salvation. How great a joy it is both for them and for us in common to come into their sight and embrace! What pleasure there in the heavenly kingdom without fear of death, and with an eternity of life the highest possible and everlasting happiness; there the glorious choir of apostles, there the throng of exultant prophets, there the innumerable multitude of martyrs wearing crowns on account of the glory and victory of their struggle and passion, triumphant virgins who have subdued the concupiscence of the flesh and body by the strength of their continency, the merciful enjoying their reward who have performed works of justice by giving food and alms to the poor, who in observing the precepts of the Lord have transferred their earthly patrimony to the treasuries of heaven! To these, beloved brethren, let us hasten with eager longing! let us pray that it may befall us speedily to be with them, speedily to come to Christ. May God see this our purpose. May Christ look upon this resolution of our mind and faith, who will give more ample rewards of His charity to those whose longings for Him have been greater.

WORKS
AND ALMSGIVING

Translated by

ROY J. DEFERRARI, Ph.D.
The Catholic University of America

WORKS AND ALMSGIVING

THE TREATISE on *Works and Almsgiving,* like that on *Mortality,* owes its origin to the pestilence which raged in Carthage and its vicinity, especially from 252 to 254, and they both appeared at about the same time. It is an exhortation to efficacious charity towards our neighbor. Many people had been impoverished and left destitute by the devastating plague. Here was an opportunity for Christian charity to help the needy, the sick, and the dying.

Cyprian develops the idea that the giving of alms is not only a duty for the Christian but also an advantage as a principle to sanctification and a leaven to divine favor. If through human weakness and frailty man has fallen into sin after baptism, almsgiving has been provided for securing salvation a second time. He supports his idea by examples and declarations taken from holy Scripture. The current maxims on the inconveniences of too great liberality are brushed aside. The ideal way of life for the Christian is that of the first community of Christians whereby, according to the Acts of Apostles, all shared whatever they possessed with one another, and all desired to possess nothing except what they had in common.

225

WORKS AND ALMSGIVING

Chapter 1

MANY AND GREAT, most beloved brethren, are the divine blessings by which the abundant and copious clemency of God the Father and of Christ has both worked and is always working for our salvation, because the Father has sent His son to preserve us and to quicken us that He might be able to restore us, and because the son wished to be sent and to be called the son of man that He might make us the sons of God. He humbled Himself that He might raise up the people who before were prostrate; He was wounded that He might cure our wounds; He served that He might draw those served away to liberty. He underwent death that He might hold forth immortality to mortals. These are the many and great gifts of divine mercy. But still further, what providence and what great clemency that is, that we are provided for by a plan of salvation so that more abundant care is taken for man's salvation who has already been redeemed! For when the Lord had come and healed the wounds which Adam had borne and had cured the old poisons of the serpent, He gave him when made whole a law not to sin anymore lest something more serious happen to him in his sinning. We were restricted and shut within a narrow limit by the prescription of innocence. And the infirmity of

227

human frailty would have no resource nor accomplish anything, unless again divine goodness came to the rescue and by pointing out the works of justice and mercy opened a way to safeguard salvation, so that by almsgiving we may wash away whatever pollutions we later contract.[1]

Chapter 2

The Holy Spirit speaks in the Scriptures, saying: 'By alms and by faith sins are cleansed.'[1] Surely not those sins which had been contracted before, for they are purged by the blood and sanctification of Christ. Likewise again he says: 'As water quenches fire, so do alms quench sin.'[2] Here also it is shown and proved that just as with laver of the waters of salvation the fire of Gehenna is extinguished, so by almsgiving and good works the flame of sins is quenched. And because the remission of sins is once granted in baptism, constant and continuous labor acting in the manner of baptism again bestows the indulgences of God. This does the Lord also teach in the Gospel. For when it was noted that His disciples were eating without first having washed their hands, He replied and said: 'He who made the inside made also the outside. Truly give alms, and behold all things are clean to you,'[3] that is, teaching and showing that not the hands but the heart ought to be washed and that the foulness within

---

1 By this time the reader must have noticed the beauty of Cyprian's exordiums and perorations, the marks of an excellent orator.

---

1 Cf. Prov. 16.6.
2 Cf. Eccli. 3.33.
3 Cf. Luke 11.40,41.

rather than without ought to be taken away, but that he who cleanses what is within has cleansed also what is without and when the mind has been made clean he has begun to be clean in skin and body. But furthermore advising and showing how we can be pure and cleansed, He added that alms must be given. The merciful One advises that mercy be shown, and, because He seeks to save those whom He redeemed at a great price, He teaches that those who have been polluted after the grace of baptism can be cleansed again.

Chapter 3

So, most beloved brethren, let us acknowledge the saving gift of divine indulgence by cleansing and purging our sins; let us, who cannot be without some wound of conscience, care for our wounds with spiritual remedies. Let no one so flatter himself on his pure and immaculate heart that relying on his innocence he think that medicine should not be applied to his wounds, since it is written: 'Who shall boast that he has a pure heart or who shall boast that he is clean from sins?'[1] and since again John lays down and says in his Epistle: 'If we say that we have no sin, we deceive ourselves and the truth is not in us.'[2] But if no one can be without sin, and whoever says that he is without fault is either proud or foolish, how necessary, how kind is the divine clemency which, since it knows that certain later wounds are not lacking to those already healed, gave salutary remedies for the care and healing of the wounds anew.

---

1 Cf. Prov. 20.9.
2 1 John 1.8,9.

Chapter 4

Finally, most beloved brethren, never has the divine admonition failed and been silent in the Old as well as the New Testament in always and everywhere urging the people of God to works of mercy, and, as the Holy Spirit prophesies and exhorts, in ordering everyone, who is being instructed unto hope of the heavenly kingdom, to practice almsgiving. The God of Isaias commands and orders: 'Cry out in strength,' he says, 'and spare not; lift up thy voices as with a trumpet; announce to my people their sins, and to the house of Jacob their crimes.'[1] And when He had ordered their sins to be charged upon them and when He had set forth their iniquities with the full force of His indignation, and had said that they could not make satisfaction for their sins, not even if they resorted to prayers, nor even if they rolled in sackcloth and ashes could they soften God's anger, yet in the last part showing that God can be placated by almsgiving alone, he added saying: 'Break thy bread with the hungry and bring into thy house those who lack a roof. If you see one naked, clothe him, and thou shalt not despise the offspring of thy seed. Then shalt thy light break forth seasonably, and thy garments shall speedily arise, and thy justice shall go before thee and the brightness of God shall surround thee. While you shall yet speak, He shall say 'Lo, here I am.'[2]

---

1 Cf. Isa. 58.1-9.
2 Cf. Isa. 58.7,8.

Chapter 5

The remedies for propitiating God have been given in the words of God himself; divine instructions have taught that God is satisfied by just works, that sins are cleansed by the merits of mercy. And in Solomon we read: 'Shut up alms in the heart of the poor, and it shall obtain help for thee against all evil.'[1] And again: 'He that stoppeth his ears lest he hear the weak, shall himself call upon God, but there will be none to hear him.'[2] For he will not be able to merit the mercy of God who himself has not been merciful, nor will gain any request from the divine love by his prayers, who has not been humane toward the prayer of the poor. This likewise the Holy Spirit declares in the Psalms and proves, saying: 'Blessed is he who thinks of the needy and the poor; the Lord will save him in the evil day:'[3] Mindful of these precepts Daniel, when king Nebuchodonosor being frightened by an unfavorable dream was worried, gave a remedy for averting evils by obtaining divine help, saying: 'Wherefore, O king, let my counsel be acceptable to thee, and redeem thy sins with alms, and thy iniquities with works of mercy to the poor, and God will be patient with thy sins.'[4] When the king did not obey him, he suffered the misfortunes and trouble which he had seen, which he might have escaped and avoided, if he had redeemed his sins by alms-giving. The angel Raphael also testifies likewise, and urges that alms-giving be practiced freely and generously, saying: 'Prayer is good with fasting and alms, for alms delivereth from death,

---

1 Eccli. 29.15.
2 Prov. 21.13.
3 Ps. 40.2.
4 Dan. 4.24.

and itself purges away sins.'[5] He shows that our prayers and fastings are of less avail, unless they are aided by almsgiving, that entreaties alone are able to obtain little, unless they are made sufficient by the addition of deeds and works. The angel reveals and makes manifest and confirms that our petitions are made efficacious by almsgiving; that by almsgiving life is redeemed from dangers; that by almsgiving souls are freed from death.

Chapter 6

Most beloved brethren, we do not so bring forth these things, so as not to approve by the testimony of truth what the angel Raphael said. In the Acts of the Apostles faith in the fact is established, and it is discovered by the proof of the accomplished and fulfilled fact that by almsgiving souls are freed not only from the second but also from the first death. When Tabitha who had been very much given to just works and almsgiving fell sick and died, Peter was summoned to the body of the lifeless one. And when he had come quickly in accord with apostolic charity, there stood around him widows weeping and beseeching, showing the cloaks and tunics and all the garments which they had previously received, and praying for the deceased not by their words but by her own works. Peter felt that what was sought in this way could be obtained and that Christ's help would not be lacking the widows as they pleaded, since He Himself was clothed in the clothing of widows. So when, falling on his knees, he had prayed and as a proper advocate of the widows and the poor had brought the prayers entrusted to him to

5 Cf. Tob. 12.8,9.

the Lord, turning to the corpse which already washed lay on
the bier, he said: 'Tabitha, arise in the name of Jesus Christ.'[1]
Nor did He fail to bring aid to Peter at once, who had said
in His Gospel that whatever should be asked in His name
was granted. Therefore, death is suspended and the spirit
is restored and, as all marvelled and were amazed, 'the body
is revived and quickens for the light of this world anew. So
powerful were the merits of mercy, so much did just works
avail! She who had conferred upon suffering widows the
assistance for living deserved to be recalled to life by the
petition of widows.

Chapter 7

Thus in the Gospel the Lord, the Teacher of our life and
Master of eternal salvation, quickening the populace of believers, and providing for them forever when quickened,
among His divine mandates and heavenly precepts, commands and prescribes nothing more frequently than that we
continue in almsgiving and not depend on earthly possessions
but rather lay up heavenly treasures. 'Sell,' He says, 'Your
possessions, and give alms';[1] and again: 'Do not lay up for
yourselves treasures on earth, where rust and moth consume,
and where thieves break in and steal; but lay up for yourselves
treasures in heaven where neither rust nor moth consumes
and where thieves do not break in. For where thy treasure is,
there also will be thy heart.'[2] And when He wished to show

---

1 Cf. Acts. 9.40

---

1 Luke 12.33.
2 Matt. 6.19-21.

the man who had been made perfect and complete by the
observance of the law, He said: 'If you wish to be perfect,
go, sell all that you have, and give to the poor, and thou
shalt have treasure in heaven, and come follow me.'[3] Likewise in another place He says that a merchant of heavenly
grace and a purchaser of eternal salvation, after ridding
himself of all his possessions, ought to purchase from the
amount of his patrimony the precious pearl, that is eternal
life, precious by the blood of Christ. He says: 'The kingdom
of heaven is like a merchant seeking good pearls. When he
finds a pearl of great price, he goes and sells all that he has
and buys it.'[4]

Chapter 8

Finally also He calls those sons of Abraham, whom He
perceives active in aiding and nourishing the poor. For when
Zachaeus said: 'Behold I give one-half of my possessions to
the poor, and if I have defrauded anyone of anything, I
restore it four-fold,' Jesus replied: 'Today salvation has come
to this house, since he, too, is a son of Abraham.'[1] For if
Abraham believed in God, and it was accounted to him unto
righteousness, surely he who gives alms according to the
precept of God believes in God; and he who possesses the
truth of faith keeps the fear of God; moreover, he who keeps
the fear of God considers God in showing mercy to the poor.
For so he labors, because he believes in God, because he
knows that those things are true which have been predicted

---

3 Matt. 19.21.
4 Matt. 13.45,46.

---

1 Luke 19.8,9.

in the words of God, and that holy Scripture cannot lie, that unfruitful trees, that is, sterile men, are cut off and cast into the fire, that the merciful are called to the kingdom. He also in another place calls the laborious and fruitful faithful, but to the unfruitful and sterile he denies the faith, saying: 'If in the wicked mammon you have not been faithful, who will entrust to you what is true? And if in the case of what belongs to another you have not been faithful, who will give you what is your own?'[2]

Chapter 9

But you are afraid and you fear lest, if you begin to act very generously, your patrimony come to an end because of your generous action and you perchance be reduced to penury; be undisturbed on this score, be secure. That cannot be ended, whence expenditure is made in the service of Christ, whence the heavenly work is celebrated. I do not promise you on my own authority but I vouch for it on the faith of holy Scriptures and on the authority of the divine promise. The Holy Spirit speaks through Solomon and says: 'He that giveth to the poor shall never be in want; but he that turns away his eyes shall be in great want,'[1] showing that the merciful and those who do good can never be in want, that rather the sparing and the sterile later come to want. Likewise the blessed apostle Paul full of the grace of the Lord's inspiration says: 'He who provides seed for the sower, also will give bread to eat and will multiply your seed

---

2 Luke 19.11,12.

---

1 Cf. Prov. 28.27.

and will increase the growth of the fruits of your justice, so that in all things you may be enriched.'[2] And again: 'The administration of this service not only will supply what the saints lack but will abound also through much action of gratitude in the Lord,'[3] because, while the action of thanks is directed to God by the prayer of the poor for our alms-giving and good works, the wealth of him who does good is increased by the retribution of God. And the Lord in the Gospel, already considering the hearts of such men and de-nouncing the faithless and unbelievers with prescient voice, bears witness and says: 'Be not anxious, saying: 'What shall we eat or what shall we drink or what shall we put on?' For after all these things the Gentiles seek. For your Father knows that you have need of all these things. But seek first the kingdom and the justice of God, and all these things shall be added to you.'[4] He says that all things are added and given over to those who seek the kingdom and the justice of God; for the Lord says that, when the day of judgment shall come they, who have labored in His Church, are ad-mitted to receive the kingdom.

Chapter 10

Your fear lest your patrimony perchance fail you, if you begin to do good generously from it, and you do not know, wretched man that you are, that, while you are afraid lest your personal wealth be failing, life itself, and salvation fail, and, while you are anxious lest any of your possessions be

---

2 Cf. 2 Cor. 9.10,11.
3 Cf. 2 Cor. 9.12.
4 Matt. 6.31-33.

diminished, you do not take notice that you yourself, a lover of mammon rather than of your soul, are being diminished, and, while you are afraid lest for your own sake you lose your patrimony, you yourself perish for the sake of your patrimony. Therefore, the Apostle well exclaims, saying: 'We brought nothing into this world, and we can take nothing out. Therefore, having food and clothing, with these let us be content. But those who seek to become rich fall into temptation and a snare, and into many harmful desires which plunge a man into destruction and damnation. For covetousness is the root of all evils and some seeking wealth have made shipwreck of their faith and have involved themselves in many troubles.'[1]

Chapter 11

Do you fear lest your patrimony perchance fail, if you begin to act generously from it? For when did it happen that resources could fail a just man, when it is written: 'The Lord will not afflict the soul of the just with famine.'[1] Elias in the desert is fed by ministering ravens, and a meal is prepared in heaven for Daniel when he was inclosed in a den of lions by order of the king; and you fear lest food be lacking for you while you do good and deserve well of the Lord, when He Himself in the Gospel bears witness for a reproach of those of doubtful mind and little faith and says: 'Look at the birds of the air; they do not sow or reap, or gather into barns; yet your heavenly Father feeds them.

---

1 1 Tim. 6.7-10.

1 Prov. 10.3.

Are not you of more value than they?"[2] God feeds the fowls, and daily sustenance is furnished the sparrows, and to those creatures who have no sense of things divine neither drink nor food is lacking. Do you think that to a Christian, do you think that to a servant of God, do you think that to one devoted to good works, do you think that to one dear to the Lord anything will be lacking?

Chapter 12

Unless you think that he who feeds Christ is not himself fed by Christ, or that earthly things will be lacking to those upon whom heavenly and divine things are bestowed, whence this incredulous thinking, whence that impious and sacrilegious contemplation? What is a faithless heart doing in a home of faith? Why is he called and spoken of as Christian who does not believe in Christ at all? The name of pharisee is more befitting you. For when the Lord in the Gospel was discoursing about almsgiving, and forewarned faithfully and for our salvation that we should make friends for ourselves of our earthly lucre by provident good works, the Scripture added after this the following words: 'Now the Pharisees, who were very fond of money, were listening to all these things, and they were sneering at him.'[1] Certain persons like these we now see in the Church, whose closed ears and blinded hearts admit no light from the spiritual and saving warnings, of whom we should not marvel that they contemn the servant in his discourses, when we see that the Lord Himself is contemned by such.

---

2 Matt. 6.26.

1 Luke 6.14.

Chapter 13

Why do you give approbation to yourself with these empty and foolish thoughts, as if you were withheld from good works by fear and solicitude for the future? Why do you hold forth certain shadows and illusions of a vain excuse? By all means confess what is the truth, and, since you cannot deceive those who know, set forth the hidden and secret things of your mind. The shadows of sterility have besieged your mind, and with the withdrawal from it of the light of truth the deep and profound darkness of avarice has blinded your carnal heart. You are the captive and slave of your money; you are tied by the chains and bonds of avarice, and you whom Christ had already freed are bound anew. You save money which, when saved, does not save you; you accumulate a patrimony which burdens you with its weight; and you do not remember what God replied to the rich man who boasts with foolish glee over the abundance of his abounding harvest. 'Thou fool,' He said, 'this night thy soul is demanded. Therefore, the things that thou hast provided, whose will they be?'[1] Why do you alone watch over your riches? Why do you pile up the burden of your patrimony, that the richer you have been in the sight of the world, the poorer you may become in the sight of God? Divide your returns with your God; share your gains with Christ; make Christ a partner in your earthly possessions, that He also may make you co-heir of His heavenly kingdom.

---

1 Luke 12.20.

Chapter 14

You err and are deceived, whoever think yourself rich in the world. Hear the voice of your Lord in the Apocalypse as He rebukes such men with just reproaches. He says: 'You say: "I am rich and have grown wealthy and I have need of nothing," and you do not know that you are wretched and poor and blind and naked. I counsel you to buy of me gold refined by fire, that you may become rich, and that you may put on a white garment, and that the shame of your nakedness may not appear; and anoint your eyes with eye-salve that you may see.'[1] You, therefore, who are wealthy and rich buy for yourself from Christ gold that has been tried by fire, that you can be pure gold, when your impurities have been burnt out as if by fire, if you are cleansed by almsgiving and just works. Buy for yourself a white garment, that you, who according to Adam had been naked and were before frightful and unseemly, may be clothed in the white raiment of Christ. And you who are a rich and wealthy matron annoint your eyes not with the stibium of the devil but with the eye-salve of Christ, that you can come to see God, when you merit God by character and good works.

Chapter 15

But you, who are such, cannot do good works in the Church; for your eyes suffused with blackness and covered with the shadows of night do not see the needy and the poor. Do you, rich and wealthy, think that you celebrate the Lord's Feast, who do not at all consider the offering,

---

1 Cf. Apoc. 3.17,18.

who come to the Lord's Feast without a sacrifice, who take
a part of the sacrifice which the poor man offered? Behold
in the Gospel the widow mindful of the heavenly precepts,
doing good in the very midst of the pressures and hardships
of poverty, casting two mites which were her only possessions
into the treasury; and when the Lord noticed and saw her,
considering and weighing her good work not as from a patrimony but as from the heart, He answered and said: 'Truly
I say to you that this widow has put more than all into the
offering for God. For all these out of their abundance have
put in as gifts to God, but she out of her want has put in
all that she had to live on.'[1] A greatly blessed and glorious
woman, who even before the day of judgment merited to
be praised by the voice of the Judge. Let the rich man be
ashamed of his sterility and his misfortunes. A widow, that
is, a poor widow is found with an offering, and, although
all things that are given are conferred upon orphans and
widows, she gives who ought to receive, that we may know
what punishment awaits the rich man, when by this teaching
the poor also should do good. And that we may understand
that these works are given to God and that he, whoever
does these, deserves well of God, Christ calls this 'gifts of
God' and points out that the widow has placed two mites
among the gifts of God, that it can be more and more
manifest that he who pities the poor lends to God.

Chapter 16

Let not this fact, dearest brethren, restrain and recall the
Christian from good and just works, that anyone think that

---

1 Luke 21.3,4.

he can be excused for the benefit of his children, since in spiritual contributions we should consider Christ who has professed that He receives them and not prefer our fellow-servants to our children but the Lord, for he instructs and warns us, saying: 'He who loves father or mother more than me is not worthy of me, and he who loves son or daughter more than me is not worthy of me.'[1] Likewise in Deuteronomy for the strengthening of the faith and the love of God, similar things are written. He says: 'Those who say to their father and mother: "I do not know you," and who have not known their children, these have kept thy precepts and observed thy covenant.'[2] For if we love God with our whole heart, we should prefer neither parents nor children to God. This also John lays down in his Epistle, that there is no love of God in those whom we see unwilling to do good to the poor. He says: 'He who has the goods of this world and sees his brother in need and closes his heart to him, how does the love of God abide in him?'[3] For if by almsgiving to the poor God is made our debtor, and when it is given to the least it is given to Christ, there is no reason for anyone preferring earthly things to heavenly, nor placing human things before divine.

Chapter 17

Thus when the widow in the third Book of Kings, after all had been consumed in the drought and the famine, had made a cake upon the ashes from the little meal and oil that was left, and after this had been eaten was about to die

---

1 Matt. 10.37.
2 Deut. 33.9.
3 1 John 3.17.

with her children, Elias came and asked that there first be given him to eat and that she with her children then eat what was left of this. She did not hesitate to obey nor did the mother put her children before Elias in the famine and want. Rather, there is done in the sight of God what pleases God; promptly and gladly what was sought is offered, and a portion is not given out of the abundance but the whole from a little, and another is fed before her hungry children, and in poverty and hunger food is not considered before mercy, so that while in a saving work life according to the flesh is contemned the soul spiritually is preserved. Thus Elias, playing the part of Christ, and showing that he returns to each according to his mercy, replied and said: 'Thus saith the Lord: the pot of meal shall not fail, nor the cruse of oil diminish until the day wherein the Lord will give rain upon the earth.'[1] According to her faith in the divine promise what she promised was multiplied and heaped high for the widow, and, as her just works and merits of mercy took on growth and increase, her vessels of meal and oil were filled. Nor did the mother deprive her children of what she gave Elias, but rather she conferred upon her children what she did kindly and piously. But she did not yet know Christ; not yet had she heard his precepts; she did not, as one redeemed by His cross and His passion, repay food and drink for His blood, so that from this it is apparent how much he sins in the world, who, placing himself and his children before Christ, preserves his wealth, and does not share his plentiful patrimony with the indigent poor.

1 3 Kings 17.14.

Chapter 18

But yet there are many children in the house, and the number of offspring prevents you from applying yourself to good works. Still by this very fact you ought the more to do good works, since you are the father of many pledges. There are more for whom you beseech the Lord; the sins of many must be redeemed; the consciences of many must be purged; the souls of many must be freed. As in this unholy life the greater the number of your children the greater is the expense for their nourishment and sustenance, so too in the spiritual and heavenly life the greater the abundance of your children, the greater also should be the outlay of good works. Thus Job offered numerous sacrifices for his children, and as great as was the number of pledges in his home, so great a number of victims also was offered to God. And since daily there cannot be lacking some sinning in the sight of God, daily sacrifices were not lacking with which the sins could be wiped away. Scripture proves this when it says: 'Job, a true and just man, had seven sons and three daughters, and he cleansed them by offering for them sacrifices to God according to their number, and for their sins one calf.'[1] If then you truly love your sons, if you show them the full and paternal sweetness of love, you should do good works more that you may commend your sons to God by your righteous works.

---

1 Cf. Job. 1.2-5.

Chapter 19

Do not consider him the father of your children who is both temporary and weak, but obtain Him who is the eternal and strong Father of spiritual children. Assign to Him your wealth which you are keeping for your heirs; let Him be your children's guardian, their caretaker, their protector with his divine majesty against all worldly injuries. When your patrimony is entrusted to God, the state does not seize it, nor does the tax-collector assail it, nor any forensic calumny overturn it. The inheritance is placed in safety, which is kept under God's care. This is to provide for the future of your dear charges; this is to provide for your future heirs with paternal love according to the faith of the holy Scripture which says: 'I have been younger and I have grown old, and I have not seen the just man foresaken nor his seed begging bread. All the day he shows mercy and lends, and his seed shall be blessed.'[1] And again: 'He who lives without reproach in justice shall leave behind him blessed children.'[2] So you as a father are a transgressor and a betrayer, unless you look out faithfully for the welfare of your children, unless you attend to their salvation with religious and true love. Why are you eager for earthly rather than heavenly patrimony? Why do you prefer to commed your children to the devil rather than to Christ? You sin twice and commit a twofold and double crime both because you do not make ready the help of God the Father for your children and because you teach your children to love their patrimony more than Christ.

---

1 Cf. Ps. 36.25,26.
2 Cf. Prov. 20.7.

Chapter 20

Be to your children such a father as was Tobias. Give useful and salutary precepts to your pledges such as he gave to his son; command your children as he too commanded saying: 'And now, sons, I command you, serve God in truth, and do before Him what pleases Him; and command your children that they do justice and almsdeeds, and that they be mindful of God, and bless His name on every occasion.'[1] And again: 'And all the days of thy life, son, have God in mind, and do not transgress His commandments. Do justice all the days of thy life, and do not walk the way of iniquity, for when you act truthfully there will be respect of your works. Give alms out of thy substance, and turn not away thy face from any poor person, for so shall it come to pass that the face of the Lord shall not be turned from thee. As you have, my son, so give: if you have an abundant supply, give alms the more from that. If you have a little, give a share from that little. Have no fear when you bestow an alms; you are storing up for yourself a good reward for the day of necessity, for alms delivers from death and does not suffer one to go into darkness. Alms provides a great confidence for all who do it before the most high God.'[2]

Chapter 21

What sort of gift is it, dearest brethren, whose setting forth is celebrated in the sight of God? If in a gift of the Gentiles it seems grand and glorious to have proconsuls or emperors

---

1 Cf. Tob. 14.10-12.
2 Cf. Tob. 4.5-12.

present, and the preparation and the expense on the part of the givers is greater that they may be able to please greater personages, how much more illustrious and greater is the glory of the giver to have God and Christ as spectators; how much richer in this case is the preparation, and extensive the expense to be set forth, when the powers of heaven assemble for the spectacle, all the angels assemble, when not a four-horsed chariot or a consulship is sought for the giver, but eternal life is presented, nor is the empty and temporary favor of the mob laid hold of, but the everlasting reward of the heavenly kingdom is received.

Chapter 22

And that the lazy and the sterile and those doing nothing about the fruit of salvation because of their covetousness for many may be more ashamed, that the blush of their shame and disgrace may the more strike upon their sordid conscience, let each one place before his eyes the devil with his servants, that is, with the people of perdition and of death springing forth into the midst, the people of Christ, with Him present and judging, calling forth in a contest of comparison, as he says: 'I, for those whom you see with me have neither received blows nor have I undergone stripes, nor carried the cross, nor poured forth blood, nor have I redeemed my family at the cost of suffering and blood; moreover, neither do I promise them a heavenly kingdom nor, after restoring immortality, do I again recall them to paradise; and what precious, what grand gifts, sought out with what excessively long labor do they prepare for me with the most sumptuous devices, after mortgaging or selling their possessions; and, unless a respectable demonstration follows, they are cast out with reproaches and hissings, and sometimes they are almost stoned to death by the fury of the populace. Point out such almsgivers of yours, O Christ, those rich men, those men affluent with abounding wealth, whether in the Church where you preside and watch they give forth a gift of this kind, after pawning and distributing their possessions, rather after transferring them to heavenly treasures by exchanging what they possess for something better. By those transitory and earthly gifts of mine no one is fed, no one is clothed, no one is sustained by the solace of any food or drink. Everything in the midst of the madness of the giver and the mistake of the spectator are perishing because of the prodigious and foolish vanity of frustrating pleasures. There among your poor You are clothed and You are fed; You promise those who give alms eternal life; and scarcely are Your people, who are honored by You with divine wages and heavenly rewards, made equal to mine.'

Chapter 23

What do you reply to all this, dearest brethren? In what manner do we defend the sacrilegious sterilities and the minds of the rich covered by a kind of night of shadows; by what excuse do we clear them, we who are less than the servants of the devil, so as not to repay Christ even in small measure for the price of His passion and blood? He has given us precepts; He has taught what His servant should do; promising a reward to those who give alms and threatening punishment to the sterile; He has set forth His sentence; He has foretold what His judgment would be. What excuse can there be for him who ceases to do so; what defense for the sterile? Unless it be that, unless the servant does what is commanded, the Lord will do what He threatens. He even says: 'When the Son of man shall come in His majesty, and all angels with Him, then He will sit on the throne of His glory; and before Him will be gathered all the nations, and He will separate them one from another, as the shepherd the sheep from the goats, and He will set the sheep on His right hand, but the goats on the left. Then the king will say to those who are on His right hand: "Come, ye blessed of my Father, take possession of the kingdom prepared for you from the foundation of the world; for I was hungry and you gave me to eat; I was thirsty and you gave me to drink; I was a stranger and you took me in; naked and you covered me; I was sick and you visited me; I was in prison and you came to me." Then the just will answer Him saying: "Lord, when did we see hungry, and feed thee; or thirsty, and give thee drink? And when did we see thee a stranger, and take thee in; or naked, and clothe thee? Or when did we see thee sick, or in prison, and come to thee?" Then the king answering will say to them, "Amen I say to you, as long as you did it for one of these, the least of my brethren, you did it for me." Then he will say to those who are on His left hand: 'Depart from me, accursed ones, into the everlasting fire which my Father has prepared for the devil and his angels. For I was hungry and you did not give me to eat; I was thirsty and you gave me no drink; I was a stranger and you did not take me in; naked, and you did not clothe me; sick, and in prison, and you did not visit me." Then they also will answer and say to Him: "Lord, when did we see Thee hungry, or thirsty, or a stranger, or naked, or sick, or in prison, and did not minister to Thee?" And He will answer them: "Amen, I say to you, as long as you did not do it for one of these least ones, you did not do it for me." And these will go away into everlasting fire, but the just into everlasting life."[1] What greater declaration could Christ have made to us? How more could He have stimulated the works of our justice and mercy than by having said that whatever is offered to the poor and the needy is offered to Him, and by having said that He is offended unless offering is made to the needy and the poor? So that he in the Church, who is not moved by consideration of his brother, may indeed be moved by contemplation of Christ, and he who does not give thought to his fellow servant in trouble and in need may indeed give thought to the Lord abiding in that very one whom he despises.

Chapter 24

And so, most beloved brethren, let us whose fear is inclined toward God, and whose minds, after spurning and trampling upon the world, are turned to heavenly and divine things to deserve well of the Lord, offer obedience with full faith, devoted minds, and continual good works. Let us give Christ earthly garments that we may receive heavenly clothing. Let us give worldly food and drink that together with Abraham and Isaac and Jacob we may come to the heavenly banquet. Lest we reap little, let us sow very much. While there is time, let us take thought for security and eternal salvation, as Paul, the Apostle, advises saying: 'Therefore, while we have time, let us do what is good to all men, but especially to those who are of the household of faith. And

---

1 Cf. Matt. 25.31-46.

in doing good let us not grow tired, for in due time we shall reap.'[1]

Chapter 25

Let us consider, most beloved brethren, what the assemblage of believers did under the Apostles, when at the very beginning the mind flourished with greater virtues, when the faith of believers was warm with a fervor of faith still new. Then they sold their homes and estates, and gladly and generously offered the proceeds to the Apostles for distribution among the poor, by selling and distributing their earthly patrimony transferring their estates there where they might receive the fruits of an eternal possession, there preparing homes where they might begin to live always. Such was their abundance in good works then as was their unity in love, as we read in the Acts of the Apostles: 'Now the multitude of those who believed were acting with one soul and one mind, nor was there any discrimination among them, nor did they judge anything their own of the goods that they had, but they had all things in common.'[1] This is truly to become a son of God by spiritual birth; this is to imitate the equity of God by the heavenly law. For whatever belongs to God, belongs to all by our appropriation of it, nor is anyone kept from his benefits and gift, nor does anything prevent the whole human race from equally enjoying God's goodness and generosity. Thus the day illuminates equally; the sun radiates, the rain moistens; the wind blows, and for those who sleep there is one sleep; and the splendor of the

---

1 Cf. Gal. 6.9,10.

---

1 Cf. Acts. 4.32.

stars and the moon is common. With this example of equality the possessor on the earth who shares his returns and fruits, while he is fair and just with his gratuitous bounties, is an imitator of God the Father.

Chapter 26

What, dearest brethren, will be that glory of the charitable; how grand and consummate the joy, when the Lord begins to number His people, and, distributing the rewards for our merits and works, to grant heavenly things for the earthly, everlasting for the temporal, great for small, to offer us to the Father to whom he restored us by His sanctification, to bestow eternal immortality on us, for which He has prepared us by the quickening of His blood, to bring us back again to paradise, to open up the kingdom of heaven by the faith and truth of His promise! Let these things cling firmly in our thoughts; let these things be understood with a full faith; let these things be lived with a whole heart; let these things be redeemed by the magnanimity of unceasing good works. Dearest brethren, a glorious and divine thing is the work of salvation [charity], a grand solace for believers, a salutary safeguard of our security, a bulwark of hope, a safeguard of faith, a cure for sin, something placed in the power of the doer, a grand and easy thing, a crown of peace without the danger of persecution, a true and very great gift of God, necessary for the weak, glorious for the strong, aided by which the Christian bears spiritual grace, deserves Christ as judge, and accounts God his debtor. Let us strive gladly and promptly for this palm of the works of salvation; let us all run in the contest of justice as God and Christ look on, and let us, who already have begun to be greater than this life and this world, not slacken our course by a desire for this life and this world. If the day of reward or of persecution comes upon us ready and swift as we run in this contest of good works, the Lord will never fail to give a reward for our merits; in peace He will give to those who conquer a white crown for their good works; in persecution He will give a second crown, a purple one, for our passion.

THE GOOD OF PATIENCE

Translated by
SISTER GEORGE EDWARD CONWAY, S. S. J.
Chestnut Hill College

THE GOOD OF PATIENCE

DE BONO PATIENTIAE is one of the minor works of Cyprian, but is was great enough, with his other works, to have circulated freely throughout East and West for hundreds of years after its author's death.[1] A century and a half later we find St. Augustine writing: 'But having considered and treated all these things, we have now come to that peaceful statement of Cyprian, at the end of the letter [73] which never tires me, though I have read and reread it many times over—so great is the charm of fraternal love which breathes forth from it, so great the sweetness of charity in which it abounds. "As for us, he [Cyprian] says, as far as in our power, we do not contend on the subject of heretics, with our colleagues and fellow bishops. We keep with them divine harmony and the peace of the Lord. . . With patience and gentleness we keep charity

---

1 The diffusion of Cyprian's writings everywhere after his death has been called almost unique in Christian literary history (J. deGhellinck, S. J., *Patristique et Moyn Age* II [Brussels, Paris, 1947] 203-204). And the unusually large number of extant early manuscripts of his works testify to this popularity. In confirmation of this prestige we have citations from St. Jerome (*Epist.* 107.12), Prudentius (*Peristeph.* 13.100-106), Cassiodorus (*De inst. div. litt.* 19), and many other Christian writers. But St. Augustine has surpassed everyone else in his praise of Cyprian. In addition to his ten sermons on St. Cyprian, he has also cited his predecessor more than a hundred times, and always refers to him in terms of the highest praise.

of spirit, the honor of the college, the bond of faith, and the harmony of the priesthood. Because of this also, we have written to the best of our poor ability and with the permission and inspiration of the Lord, a treatise, *The Good of Patience,* which we sent to you, in token of mutual affection." [2] If the letter introducing *The Good of Patience* could evoke such a eulogy, how much more inspiring the work that was composed specifically for the spread of love and patience!

In the ever-present Christian paradox it was an occasion of dispute and rising tension which ensured for us the possession of this appealing work on patience. The simple, but at that time enigmatical, question: "Should a person who has been baptized by a heretic be rebaptized on coming into the Catholic Church?" was the source of all Cyprian's difficulty. This was the subject which brought him almost to the point of rupture with Rome, which severely tested his genuine Christian love, faith, humility, and patience, which so aroused the concern of his priests and people that he found it wise to publish *The Good of Patience* in an effort to 'keep, with gentleness and patience, charity of spirit.'

In the first ages of the Church this question had caused no trouble, but in the beginning of the third century the practice of rebaptizing converts from heresy was adopted in Africa and in Asia Minor.[3] This practice was commended by Tertullian,[4] and, therefore, naturally influenced Cyprian. In the course of the succeeding years the same practice was recommended by councils in Carthage[5] and in Asia Minor.[6] Rome,

---

2 St. Augustine, *De baptismo* 5.22.
3 A. d'Alès, *La théologie* 237, and also in DAFC 1.390-418; P. Godet, *DTC* 3.2460.
4 Tertullian, *De baptismo* 15.
5 c. 220.
6 Councils of Iconium and Synnada, c. 222-235.

however, and Alexandria never fell into the error, but kept
to the primitive practice of simple laying hands on such
converts. The differing practices of East and West spread,
came into conflict, and finally flared into a wide controversy
during the pontificate of Pope Stephen (254-257).

Cyprian's letters concerning the controversy[7] offer enlighten-
ing information on the state of the question and on the concern felt by many because of the differing opinions and
practices, and give, also, his own adamant opinion. In Letter
69, written in the first months of 255, Cyprian answers a
certain Magnus, who had written him asking for a definite
answer on the problem of the validity of the baptism
administered by the followers of Novatian. In this letter,
Cyprian definitely holds that, since Novitian has no power
or authority to confer the sacrament, rebaptism[8] would be
necessary for such converts. Letter 70, a synodal letter of
the same year from thirty-one bishops of Proconsular Africa
to eighteen Numidian bishops, answering their question on
the validity of the baptism administered by heretics or schismatics, restates the view that no one can be baptized outside the Church. In Letter 71, also from the year 255, Cyprian
answers Quintus, a bishop of Mauretania, who had requested
from him the correct teaching on the baptism of heretics and
schismatics, by reiterating his view that the Church is one
and that baptism cannot be outside the Church. Letter 72,
written in the spring of the following year (256), is a synodal
letter from seventy-one bishops of Proconsular Africa and

---

7 Letters 69-75.
8 It must be remarked that Cyprian studiously avoided the use of the
  word 'rebaptism,' in accordance with his belief that, since heretical
  baptism was not baptism, there could not be a rebaptism. Cf. his
  Epist. 71.1: '*Nos autem dicimus eos qui inde veniunt non rebaptizari
  apud nos sed baptizari.*'

Numidia to Pope Stephen. This letter definitely holds their concerted opinion that when a person has been baptized by a heretic admission into the Church demands rebaptism. Letter 73 (spring of 256), a lengthy and important letter on the same topic, is written in answer to Bishop Jubaianus of Mauretania. While answering the bishop's questions, Cyprian gives full and detailed reasons for his belief. This letter, arguing so strongly for his position, yet strives at its close to infuse sentiments of charity and patience in his own heart and those of his fellows. Of the closing paragraph of this letter St. Augustine could say: 'There are many things to be considered in these words, wherein the brightness of Christian charity shines forth in this man who loved the beauty of the Lord's house, and the place where His glory dwelt.'[9] Thus, into the growing uncertainty of many in Africa concerning the proper procedure, and the consequent shortness of temper, Cyprian circulated *The Good of Patience*.

We say circulated because, although Cyprian acknowledges his work to be a *libellus,* a treatise, it contains many of the elements of an early Christian homily or sermon, and, without doubt, was used as sermon material. His frequent use of the title 'beloved brethren,' the repeated and emphatic use of verbs of hearing and speaking in the introductory paragraph, the consistent use of the plural number, the abundant use of examples of a broad, general nature, all point to the theory that probably this was originally a sermon delivered by Cyprian to his flock, which later, in the heat of the baptismal controversy, was adapted and sent by him to Bishop Jubaianus. The treatise was an admirable effort to check his own growing obstinacy and to spread love and patience.

9 St. Augustine, *op. cit.* 5.23.

Looking into the decade of Cyprian's episcopate, and noting the variety and seriousness of the problems which beset him, we find ample justification for his use of the virtue of patience as meditation and sermon material. Two persecutions,[10] almost three,[11] the schism of Novatian,[12] the problem of the lapsed,[13] at least seven provincial councils,[14] the widespread physical and spiritual harm of the plague,[15] the exile and martyrdoms of the Popes,[16] and the grave disagreement on the question of the baptism of heretics—such problems were the proving-grounds of Cyprian's own patience and gave him the right to preach it. Thus his teaching of patience is based not only on the work of Tertullian, but also on his own conviction, experience, and practice.

As with his *The Lord's Prayer* and *The Dress of Virgins*,

---

10 Decian (249-251) ; Valerian (257-260).

11 The edict of Gallus and Volusianus did not bring about the severe persecution which had been feared in 252, although even in the short-lived struggle Pope Cornelius was exiled (Fliche-Martin II 151).

12 The very serious schism which developed when Novatian tried to claim for himself the throne of Peter affected the whole Church.

13 In the Decian persecution many weak Christians denied their faith in Christ, but afterwards repented and sought reconciliation with the Church. The delicate balance of judgment needed in determining the varying degrees of guilt of these lapsed Christians was one of Cyprian's difficult problems.

14 In 251, 252, 253, 254, 255; two in 256. These dates are those of L. Bayard, trans., *Saint Cyprien, Correspondence* (2 vols., Paris 1925) liii.

15 The plague which ravaged the Roman Empire from 251 to 255 tested and found wanting the charity and faith of many weak Christians. Cyprian strove to strengthen their faith and love by his *De mortalitate* and by his own generous example.

16 Pope Fabian was martyred in 250, and Pope Cornelius died in exile in 253. Lucius, who was in charge for less than a year, disappeared in March, 254. St. Stephen ascended the throne of Peter on May 12, 254 and was martyred in August, 257. Sixtus II, Pope for less than a year, was martyred on August 6, 258, just a month before Cyprian. The papal throne was vacant for nearly a year until the Valerian persecution began to subside, when Dionysius of Rome was raised to the office on July 22, 259.

so also with *The Good of Patience,* Cyprian leaned heavily on Tertullian for some of his basic ideas. However, the similarity ends there, for Cyprian's originality is evident in the structure, style, spirit, and vocabulary of his own work. In developing this theme, Cyprian follows the same plan which characterizes his other homiletic treatises like *Mortality,* that is, quotation from Scripture, commentary on it, and application of the lesson to the current circumstances. His treatment of this spiritual work of mercy involves its differentiation from the pagan concept of patience, its origin in God, its practice by Christ and the saints, and its necessity in our lives; its practicality from the moment of birth to death in circumstances physical, moral, spiritual. He urges his people to practice patience with a sweetness, gentleness, strength, and persuasiveness that mark his own possession of it. For him it is a basic virtue. It is the 'pith and marrow' of his concept of Christianity, and can be found hidden or expressed, in all his exhortations.

THE GOOD OF PATIENCE

Chapter 1

IN SPEAKING OF PATIENCE, beloved brethren, and in preaching on its benefits and advantages, how can I better begin than by pointing out the fact that now, just for you to listen to me, I see that patience is necessary, as you could not even do this, namely, listen and learn, without patience. For only then is the word of God and way of salvation effectively learned, if one listens with patience to what is being said. Nor do I find, beloved brethren, among all the ways of heavenly discipline whereby we Christians are directed to seek the God-given rewards of our hope and faith, any other thing that is preferable, whether as more useful for life or more significant in attaining glory, than that we who are subject to the precepts of the Lord with an obedient fear and devotion should maintain patience especially and with extreme care.

Chapter 2

Philosophers also declare that they pursue this virtue, but their patience is as false as is their wisdom, for how can anyone be either wise or patient unless he knows the wisdom and patience of God? For He Himself warns and states concerning those who think that they are wise in this world: 'I will destroy the wisdom of the wise and the prudence of the prudent I will reject.'[1] Likewise the blessed Apostle Paul, filled with the Holy Spirit and sent to call and to form the Gentiles in the faith, declares and teaches, saying: 'See to it that no one ravages you by philosophy and vain deceit, according to human traditions, according to the elements of the world and not according to Christ, for in Him dwells all the fullness of the Godhead.'[2] And in another place he says: 'Let no one deceive himself. If anyone of you thinks he is wise, let him become foolish in the eyes of this world that he may become wise, for the wisdom of this world is foolishness in God's sight. For it is written: I will catch the wise in their craftiness, and again: God knows the thoughts of the wise that they are foolish.'[3] Therefore, if their wisdom is not true, their patience cannot be true either. For if that man who is humble and meek is patient, and yet we see that the philosophers are not humble or meek, but very pleasing to themselves, and displeasing to God by the very fact that they are pleasing to themselves, it is evident that patience is not found where there is the arrogant boldness of an affected freedom and the shameless boasting of the proud and half-naked breast.

Chapter 3

We, however, beloved brethren, are philosophers not in words but in deeds; we exhibit our wisdom not by our dress,

---

1 1 Cor. 1.19 (Isa. 29.14).
2 Col. 2.8,9.
3 1 Cor. 3.18-20 (Job. 5.13; Ps 93.11).

but by truth; we know virtues by their practice rather than through boasting of them; we do not speak great things but we live them. Therefore, as servants and worshipers of God, let us show by spiritual homage the patience that we learn from heavenly teachings. For that virtue we have in common with God. In Him patience has its beginning, and from Him as its source it takes its splendor and dignity. The origin and greatness of patience proceeds from God its Author. The quality that is dear to God ought to be loved by man. The Divine Majesty commends the good which He loves. If God is our Master and our Father, let us strive after the patience of Him who is both our Master and our Father, because it is fitting that servants be obedient and it is not proper that sons be unworthy.

Chapter 4

But how wonderful and how great is the patience of God! He endures most patiently the profane temples, the earthly images and idolatrous rites that have been set up by men in insult to His majesty and honor. He makes the day to rise and the sun to shine equally over the good and the evil.[1] When He waters the earth with showers no one is excluded from His benefits, but He bestows His rains without distinction on the just and the unjust alike. We see that, at the will of God, with an indivisible uniformity of patience toward the guilty and the innocent, the religious and the impious, the grateful and the ungrateful, the seasons obey and the elements serve, the winds blow, fountains flow, harvests increase in abundance, the fruits of the vines ripen, trees are heavy with fruit, the groves become green, and the meadows burst into

---

1 Cf. Matt. 5.45.

flower. And although God is provoked by frequent, yes even continual, offenses, He tempers His anger and patiently waits for the day of retribution which He once foreordained. And although vengeance is in His power, He prefers to be long-suffering in His patience, that is, waiting steadfastly and delaying in His mercy, so that, if it is at all possible, the long career of malice at some time may change, and man, however deeply he is infected with the contagion of error and crime, may be converted to God even at a late hour, as He Himself warns and says: 'I desire not the death of him that dieth, as much as that he return and live.'[2] [And again: 'Return to Me, saith the Lord.'] And again: 'Return to the Lord your God for He is merciful and loving and patient and rich in pity, and one who turns aside His judgment in respect to the evils proposed.'[4] The blessed apostle Paul, calling back the sinner to penance by reminding him of this, putting the question says: 'Or do you despise the wealth of His goodness and His long-suffering and patience? Dost thou not know that the patience and goodness of God is meant to lead you to repentance? But thou, according to thy hardness and thy unrepentant heart, dost treasure up to thyself wrath on the day of wrath and of the revelation of the just judgment of God who will render to every man according to his works.'[5] He said that the judgment of God is just, because it is delayed; because it is postponed repeatedly and for a long time, so that care and thought may be taken for man's eternal life by the long-enduring patience of God. Punishment is finally paid by the impious and the sinner when repentance of the sin can no longer avail.

---

2 Ezech. 18.32.
3 Mal. 3.7.
4 Joel 2.13.
5 Rom. 2.4-6.

Chapter 5

And in order that we may be able to understand more fully, beloved brethren, that patience is an attribute of God and that whoever is gentle, patient, and meek is an imitator of God the Father, when in His gospel the Lord was giving salutary precepts and in revealing the divine counsels was instructing His disciples unto perfection, He made this pronouncement: 'You have heard that it was said: "Thou shalt love thy neighbor and shalt hate thy enemy." But I say to you, love your enemies and pray for those who persecute you, so that you may be the children of your father in heaven, who makes his sun to rise on the good and evil and sends rain on the just and the unjust. For if you love those who love you, what reward shall you have? Do not even the publicans act thus? And if you salute your brethren only, what are you doing more than others? Do not even the Gentiles do that? You, therefore, will be perfect as your heavenly Father is perfect.'[1] He said that it is in this way that the sons of God are made perfect; He showed that it is in this way that we attain our goal, and He taught that we are restored by a heavenly birth, if the patience of God the Father abide in us, if the divine likeness which Adam lost[2] by sin be manifested and shine in our actions. What glory it is to become like God! What wonderful and what great happiness it is to possess among our virtues what can be put on a par with the divine merits!

1 Matt. 5.43-48.
2 Cf. Gen. 3.

Chapter 6

And this, beloved brethren, Jesus Christ, our Lord and our God, did not teach by words only, but He also fulfilled it by His deeds. And He who said that He came down for this purpose, namely, to do the will of His Father,[1] among the other miracles of virtue by which He gave proof of His divine majesty, also preserved and exemplified His Father's patience by His habitual forbearance. Accordingly, His every act right from the very outset of His coming is marked by an accompanying patience;[2] for from the first moment of His descent from the sublimity of heaven to earthly things, He did not disdain, though the Son of God, to put on man's flesh, and although He Himself was not a sinner, to bear the sins of others.[3] Having put aside His immortality for a time, He suffered Himself to become mortal, in order that, though innocent, He might be slain for the salvation of the guilty.[4] The Lord was baptized by His servant, and He, although destined to grant the remission of sins, did not Himself disdain to have His body cleansed with the water of regeneration.[5] He, through whom others are fed, fasted for forty days; He felt hunger and starvation so that those who were famished for the Word of God and grace might be filled with the Bread of Heaven; He engaged in conflict with the devil who tempted Him, and content with having vanquished so formidable an enemy, He did not carry the fight beyond words.[6] He did not rule His disciples as a master

---

1 Cf. John 6.38.
2 Cf. Math. 1.18.
3 Cf. 1 Peter 2.24.
4 Cf. Matt. 1.21.
5 Cf. Matt. 3.13-17; Mark 1.9-11; Luke 3.21-23.
6 Cf. Matt. 4.1-10; Mark 1.12,13; Luke 4.1-13.

rules his slaves, but being both kind and gentle, He loved them as a brother, even deigning to wash the feet of His apostles, so that, while He was such a Master to His servants, He might teach by His example the attitude that a fellow servant ought to have toward his companions and equals.[7] We should not wonder then that He was such a one among His disciples, who was able to tolerate Judas, even to the end, with enduring patience, who could eat with His enemy, who could know the foe in His household and not reveal him,[8] who could not refuse the kiss of His betrayer.[9] But what wonderful equanimity in bearing with the Jews, and what wonderful patience in persuading the unbelieving to accept the faith, in winning the ungrateful by kindness, in responding gently to those who contradicted Him, in enduring the proud with mercy, in yielding with humility to persecutors, in wishing to win over the murderers of the prophets and those persistently rebellious against God even to the very hour of His passion and cross!

Chapter 7

But in that very hour of His passion and cross, before they had come to the cruel act of His slaughter and the shedding of His blood, what violent abuses He listened to with patience, and what shameful insults He endured! He was even covered with the spittle of His revilers,[1] when, but a short time before, with His own spittle He had cured

---

7 Cf. John 13.1-20.
8 Cf. John 13.1-30; Matt. 26.20-25.
9 Cf. Matt. 26.48,49; Mark 14.44,45; Luke 22.47,48.

---

1 Cf. Matt. 26.67,27,30; Mark 15.19.

the eyes of the blind man.[2] He Himself suffered the lash, in whose name His servants now scourge the devil and His angels.[3] He who now crowns the martyrs with eternal garlands was Himself crowned with thorns;[4] He who now gives true palms to the victors was beaten in the face with hostile palms;[5] He who clothes all others with the garment of immortality was stripped of His earthly garment;[6] He who has given the food of heaven was fed with gall;[7] He who has offered us the cup of salvation was given vinegar to drink.[8] He the innocent, He the just, nay rather, Innocence Itself and Justice Itself is counted among criminals,[9] and Truth is concealed by false testimonies. He who is to judge is judged, and the Word of God, silent, is led to the cross. And although the stars are confounded at the crucifixion of the Lord, the elements are disturbed, the earth trembles, night blots out the day,[10] the sun withdraws both its rays[11] and its eyes lest it be forced to gaze upon the crime of the Jews, yet He does not speak, nor is He moved, nor does He proclaim His majesty, even during the suffering itself. He endures all things even to the end with constant perseverance so that in Christ a full and perfect patience may find its realization.

2 Cf. Mark 8.23; John 9.6.
3 Cf. Matt. 27.26; Mark 15.15; John 19.1.
4 Cf. Matt. 27.29; Mark 15.17; John 19.2.
5 Cf. Matt. 26.67; Mark 14.65; Luke 22.64; John 19.3.
6 Cf. Matt. 27.35; Mark 15.24; Luke 23.34; John 19.23..
7 Cf. Matt. 27.34.
8 Cf. Luke 23.36; Matt. 27.48.
9 Cf. Matt. 27.38; Mark 15.27; John 19.18.
10 Cf. Matt. 27.45; Mark 15.33; Luke 23.44.
11 Cf. Matt. 23.45.

Chapter 8

And after such sufferings, He even still receives His murderers if they are converted and come to Him, and with a patience instrumental in saving man, this kind Master closes His Church to no one. Those adversaries, those blasphemers, those persistent enemies of His name, provided they do penance for their offense, provided they acknowledge the crime committed, He not only receives and pardons, but admits to the reward of the kingdom of heaven. What can be called more patient, what more kind? Even he who shed the blood of Christ is given life by the blood of Christ. Such is the wonderful patience of Christ. And unless it were so wonderful in character, the Church would not have Paul the great Apostle.

Church 9

But if we also, beloved brethren, are in Christ, if we put Him on, if He Himself is the way of our salvation, let us who follow in the salutary footsteps of Christ walk by the example of Christ as John the Apostle teaches, saying: 'He who says that he abides in Christ ought himself also to walk just as He walked.'[1] Likewise Peter, on whom the Lord had deemed it worthy for His Church to be founded, writes in his letter and says: 'Christ also has suffered for you, leaving you an example that you may follow in His steps, "Who did no sin, neither was deceit found in His mouth,"

---

1 1 John 2.6.

who when He was reviled, did not revile in turn, when He suffered did not threaten, but yielded Himself to Him who judged Him unjustly.'[2]

Chapter 10

We find accordingly that the patriarchs and prophets and all the just, who set up in their persons the type of Christ as a prefiguration, have treasured nothing in the estimation of their virtues more than the fact that they preserved patience with a strong and stable equanimity. So Abel, as the first one to inaugurate and dedicate martyrdom and the suffering of the just, did not resist or struggle against his brother the parricide, but in humble and gentle patience allowed himself to be killed.[1] So Abraham, trusting God and being the first to establish the root and foundation of faith, when he was tempted in regard to his son, did not hesitate or delay but obeyed the commands of God with a full and devoted patience. And Isaac, prefigured in the likeness of the Lord as victim, was found to be patient when he was offered by his father to be sacrificed.[2] When Jacob was driven from his own land on account of his brother, he departed patiently and, with greater patience afterward, humbly petitioning by means of peaceful gifts, he restored to harmony his still more impious brother and persecutor.[3] Joseph, sold by his brothers and banished, not only patiently forgave but even generously

---

2 1 Peter 2.21-23.

1 Cf. Gen. 4.
2 Cf. Gen. 22.
3 Cf. Gen. 28,33.

and kindly bestowed free grain on them when they came to him.[4] Moses was often scorned by an ungrateful and faithless people and almost stoned, and yet with mildness and patience he prayed to the Lord in their behalf.[5] But what great and wonderful and Christian patience is to be found in David, from whom Christ descended according to the flesh! David often had the opportunity to kill King Saul, his persecutor, who was eager to destroy him. Yet when Saul was subject to him and in his power, David preferred to save his life and did not retaliate on his enemy but, on the contrary, even avenged him when he was killed.[6] In short, many prophets have been killed, many martyrs have been honored with glorious deaths, and all have attained their heavenly crowns through the merit of patience, for a crown for sorrow and suffering cannot be obtained unless patience in sorrow and suffering precede.

Chapter 11

But in order that it can be more manifestly and more fully known, beloved brethren, how useful and necessary patience is, let us consider the judgment of God which, at the very beginning of the world and of the human race, was passed upon Adam who was unmindful of God's command and a transgressor of the law that was imposed.[1] Then we shall know how patient we ought to be in this world, we who are born under the condition that we must struggle here

---

4 Cf. Gen. 37.45.
5 Cf. Num. 14.9.
6 Cf. 1 Kings 26.

---

1 Cf. Gen. 3.17.

under trials and conflicts. 'Because you have listened,' He said, 'to the voice of your wife and you have eaten of that tree from which alone I commanded you not to eat, cursed will be the earth in all your works; in sorrow and mourning you shall eat from it all the days of your life. Thorns and thistles shall it bring forth to you and you shall eat of the food of the field. In the sweat of your brow you shall eat your bread till you return from the ground from which you were taken, since you are earth and shall return to earth.'[2] We are all bound and confined by the bond of this sentence until, having paid the debt of death, we leave this world. We must be in sorrow and lamentation all the days of our life. And we must eat our bread with sweat and labor.

Chapter 12

Hence when anyone is born and enters the abode of this world, he begins with tears. Although even then inexperienced and ignorant of all things, he can do nothing else at his birth except weep. With natural foresight he laments the anxieties and labors of this mortal life, and at its very beginning, by weeping and lamentations his young soul testifies to the trials of the world which he is entering. For he toils and labors as long as he lives here. Nothing else can relieve those who labor and toil more than the consolation derived from patience. This is not only proper and necessary for everyone in this world, but even more for us who, through the onslaughts of the devil, are more harassed; who, standing daily in the front of the battle, are wearied by our combats with an old and well-trained enemy; who, in addition to the various and

---

2 Gen. 3.17-19.

constant attacks of temptations and in the struggle of persecution, must relinquish our patrimonies, who must endure prison, bear chains, give up our lives, who must undergo the sword, beasts, fire, the cross, in short, all kinds of tortures and punishments, relying on our faith and the virtue of patience, for the Lord Himself teaches and says: 'These things I have spoken to you that in Me you may have peace; in the world, however, you will have affliction; but take courage: I have overcome the world.'[1] If, however, we who have renounced the devil and the world suffer trials and the attacks of the devil and the world more frequently and more violently, how much more ought we to maintain patience, with which, as our helper and companion, we may endure all afflictions.

Chapter 13

It is a salutary precept of our Lord and Master: 'He who has endured even to the end will be saved.'[1] And again: 'If you abide in My word, you are My disciples indeed, and you shall know the truth and the truth shall make you free.'[2] We must endure and persevere, beloved brethren, so that, having been admitted to the hope of truth and liberty, we can finally attain that same truth and liberty, because the very fact that we are Christians is a source of faith and hope. However, in order that hope and faith may reach their fruition, there is need of patience. For we do not strive for

---

1 John 16.33.

---

1 Matt. 10.22.
2 John 8.31,32.

present glory, but for a future one, according to what Paul the Apostle teaches, saying: 'For in hope we were saved. But hope that is seen is not hope. For how can a man hope for what he sees? But if we hope for what we do not see, we wait for it with patience.'[3] Patient waiting is necessary that we may fulfill what we have begun to be, and through God's help, that we may obtain what we hope for and believe. Accordingly, in another place, that same Apostle instructs and teaches the just and those who do works and those who lay up for themselves heavenly treasures from the increase of divine interest to be patient also, for he says: 'Therefore while we have time, let us do good to all men, but especially to those who are of the household of faith. And in doing good let us not grow tired, for in due time we shall reap.'[4] He warns lest anyone, through lack of patience, grow tired in his good work; lest anyone, either diverted or overcome by temptations, should stop in the middle of his course of praise and glory and his past works be lost, while those things which had begun to be perfect, cease, as it is written: 'The justice of the just shall not deliver him in what day soever he shall err.'[5] And again: 'Hold fast what thou hast, that no other receive thy crown.'[6] And these words urge patient and resolute perseverance, so that he who strives for a crown, now with praise already near, may be crowned because his patience endures.

---

3 Rom. 8.24-25.
4 Gal. 6.10,9.
5 Ezech. 33.12.
6 Apoc. 3.11.

Chapter 14

Patience, however, beloved brethren, not only preserves what is good, but also repels what is evil. Devoted to the Holy Spirit and cleaving to heavenly and divine things, it struggles with the bulwark of its virtues against the acts of the flesh and the body whereby the soul is stormed and captured. Accordingly, let us look at a few out of many of these acts, so that from these few, all the rest may be understood. Adultery, deceit, homicide, are mortal sins. Let patience be strong and stable in the heart, and then the sanctified body and temple of God will not be corrupted by adultery, innocence dedicated to justice will not be infected by the contagion of deceit, and the hand that has held the Eucharist[1] will not be sullied by the blood-stained sword.

Chapter 15

Charity is the bond of brotherhood, the foundation of peace, the steadfastness and firmness of unity; it is greater than both hope and faith;[1] it excels both good works and suffering of the faith; and, as an eternal virtue, it will abide with us forever in the kingdom of heaven. Take patience away from it, and thus forsaken, it will not last; take away

---

1 In the early ages of the Church it was customary for the faithful to receive the consecrated bread, the Body of the Lord, in their hands and thus to administer Communion to themselves. Cyprian refers to this custom also in *De lapsis* 16.22.26; *Epist.* 58.9. For a detailed account see J. A. Jungmann, S. J., *The Mass of the Roman Rite, Its Origins and Developments* (translated by F. A. Brunner, C. SS. R. [New York 1955]) especially 2 378-386; H. Leclercq, 'Communion,' *DACL* 3.2428-2438; H. Moreau, 'Communion,' *DTC* 3.418-514.

---

1 Cf. 1 Cor. 13.13.

the substance of enduring and tolerating, and it attempts to last with no roots or strength. Accordingly, the Apostle when he was speaking about charity joined tolerance and patience to it, saying: 'Charity is magnanimous, charity is kind, charity does not envy, is not puffed up, is not provoked, thinks no evil, loves all things, believes all things, hopes all things, endures all things.'[2] By this he showed that charity can persevere steadfastly because it has learned how to endure all things. And in another place he says: 'bearing with one another in love, taking every care to preserve the unity of the Spirit in the union of peace.'[3] He proved that neither unity nor peace can be preserved unless brothers cherish one another with mutual forbearance and preserve the bond of unity with patience as intermediary.

Chapter 16

How then will you be able to endure these things—not to swear or curse, not to seek again what has been taken away from you,[1] on receiving a blow to offer the other cheek also to your assailant,[2] to forgive your brother who offends you not only seventy times seven times, but all his offenses without exception,[3] to love your enemies, to pray for your adversaries and persecutors,[4] if you do not have the steadfastness of patience and forbearance? We see what happened in the

2 1 Cor. 13.4,5,7.
3 Eph. 4.2,3.

1 Cf. Luke 6.30.
2 Cf. Matt. 5.39; Luke 6.30.
3 Cf. Matt. 18.21,22.
4 Cf. Matt. 5.44; Luke 6.27,28.

case of Stephen. When he was being killed by the violence and stones of the Jews, he did not ask for vengeance but for-giveness for his murderers, saying: 'O Lord, do not lay this sin against them.'[5] So it was most fitting that the first martyr for Christ who, in preceding by his glorious death the martyrs that were to come, was not only a preacher of the Lord's suffering but also an imitator of His most patient gentleness. What shall I say of anger, of discord, of contention, evils which a Christian ought not to have? Let there be patience in the heart and these evil things can not have a place there; or if they attempt to enter, on being quickly driven out, they depart, so that the heart may continue to be a peaceful dwelling where the God of peace may delight to abide. Accordingly, the Apostle admonishes and teaches, saying: 'Do not grieve the Holy Spirit of God, in whom you were sealed for the day of redemption. Let all bitterness, and wrath, and indignation, and clamor, and reviling, be removed from you.'[6] For if a Christian has withdrawn from the fury and contention of the flesh as from the storms of the sea, and has now begun to be tranquil and gentle in the harbor of Christ, he ought not to admit into his heart either anger or discord, for it is not right for him to render evil for evil or to hate.

Chapter 17

Likewise, patience is also necessary in respect to the various hardships of the flesh and frequent and cruel torments of the body by which the human race is daily wearied and oppressed. For since in that first transgression of God's command

5 Cf. Acts 7.58-60.
6 Eph. 4.30,31.

strength of body departed with immortality, and infirmity entered the body by death, and since strength cannot be regained except when immortality shall have been regained, it is necessary to keep struggling and contending in this state of bodily weakness and infirmity; and this struggle and strife can not be endured without the strength of patience. But different kinds of sufferings are imposed on us to test and prove us, and many forms of temptations are inflicted upon us by loss of wealth, burning fevers, torments of wounds, by the death of dear ones. Nothing else distinguishes the unjust and just the more than this, that in adversities the unjust man complains and blasphemes because of impatience, while the just man is proved by patience, as it is written: 'In thy sorrow endure and in thy humiliation keep patience, for gold and silver are tried in the fire.'[1]

Chapter 18

Thus Job was examined and proved and raised to the pinnacle of praise because of the virtue of patience. How many weapons of the devil were hurled against him! How many torments were inflicted on him! He suffered the loss of his property, he was bereft of his numerous progeny; a master rich in wealth and a father richer in children was suddenly neither master nor father. Cruel wounds attacked his body and a scourge of devouring worms consumed his dissolving and decaying limbs. And lest anything at all might remain which Job had not experienced in his trials, the devil even armed his wife against him, using that ancient device of his wickedness, as if he could deceive and cheat all men

1 Eccli. 2.4,5.

through a woman as he did in the beginning. Nevertheless, Job was not broken by these heavy and continuous assaults, and in spite of these trials and afflictions he extolled the praise of God by his victorious patience. Tobias also, who after his magnificent work of justice and mercy was tempted by the loss of his eyes, endured his blindness with great patience and gained outstanding merit with God through the renown of his patience.

Chapter 19

And, beloved brethren, that the good of patience may shine forth more brightly, let us consider, on the other hand, what evil impatience causes. For as patience is a good of Christ, so, on the contrary, impatience is an evil of the devil; and as the man in whom Christ lives and abides is found to be a patient man, so he is always impatient whose mind is possessed by the wickedness of the devil. Accordingly, let us consider the origins of impatience. The devil bore with impatience the fact that man was made to the image of God, and for this reason was the first to perish and cause to perish. Adam, in violation of the heavenly command, was incapable of resisting the desire of the deadly food and fell into the death of sin; he did not preserve, under the guardianship of patience, the grace received from God. Cain was impatient of his brother's sacrifice and gift and killed him.[1] Because Esau put lower things before higher, he lost his birthright through impatience for the lentils.[2] Why was the Jewish people faithless and ungrateful toward the divine blessings?

---

1 Cf. Gen. 3,4.
2 Cf. Gen. 25.29-34.

Was it not that this crime of impatience first drew them away from God? When they could not bear the delay of Moses speaking with God they dared to demand profane gods, and to proclaim as leader of their journey the head of a calf and an earthly image.[3] They never abandoned this same fault of impatience, but always impatient of the divine teaching and guidance, by killing all their prophets and all just men, they hastened to the cross and to the shedding of the blood of the Lord. Impatience also produces heretics in the Church, and, after the manner of the Jews, it drives them, as rebels against the peace and charity of Christ, to hostile acts and furious hates. And not to be tedious by giving details, all things without exception which patience by its works builds unto glory, impatience reduces to ruin.

Chapter 20

And so, beloved brethren, after the benefits of patience and the evils of impatience have been carefully weighed, let us observe fully and maintain the patience through which we abide in Christ and with Christ are able to come to God. That patience, rich and manifold, is not confined within a narrow compass or restrained by bounds of small extent. The virtue of patience extends widely and its wealth and abundance proceed from a source that has indeed a single name, but with its full-flowing streams it is diffused through many glorious courses, and nothing in our actions can avail towards the full realization of merit which does not take the power for its accomplishment from that source. It is patience that both commends us to God and saves us for God. It is

---

3 Cf. Exod. 32.

that same patience which tempers anger, bridles the tongue, governs the mind, guards peace, rules discipline, breaks the onslaught of lust, suppresses the violence of pride, extinguishes the fire of dissension, restrains the power of the wealthy, renews the endurance of the poor in bearing their lot, guards the blessed integrity of virgins, the difficult chastity of widows, and the indivisible love of husbands and wives. It makes men humble in prosperity, brave in adversity, meek in the face of injuries and insults. It teaches us to pardon our offenders quickly; if you yourself should offend, it teaches you to ask pardon often and with perseverance. It vanquishes temptations, sustains persecutions, endures sufferings and martyrdoms to the end. It is this patience which strongly fortifies the foundations of our faith. It is this patience which sublimely promotes the growth of hope. It directs our action, so that we can keep to the way of Christ while we make progress because of His forbearance. It ensures our perseverance as sons of God while we imitate the patience of the Father.

Chapter 21

And since I know, beloved brethren, that very many, either because of the weight of their pressing injuries or because of resentment toward those who attack them and rage against them, wish to be revenged quickly, I must warn you before I close, that finding ourselves in these storms of a turbulent world and in the midst of the persecutions of the Jews or of the Gentiles or of the heretics, we should patiently await the day of vengeance. We should not hasten to revenge our pain with an angry speed, since it is written: 'Expect Me, saith the Lord, in the day of My resurrection for a testimony, since My judgment is to the congregations of nations that I may receive kings and pour out My anger over them.'[1] The Lord commands us to wait and to endure with a strong patience the day of future vengeance, and He also speaks in the Apocalypse, saying: 'Do not seal up the words of the prophecy of this book, because now the time is close at hand and those who persevere in doing wrong, let them do wrong, and he who is filthy, let him be filthy still, but let the just man still do more just things, and likewise the holy man, holier things. Behold I come quickly! and My reward is with Me, to render to each according to his works.'[2] Therefore, even the martyrs as they cry out and as they hasten to their punishment in the intensity of their suffering are still ordered to wait and to show patience until the appointed time is fulfilled and the number of martyrs is complete. And He said: 'When he opened the fifth seal, I saw under the altar of God the souls of those who had been slain for the Word of God and for their own testimony and they cried with a loud voice saying: How long, O Lord, Holy and True, dost thou refrain from judging and avenging our blood on those who dwell on the earth. And a white stole was given to each of them and they were told to rest for a little while longer until the number of their fellow-servants and brothers, who are to be slain later even as they had been, should be complete.'[3]

---

1 Soph. 3.8.
2 Apoc. 22.10-12..
3 Apoc. 6.9-11.

Chapter 22

But when the divine vengeance for the blood of the just will come, the Holy Spirit declares through the prophet Malachias, saying: 'Behold the day of the Lord comes glowing as a furnace and all the strangers and all the unjust will be as stubble and the coming day shall set them on fire, saith the Lord.'[1] And we read likewise in the psalms, where it is announced that the coming of God the Judge must be venerated because of the majesty of His judgment: 'God our God shall come revealing Himself and He shall not be silent. A fire shall burn before Him and a mighty tempest shall be about Him. He shall call Heaven on high and earth that he may separate His people. Collect for Him His just men, those who place His testimony in sacrifices and the heavens will announce His justice, for God is the Judge.'[2] And Isaias prophesies the same things, saying: 'For behold the Lord will come like a fire and, like a whirlwind, His carriage, to repay vengeance in anger. For in the fire of the Lord they will be judged and by his sword they will be wounded.'[3] And again: 'The Lord God of Hosts shall go forth and shall threaten war; He shall stir up battle and shall cry over his enemies with strength; I have been silent, shall I be silent always?'[4]

---

1 Mal. 4.1.
2 Ps. 49.3-6.
3 Isa. 66.15,16.
4 Isa. 42.13,14.

Chapter 23

But who is He who says that He was silent formerly and will not always be silent? It is surely He who was led as a sheep to the slaughter and who, like a lamb without making a sound before its shearer, did not open His mouth.'[1] Surely it is He who did not cry out and whose voice was not heard in the streets. Surely it is He who was not stubborn and who did not contradict when He offered His back to the scourges and His cheeks to blows and did not turn away His face from their filthy spittle;[3] He, who when He was accused by the priests and elders, answered nothing[4] and, to the amazement of Pilate, kept a most patient silence.[5] He is the One who, although He was silent in His passion, will not be silent later in the day of reckoning. He is our God, that is, the God not recognized by all but by the faithful and those who believe, and when He comes manifesting Himself in His second coming, He will not be silent. For although He was formerly hidden in humility, He will come manifested in power.

Chapter 24

This is the Judge and the Avenger, beloved brethren, that we are to await who, when He revenges Himself, is destined to revenge us, the people of His Church and the number of all the just from the beginning of the world. Let him who

1 Cf. Isa. 53.7.
2 Cf. Isa. 42.2.
3 Cf. Isa. 50.5,6.
4 Cf. Matt. 26.63; Mark 14.61.
5 Cf. Matt. 27.14; Mark 15.5.

hastens and hurries too much to his own revenge consider that He alone who avenges has not yet avenged Himself. [God the Father commanded that His Son be adored and the Apostle Paul, mindful of the divine precept, declares this and says: 'God has exalted Him and has bestowed upon Him that name that is above every name, so that at the name of Jesus all should bend the knee, of those in heaven, on earth, and of those under the earth';[1] and] in the Apocalypse, when John wishes to adore him, the Angel resists him and says: 'Thou must not do this because I am a fellow servant of you and of your brothers. Adore Jesus the Lord.'[2] How wonderful then is Jesus our Lord, and what great patience this is that He who is adored in heaven is not yet avenged on earth! Let us think of His patience, beloved brethren, in our persecutions and sufferings. Let us show the full obedience that is inspired by our expectation of His coming, and let us not hasten with the impious and shameless haste of a servant to defend ourselves before the Lord. Let us rather persevere and let us labor, and watchful with all our heart and steadfast even to total resignation, let us guard the precepts of the Lord, so that when the day of wrath and vengeance comes, we may not be punished with the impious and sinners but may be honored with the just and those who fear God.

---

1 Phil. 2.9,10.
2 Apoc. 22.9.

JEALOUSY AND ENVY

Translated by

ROY J. DEFERRARI, Ph.D.
The Catholic University of America

JEALOUSY AND ENVY

EALOUSY AND ENVY has frequently been associated with *The Advantage of Patience*. In fact, it has been called a companion treatise and intended to complete the discussion of patience. If this is true, its was probably written late in 256 or in the beginning of 257. Pontius, Cyprian's biographer and author of a list of Cyprian's works, places it directly after the treatise on patience, and so seems to support this opinion. However, the so-called Cheltenham list places *Jealousy and Envy* after the *Unity of the Church,* and H. Koch[1] insists that is more closely associated with this and *The Lapsed*, since the Carthaginian and Roman schisms rather than the sacramental controversy form its background. Accordingly, Koch suggests 251 or 252 as the more probable date of composition.

Cyprian first points out that jealousy or envy is a sin, especially grievous since its wickedness is hidden. Its origin is to be traced to the devil. In his usual manner he supports his arguments by quotations from the Bible, in this instance from the Old Testament. Envy and jealousy are poisonous growths that often take root in the Church, and bring forth the fruits of hatred, schism, dissatisfaction, and insubordination. Very properly was hatred of one's fellow man forbidden

---

1 *Cyprianische Untersuchungen* (Bonn 1926) 132-136.

again and again by Christ and His Apostles. Finally, Cyprian exhorts all to love of enemies, setting forth God as an example. He dissuades from the sin of envy by urging the rewards of a united love and a bond of brotherhood.

JEALOUSY AND ENVY

Chapter 1

O BE JEALOUS of the good that you see and to be envious of those better than one's self seems in the eyes of some to be a slight and moderate wrong, most beloved brothers, and, when it is thought to be light and moderate, it is not feared; when it is not feared, it is contemned; when it is contemned, it is not easily avoided; and it becomes a dark and hidden source of destruction, which, when it is not perceived so that it can be avoided by the provident, secretly afflicts improvident minds. But furthermore, the Lord has ordered us to be prudent, and He bade us to be watchful with cautious solicitude, lest the adversary himself ever watchful and always lying in wait, when he has crept into the heart, blow up flames from sparks, make very great things from small ones, and, when he soothes the relaxed and the incautious with a milder air and a softer breeze, after stirring up storms and whirlwinds, contrive the ruin of faith and the shipwreck of salvation and life. So, most beloved brethren, we must be on our guard, and strive with all our strength, so that we may with watchful and full diligence repulse the enemy who rages and directs his shafts against every part of the body where we can be struck or wounded, as Peter the Apostle in his Epistle forewarns and

293

teaches, saying: 'Be sober, be watchful! For your adversary the devil, as a roaring lion, goes about seeking something to devour.'[1]

Chapter 2

He encircles us individually and, like an enemy besieging those enclosed explores the walls, tries whether any part of the members is less stable and less trustworthy, by whose approach penetration to the interior may be effected. He offers to the eyes seductive forms and easy pleasures, so that by sight he may destroy chastity. He tempts the ears with melodious music, that by the hearing of sweet sounds he may relax and enervate Christian vigor. He provokes the tongue by abuse; he instigates the hand by irritating injuries to the viciousness of murder. To make the defrauder, he presents unjust gains; to capture the soul with money, he brings in harmful gains; he promises earthly honors, to destroy heavenly ones; he displays the false, to take away the true; and when he cannot deceive secretly, he threatens boldly and openly, holding out the terror of a turbulent persecution, always restless to conquer the servants of God, and always hostile, crafty in peace, violent in persecution.

Chapter 3

Therefore, most beloved brethren, the mind stands ready and armed against all the deceitful plots or the open threats of the devil, always as prepared to repulse, as the enemy is always prepared to attack. And since his missiles which steal

---

1 Cf. Peter 5.8.

upon us secretly are more frequent and his casting of them more concealed and clandestine, and to the extent that this is not perceived, this attack is the more effectual and more frequent to our injury, let us also be alert to understand and repel these. Among these is the devil of jealousy and envy. If anyone should look deeply into this, he will discover that nothing should be avoided more by a Christian, nothing provided for more cautiously than that one be not caught by envy and malice, that one, being entangled in the blind snares of a deceitful enemy, when brother by envy turns to hatred of brother, not himself unwittingly perish by his own sword. That we may be able to gather this more fully and perceive it more clearly, let us recur to its source and origin. Let us see from what jealousy begins, both when and how. For more easily will so pernicious an evil be avoided, if both the origin and magnitude of the same is known.

Chapter 4

For this reason the devil at the very beginnings of the world was both the first to perish and to ruin [others]. He supported by his angelic majesty, acceptable and dear to God, after he had seen man made to the image of God, with malevolent envy plunged into jealousy, not casting down another by the instinct of jealousy before he himself was cast down by jealousy, a captive before capturing, ruined before ruining; when at the instigation of envy he deprived man of the grace of immortality which had been given him, he himself lost that which he had been before. Of such a nature is the evil, most beloved brethren, by which an angel fell, by which that high and glorious sublimity could have been circumvented, and overturned, by which he who deceived was deceived. Therefore, envy rages on earth, when he who is about to perish from jealousy obeys the master of perdition, when he who becomes jealous imitates the devil, just as it is written: 'But by the envy of the devil, death came into world.' So they who are on his side imitate him.

Chapter 5

Hence finally begin the first hatreds of the new brotherhood; hence the abominable parricides, when the unjust Cain is jealous of the just Abel, when the evil persecutes the good out of jealousy and envy. So strong was the fury of emulation for the consummation of the crime, that neither love of brother nor the enormity of the crime nor fear of God nor the punishment of the sin was considered. He was unjustly oppressed who had been the first to show justice; he endured hatred who did not know how to hate; he was slain impiously who while dying did not fight back. Jealousy was the cause of Esau having been hostile to his brother Jacob, for because Jacob had received the blessing of his father, Esau burned with the firebrands of envy into a persecuting hatred. As for Joseph's having been sold by his brothers, the cause for the selling came from jealousy. After he set forth simply, as brother to brothers, the prosperity which had been shown him in visions, their malevolent minds erupted into envy. What other than the stimulus of jealousy provoked Saul the king also to hate David, to desire to kill that innocent, merciful man, patient with a gentle mildness, by often repeated persecutions? Because, when Goliath had been killed and so great an enemy had been slain by divine assistance and condescension, the admiring people burst forth into approbation unto praise of David, Saul through envy conceived the furies of hatred and persecution. Not to make my account long by naming individuals, let us consider the destruction of a people that perished once and for all. Did not the Jews perish on this account, since they preferred to envy rather than to believe in Christ? Disparaging the great things that He did, they were deceived by a blinding jealousy and they were unable to open the eyes of their hearts so as to recognize His divine works.

Chapter 6

Now considering these matters, most beloved brethren, let us vigilantly and courageously fortify our hearts, which have been dedicated to God, against so great an evil destructiveness. Let the death of others be of advantage for our salvation; let the punishment of the imprudent confer health upon the cautious. There is, however, no ground for anyone thinking that such an evil as that is contained under one form or is confined to brief limits and within a narrow territory. The manifold and fruitful destruction of jealousy is widely spread. It is the root of all evils, the source of disasters, the nursery of sins, the substance of transgressions. From it hatred arises; animosity proceeds from it. Jealousy inflames avarice, when one cannot be content with its own on seeing another richer. Jealousy incites ambition when one sees another more exalted in honors. When jealousy blinds our senses and reduces the secrets of the mind to its sway, fear of God is scorned, the teaching of Christ is neglected, the day of judgment is not provided for. Pride inflates; cruelty embitters; faithlessness prevaricates; impatience agitates; discord infuriates; anger grows hot; nor can he who has become a subject of an alien power restrain or rule himself. Hence the bond of the Lord's peace is broken; hence fraternal charity is violated; hence truth is adulterated, unity is broken, there is a plunging into heresies and schisms, when priests are disparaged, when bishops are envied, when one complains that he himself rather has not been ordained or disdains to tolerate another who has been placed over him. Hence the proud man is recalcitrant and rebellious out of jealousy, perverse out of envy, out of animosity and jealousy an enemy not of the man but of the honor.

Chapter 7

Of such a sort, indeed, is the gnawing worm of the soul. What a plague of one's thoughts, how great a rust of the heart to be jealous either of the virtue or of the happiness of another, that is, to hate in him either his own merits or divine blessings, to turn the good things of another to one's own evil, to be tormented by the prosperity of illustrious men, to make the glory of others one's own punishment, to apply, as it were, hangmen to one's own heart, to bring tortures to one's own thoughts and feelings to lacerate us with intestinal tortures, to beat the secret places of the heart with the claws of malevolence! No food can be delightful to such men, no drink pleasing. There is always sighing and groaning and suffering, and, since jealousy is never set forth by the envious, day and night the heart is besieged and torn with intermission. Other evils have a terminus, and whatever sin is committed is brought to an end by its consummation. In the adulterer the crime ceased when the act of lust has been perpetrated, in the killer the crime rests when the homicide has been committed; and the possession of the booty brings the rapacity of the thief to an end; and the completion of the deception places moderation on the deceiver. Jealousy has no terminus; it is a continually abiding evil and a sin without end, and as he who is envied proceeds with greater success, to this extent does the envious one burn to a greater heat with the fires of envy.

Chapter 8

Hence the threatening look, the savage appearance, pallor in the face, trembling of the lips, gnashing of teeth, mad words, unbridled insults, a hand prompt for the violence of murder, and even if the hand is for the time without a sword, yet it is armed with the hatred of an infuriated mind. And thus the Holy Spirit says in the psalms: 'Be not jealous of him who walks well in his way.'[1] And again: 'The wicked man plots against the just man and gnashes his teeth against him. But God will laugh at him, for He sees that his day will come.'[2] The blessed Apostle Paul designates and notes these when he says: 'The venom of asps is under their lips: and their mouth is full of cursing and bitterness. Their feet are swift to shed blood; contrition and calamity are in their ways, for they have not known the way of peace, nor is the fear of God before their eyes.'[3]

---

1 Cf. Ps. 36.7.
2 Cf. Ps. 16.12,13.
3 Cf. Rom. 3.13-18.

Chapter 9

The evil is much lighter and the danger less, when the limbs are wounded by a sword. The cure is easy where the wound is manifest, and when a remedy comes to its assistance what is seen is quickly brought to health. The wounds of jealousy are concealed and hidden, nor do they admit the remedy of a healing cure, which have concealed themselves with blind pain within the lurking places of the conscience. Whoever of you are envious and malignant, you are seen as you are, crafty, pernicious, and hostile to those whom you hate. You are the enemy of no one's well-being more than of your own. Whoever he is whom you persecute with jealousy, will be able to escape and avoid you. You cannot escape yourself. Wherever you are, your adversary is with you; the enemy is always in your heart; destruction is shut up within; you are tied and bound with an inescapable chain of links; you are captive with jealousy as your master; and no solaces come to your relief. It is a persevering evil to persecute a man who belongs to the grace of God; it is a calamity without a remedy to hate one who is happy.

Chapter 10

And therefore, most beloved brethren; the Lord, having regard for this danger, lest anyone out of jealousy of his brother fall into the snare of death, when the disciples asked him who among them was the greatest, said: 'He who will be the least among all you, this one shall be the greatest.'[1] He cut off all jealousy by His reply; He eradicated and tore

---

1 Cf. Luke 9.48.

away every cause and basis for envy. It is not permitted him to be envious. There can be no contention among us for exaltation. From humility we grow to the highest accomplishments; we have learned how we may be pleasing. Finally also the Apostle Paul, when instructing and advising how we who, being illuminated by the light of Christ, have evaded the darkness of the conversation of night, may walk in the deeds and in the works of light, writes and says: 'The night is far advanced; but the day is at hand. Let us, therefore, lay aside the works of darkness, and put on the armor of light. Let us walk becomingly as in the day, not in revelry and drunkenness, not in debauchery and wantonness, not in strife and jealousy.' If the shades have receded from your heart, if the night is scattered from it, if gloom has been wiped away, if the splendor of the day has illuminated your senses, if you have begun to be a man of light, carry on the things that are of Christ, because Christ is the Light and the Day.

Chapter 11

Why do you rush into the darkness of jealousy? Why do you involve yourself in a cloud of envy? Why do you extinguish all the light of peace and love by the blindness of ill-will? Why do you return to the devil, whom you had renounced? Why have you become like Cain? For that he is bound by the crime of homicide, whoever has become envious of his brother and holds him in hatred, the Apostle John declares in his letter, saying: 'He who hates his brother is a murderer. And you know that no murderer has life abiding in him.'[1] And again: 'He who says that he is in the light

---

1 Cf. Rom. 13.12,13.

and hates his brother is in the darkness until now, and walks in the darkness and does not know whither he goes because the darkness has blinded his eyes.'[2] He who hates his brother walks in the darkness and does not know where he goes, he says. For he unwittingly goes to Gehenna; ignorant and blind he plunges himself into punishment; withdrawing, that is, from the light of Christ who warns and says: 'I am the light of the world. He who follows me shall not walk in darkness, but will have the light of life.'[3]

But he follows Christ who abides by His precepts, who walks in the way of His teaching, who follows in His footsteps and ways, who imitates what Christ both taught and did, according as Peter also urges and advises, saying: 'Christ has suffered for you, leaving you an example, that you may follow in His steps.'[4]

Chapter 12

We. ought to remember by what name Christ calls His people, by what title He names His flock. He calls them sheep, that Christian innocence may be equated with sheep; He calls them lambs, so that their simplicity of mind may imitate the simple nature of lambs. Why does the wolf lie hidden under sheeps' clothing; why does he who falsely calls himself a Christian dishonor the flock of Christ? What else is the putting on of the name of Christ and not going over the way of Christ than a prevarication of the divine name, than the abandonment of the way of salvation? Since

---

1 Cf. 1 John 3.15.
2 Cf. 1 John 2.9-11.
3 John 8.12.
4 I Peter 2.21.

He himself teaches and says that he comes unto life who has kept the commandments, and he is wise who has heard and done His words, that He also is called the greatest teacher in the kingdom of heaven who has so taught and done, then that will profit the preacher which has been well and usefully preached, if that which is uttered from the mouth is fulfilled by the deeds that follow. But what did the Lord urge more upon His disciples, what among His salutary counsels and heavenly precepts should be guarded and kept more than that with the same love with which He himself loved the disciples, we should also love each other? How, moreover, does he keep either the peace or the love of the Lord, who, because of the intervention of jealousy, can neither be peaceful nor loving?

Chapter 13

So also the Apostle Paul, when he was bringing out merits of peace and love, and when he was strongly asserting that neither almsgivings nor also the passion itself of a confessor and martyr would avail him, unless he had kept the requirements whole and inviolate, added, and said: 'Charity is magnanimous, charity is kind, charity is not jealous,'[1] that is, teaching and showing that he can maintain charity, whoever is magnanimous and kind and free from jealousy and envy. Likewise in another place, when he was advising that a man who has already become full of the Holy Spirit, and a son of God by heavenly birth, should follow nothing but spiritual and divine things, he lays it down and says: 'And I indeed, brethren, could not have spoken to you as to spiritual men, but as to carnal, as to little ones in Christ.

---

1 Cf. 1 Cor. 13.4.

I fed you with milk, not with solid food. For you were not yet ready for it. Nor are you now ready for it, for you are still carnal. For since there are jealousy and strife and dissensions among you, are you not carnal, and are you not walking according to man?'[2]

Chapter 14

Dearest brethren, vices and carnal sins must be crushed, and the infestuous plague of the earthly body must be trampled upon with spiritual vigor, lest, when we again are turned back to the conversation of the old man, we become entangled in deadly snares, as the Apostle providently and beneficially forewarns. He says: 'Therefore, brethren, let us live not according to the flesh, for if you live according to the flesh, you shall begin to die; but if by the spirit you put to death the deeds of the flesh, you shall live. For as many as are led by the Spirit of God, these are the sons of God.'[1] If we are the sons of God, if already we begin to be His temples, if, after receiving the Holy Spirit, we live holily and spiritually, if we have lifted our eyes from the earth toward heaven, if we have raised our heart full of God and Christ to supernal and divine things, let us do nothing which is not worthy of God and Christ, as the apostle arouses and urges us. 'If you have risen with Christ,' he says, 'seek the things that are above, where Christ is seated at the right hand of God. Mind the things that are above, not the things that are of the earth. For you have died and your

2 Cf. 1 Cor. 3.1-13.

1 Cf. Rom. 8.12-14.

life is hidden with Christ in God. When Christ, your life, shall appear, then you too shall appear with Him in glory.'[2] Let us, therefore, who in baptism have both died and been buried according to the carnal sins of the old man, who have risen with Christ in the heavenly regeneration, both consider and do equally the things that are of Christ, as the same Apostle again teaches and advises, saying: 'The first man was of earth, earthy; the second man is from heaven. As was that one from earth, so are those who are from earth; and as is the heavenly, so are also the heavenly. Just as we have borne the likeness of him who is of the earth, so let us bear the likeness of him who is of heaven.'[3] Moreover, we cannot bear the heavenly images, unless, in that condition in which we have now begun to be, we show the likeness of Christ.

Chapter 15

For this is to have changed what you had been, and to begin to be what you were not, so that the divine birth shine in you, so that the divine discipline may respond to God the Father, so that, in the honor and praise of living, God may shine in man, as He Himself exhorts and advises, and as He promises to those who glorify Him a reward in their turn. He says: 'Those who glorify me, I shall glorify, and him who despises me shall be despised.'[1] The Lord, forming and preparing us for this glorification, and the Son of God, instilling the likeness of God the Father, says in His Gospel: 'You have heard that it was said: "Thou shalt love thy neighbor,

---

2 Col. 3.1-4.
3 Cf. 1 Cor. 15.47-49.

---

1 1 Kings 2.30.

and shalt hate thy enemies." But I say to you, Love your enemies and pray for those who persecute you, so that you may be like your Father who is in heaven, who makes his sun to rise on the good and the evil, and sends rain on the just and the unjust.'[2] If it is a joy and a glory for men to have children like themselves, and it delights them to have begotten them when the remaining offspring with like lineaments corresponds to the father, how much greater is the joy in God the Father, when one is so born spiritually that in his acts and praises divine goodness is proclaimed. What a palm of justice it is, what a crown for you to be such that God does not say about you: 'I have brought up children, and exalted them, but they have despised me.'[3] Let Christ rather praise you and invite you to the reward, saying: 'Come blessed of my Father, take possession of the kingdom which has been prepared for you from the origin of the world.'[4]

Chapter 16

The mind, dearest brethren, must be strengthened by these meditations: it must be confirmed against all the darts of the devil by exercises of this kind. Let divine reading be in the hands; let thoughts of the Lord be in the senses; let prayer never cease at all; let saving labor persevere. Let us all be occupied by spiritual actions, so that, as often as the enemy approaches, as often as he tries to come near, he may find the heart closed and armed against him. For the crown of the Christian man is not the one which is received at the time of persecution. Peace also has its crown, by which we are

2 Cf. Matt. 5.43-45.
3 Isa. 1.2.
4 Cf. Matt. 25.34.

crowned as the victor of many a varied combat, after the adversary has been laid low and subdued. To have overcome lust is the palm of continence. To have resisted wrath and injury is the crown of patience. Triumph over avarice is to spurn money. Praise of faith is to endure the adversities of the world by faith in the future. And he who is not proud in prosperity obtains the glory of humility. And he who is inclined to the mercifulness of befriending the poor gains the retribution of a heavenly treasure. And he knows not how to be jealous and, being of one mind and kind, loves his brethren, is honored with the reward of love and peace. We run daily in this contest of virtues; we arrive at these palms and crowns of justice without interruption of time.

Chapter 17

That you also may be able to arrive at these crowns, you who had been possessed by jealousy and zeal, abandon all that malice with which you were formerly held, and reform yourself to the way of eternal life with the footsteps of salvation. Tear out of your heart the thorns and the thistles, that the Lord's seed may enrich you with a fertile fruit, that the divine and spiritual crop may burst forth into the plenty of a rich harvest. Expel the venom of gall; cast out the virus of discords; let the mind which the jealousy of the serpent had infected be cleansed; let all the bitterness which had settled within be softened by the sweetness of Christ. From the sacrament of the cross you receive both food and drink; let the wood, which availed at Mara in a figure for sweetening the taste, avail you in truth for soothing the softened breast, and you will not labor for the remedy for increasing the health. Cure yourself at the source from which you had been wounded. Love those whom you hated before; esteem those whom you envied with unjust disparagements. Imitate the good, if you can follow them; if you cannot follow them, surely rejoice with them and congratulate your betters. Make yourself a sharer with them in a united love; make yourself an associate in a fellowship of charity and in a bond of brotherhood. Your debts will be forgiven you, when you yourself shall forgive; your sacrifices will be accepted, when you shall come to God as a peace-maker. Your thoughts and actions will be directed by God, when you ponder the things that are divine and just, as it is written: 'Let the heart of man ponder just things, so that his steps may be directed by God.'[1]

Chapter 18

Moreover, you have many things to ponder. Ponder paradise, where Cain, who destroyed his brother through jealousy, does not return. Ponder the kingdom of heaven to which the Lord admits only those of one heart and mind. Ponder the fact that only those can be called the sons of God who are peace-makers, who, united by divine birth and law, correspond to the likeness of God the Father and Christ. Ponder that we are under God's eyes, that we are running the course of our conversation, and life with God Himself looking on and judging, that then finally we can arrive at the point of succeeding in seeing Him, if we delight Him as He now observes us by our actions, if we shows ourselves worthy of His grace and indulgence, if we, who are to please Him forever in heaven, please Him first in this world.

---

1 Cf. Prov. 16.1.

EXHORTATION TO MARTYRDOM, TO FORTUNATUS

ROY J. DEFERRARI, Ph.D.
The Catholic University of America

EXHORTATION TO MARTYRDOM,
TO FORTUNATUS

WE HAVE HERE only the material, not a finished work, on the subject of martyrdom. Cyprian explains his plan in detail in the preface. Thirteen theses regarding the trials of persecution are presented, each serving as a peg on which to hang appropriate quotations from the Bible interspersed with Cyprian's own observations. It thus becomes the most important of Cyprian's work, next to *Three Books of Testimonies against the Jews,* for the study of the oldest Latin versions of the Bible. The specific purpose of the treatise is to prepare the soldiers of Christ for the struggles which they may have to endure in an approaching persecution.

The question of the date of composition to be assigned to this work hinges chiefly on what persecution Cyprian had in mind. While H. Kock places the treatise in the spring of 253, when the persecution of Gallus was at hand, most opinions are divided between that of Decius (250-251) and that of Valerius (257). But Cyprian addresses the preface to a Fortunatus, who is generally thought to be the Bishop of Thuccalori and who we know took part in the African Synod of September, 256. If the last is correct, the year 257 is the most probable date of composition.

We have already called attention to the eloquent peroration with which Cyprian concludes his treatises. The peroration of the present work, in which the signal honor of martyrdom is set forth, is one of the finest pieces of writing in all Cyprian's works.

311

EXHORTATION TO MARTYRDOM,
TO FORTUNATUS

Chapter 1

YOU HAVE DESIRED, my very dear Fortunatus,[1] that since the weight of afflictions and persecutions lies heavy upon us, and at the end and at the consummation of the world the hostile time of antichrist has already begun to draw near, I bring together from the sacred Scripture exhortations for the preparation and strengthening of the minds of the brethren, with which I might animate the soldiers of Christ for the spiritual and heavenly struggle. I have felt obliged to obey your so compelling wish, so that, in so far as our mediocrity is able, prepared with the aid of divine inspiration, certain arms, as it were, and defenses might be brought forth from the Lord's precepts for the brethren who are about to fight. For it is a minor matter that we arouse the people of God with the trumpet call of our voice, unless we confirm by divine reading the faith of believers and their courage dedicated and devoted to God.

---

1 A bishop of Tucca with the name of Fortunatus is mentioned in the Council of Carthage (256).

Chapter 2

For what more fitly or more fully befits our care and solicitude than to prepare the people divinely committed to us and the army established in the heavenly camp with constant exhortations against the weapons and darts of the devil? For he cannot be a soldier fit for war who has not first been trained in the field, nor will he who seeks to obtain the contestant's crown be crowned in the stadium, unless he first gives thought to the practice and skill of his powers. He is an old adversary and an ancient enemy with whom we wage battle. Almost six thousand years are now being fulfilled since the devil first attacked man. All kinds of tempting and arts and plots for his overthrow has he learned by the very practice of a long time. If he finds a soldier of Christ unprepared, if untrained, if he does not find him vigilant with a solicitous and whole heart, he besets him in ignorance, he deceives him incautious, he entraps him inexperienced. But if anyone guards the precepts of the Lord, and bravely adhering to Christ stands against the devil, he must be conquered, since Christ whom we confess is invincible.

Chapter 3

And not to extend my talk at length, dearest brother, and not to fatigue my listener or reader by the abundance of a rather diffuse style, I have made a summary, so that, after setting forth the headings first, which each one ought to know and retain, I might add passages of the Lord, and might establish what I had set forth by the authority of the divine words, thus seeming not so much to have sent you a treatise of mine as to have furnished material for those who make treatises. This plan is of greater utility to individuals in practice. For if I gave away a garment already finished and prepared, it would be my garment which another would use and perhaps the thing having been made according to the contour of the stature and the body of another would he held little fitting. But now I have sent the very wool and purple of the lamb through whom we have been redeemed and quickened, and when you receive it, you will make a tunic according to your wish, and you will rejoice the more in it as in your own private and personal garment, and you will also show others what we have sent, that they too may be able to make garments according to their judgment; thus covering that old nakedness, they may all bear the garments of Christ, dressed in the sanctification of heavenly grace.

Chapter 4

Furthermore also, most beloved brother, I have viewed the plan as useful and salutary in so necessary an exhortation as to make martyrs, that all delays and tardiness of our words must be cut out, and that the meanderings of human speech must be put aside, that those words alone must be set down which God speaks, by which Christ exhorts His servants to martyrdom. The divine precepts themselves must be supplied as arms for those who fight. Let those be the incitements of the military trumpet; let those be the clarion call for those who fight. By those let the ears be made erect; by these let the minds be made ready; by these also let the powers of mind and body be strengthened for the endurance of every suffering. Let us only, who with the Lord's permission gave the first baptism to believers, prepare each one for another baptism also, urging and teaching that this baptism is greater in grace, more sublime in power, more precious in honor, a baptism in which the angels baptize, a baptism in which God and His Christ exult, a baptism after which no one sins again, a baptism which brings to completion the increases of our faith, a baptism which immediately joins us with God as we withdraw from the world. In the baptism of water is received the remission of sins; in that of blood the crown of virtues. This thing is to be embraced and longed for and sought after with all entreaties of our prayers, so that we who were servants of God may also be His friends.

Chapter 5

Thus exhorting and preparing our brethren, and in arming them with the strength of virtue and faith for the proclaiming of their confession of the Lord and for the battle of persecution and suffering, it must be said in the first place:

I. That the idols which man makes for himself are not gods—for neither are the things which are made greater than their maker and fashioner, nor can they protect and save anyone, who themselves perish from their temples, unless they are saved by man—but that neither are the elements to be worshipped, which serve man according to the disposition and precepts of God.

II. That, after the idols have been destroyed and the plan of the elements has been demonstrated, it must be shown that God alone is to be worshipped.

III. That then there must be added what the threat of God is against those who sacrifice to idols.

IV. That besides it must be taught that God does not easily pardon idolaters.

V. And that God is so angry with idolatry that He has even ordered those to be killed who have persuaded to sacrifice to and serve idols.

VI. That after this there must be added that we, redeemed and quickened by the blood of Christ, should place nothing before Christ, because neither did He place anything before us and He on account of us preferred evil things to good things, poverty to riches, servitude to domination, death to immortality, and that we, on the other hand, in our sufferings prefer the riches and joys of paradise to the poverty of the world, eternal sovereignty and rule to the slavery of time, immortality to death, God and Christ to the devil and antichrist.

VII. That it must also be insisted upon that, after being snatched from the jaws of the devil and freed from the snares of the world, if they begin to be in straitened circumstances and troubles, they do not wish to return anew to the world and lose the benefit of having escaped.

VIII. That it must be urged too that that they persevere in faith and virtue and in the consummation of heavenly and spiritual grace, in order that they may arrive at the palm and the crown.

IX. That difficulties and persecutions take place that we may be proved.

X. That the injuries and punishments of persecutions are not to be feared, because the Lord is greater at protecting than the devil at attacking.

XI. And lest anyone become frightened and disturbed at the difficulties and persecutions which we suffer in this world, it must be proved that it was formerly predicted that the world would hold us in hatred and would stir up persecutions against us, so that from the very fact that these things happen the faith of the divine promise is manifest in the benefits and the rewards to follow afterwards, and that whatever happens to Christians is nothing new, since from the beginning of the world the good have labored and the just have been oppressed and slain by the unjust.

XII. That in the last part there must be laid down what hope and what benefit await the just and the martyrs after the conflicts and sufferings of this time.

XIII. And that we are to receive more in the reward for our suffering than what we endure here in the suffering itself.

I. That idols are not gods and that the elements are not to be worshipped in place of gods.[1]

In Psalm 134: 'The idols of the nations are silver and gold, the work of man's hands. They have a mouth but speak not; they have eyes but see not; they have ears, but hear not; for there is no breath in their mouths. Like unto them become all who make them.'[2] Likewise in the Wisdom of Solomon: 'For they have esteemed all the idols of the heathens as gods, which have neither the use of eyes to see, nor noses to draw breath, nor ears to hear, nor fingers on the hands to handle, and as for their feet they are slow to walk. For man made them, and he that borroweth his own breath, fashioned them. For no man can make a god like himself. For, being a mortal himself, he formeth a dead thing with his wicked hands. For he is better than they whom he worship-

---

1 Astronomical idols seem to have been the earlist adopted by man (cf. Job 31.27), but the soul soon degraded itself to lower forms (cf. Rom. 1.21,23).
2 Ps. 134 (5) .15-18.

peth, because he indeed hath lived, but they never.'[3] Likewise in Exodus: 'Thou shalt not make to thyself a graven thing, nor the likeness of anything.'[4] Likewise in Solomon (concerning the elements): 'Neither by attending to the works have they acknowledged who was the workman, but have imagined either the fire, or the wind, or the swift air, or the circle of the stars, or the great water, or the sun, or the moon to be gods. And if on account of their beauty they have thought this, let them know how much the Lord is more beautiful than they. Or, if they admire their power and their effects, let them understand by them that He that made them mighty is mightier than they.'[5]

II. That God alone is to be worshipped.

As it is written: 'Thou shalt worship the Lord Thy God, and Him only shalt thou serve.'[1] Likewise in Exodus: 'Thou shalt not have strange gods before me.'[2] Also in Deuteronomy: 'See, see that I am, and there is no God beside me. I will kill and I will make to live. I will strike and I will heal, and there is none who can deliver out of my hands.'[3] Likewise in the Apocalypse: 'And I saw another angel flying in mid heaven having an eternal gospel to preach upon the earth to every nation and tribe and people, saying with a loud voice: "Fear rather God, and give him honor, for the hour of his judgment has come; and worship him who made the heaven and the earth and the sea, and all things that are

---

3 Wisd. 15.15-17.
4 Exod. 20.14.
5 Cf. Wisd. 13.1-4.

1 Deut. 6.13.
2 Exod. 20.3.
3 Deut. 32.39.

in them." '[4] Thus also the Lord in the Gospel makes mention of the first and second commandments, saying: 'Hear, O Israel, the Lord thy God is one Lord,'[5] and 'Thou shalt love the Lord thy God with thy whole heart, and with thy whole soul, and with thy whole strength. This is the first commandment. And the second is like it: Thou shalt love thy neighbor as thyself. On these two commandments depend the whole law and the prophets.'[6] And again: 'Now this is life everlasting, that they may know thee, the only true God, and him whom thou hast sent, Jesus Christ.'[7]

III. What is God's threat against those who sacrifice to idols?

In Exodus: 'He that sacrificeth to gods shall be put to death, save only to the Lord.'[1] Likewise in Deuteronomy: 'They sacrifice to devils and not to God.'[2] Again in Isaias: 'They have adored what their hands have made. And man hath bowed himself down, and man hath been debased, and I shall not forgive them.'[3] And again: 'Thou hast poured out libations to them and thou hast offered sacrifices to them. Shall I not be angry at these things? says the Lord.'[4] Likewise in Jeremias: 'And go not after strange gods to serve them, nor to adore them, nor to provoke me by the works of your hands to afflict you.'[5] Also in the Apocalypse: 'If anyone worships the beast and its image and receives a mark

---

4 Apoc. 14.6,7.
5 Mark 12.29.
6 Cf. Mark 12.29; Matt. 22.37-40.
7 John 17.3.

---

1 Exod. 22.20.
2 Deut. 32.17.
3 Isa. 2.8,9.
4 Isa. 57.6.

upon his forehead and in his hand, he also shall drink of the wine of the wrath of God which is mixed in the cup of his wrath; and he shall be tormented with fire and brimstone in the sight of the holy angels and in the sight of the Lamb. And the smoke of their torments goes up forever and ever. And they have rest neither day nor night, whoever worship the beast and its image.'[6]

IV. It is not easy for God to pardon idolaters.

Moses in Exodus prays for the people and does not obtain his prayer. 'I beseech thee, O Lord,' he says, 'this people hath sinned a heinous sin, and they have made to themselves gods of gold and silver; either forgive them this trespass, or, if thou do not, strike me out of the book that thou hast written. And the Lord said to Moses: "If anyone sin against me, I shall destroy him out of my book."'[1] Likewise when Jeremias was interceding for the people, the Lord spoke to him saying: Do not thou pray for this people, and do not make demands for them in praise and prayer, for I shall not hear in the the time when they cry unto me, in the time of their affliction.'[2] Ezechiel also denounces this same wrath of God upon those who sin against God. He says: 'And the word of the Lord came to me saying: 'Son of man, when a land shall sin against me so as to transgress grievously, I will stretch forth my hand upon it, and will break the staff of the bread thereof; and I will send famine upon it, and destroy man and beast out of it. And if these three men, Noe, Daniel, and Job, shall be in it, they will not deliver

5 Jer. 25.6.
6 Apoc. 14.9-11.

1 Exod. 32.31-33.
2 Jer. 11.14.

sons nor daughters; themselves alone shall be saved."[3] Likewise, in the first Book of Kings: 'If a man by sinning, sin against a man, they will pray for him to the Lord; but if a man shall sin against God, who will pray for him?'[4]

V. That God is so angry at idolatry that He has ordered those also to be killed, who have persuaded others to sacrifice and be subservient to idols.

In Deuteronomy: 'But if thy brother, or thy son, or thy daughter, or thy wife that is in thy bosom, or thy friend who is as thy own soul, should ask thee secretly saying: "let us go and serve strange gods, the gods of the heathen," thou shalt not consent to him, nor hear him, neither shall thine eye spare him, nor shalt thou conceal him, but thou shalt make public announcement concerning him. Thy hand shall be upon him first to kill him, and afterwards the hand of all the people. And they shall stone him, and he shall die, because he sought to turn thee from the Lord thy God.'[1] And the Lord again speaks and says that neither must a city be spared, even if it entirely consents to idolatry: 'Or if in one of the cities which the Lord thy God shall give thee to dwell in, thou hear some saying: "Let us go and serve strange gods which you know not," thou shalt forthwith kill all who are in the city with the edge of the sword, and shall burn the city with fire, and it shall be without habitation forever. It shall be rebuilt no more, that the Lord may turn from the wrath of his fury, and he will show thee mercy and will have pity on thee and will multiply thee, if thou shalt hear the

---

3 Ezech. 14.12-14.
4 1 Kings 2.25 (1 Sam. 2.25).

1 Cf. Deut. 13.6-10.

voice of the Lord thy God, and observe his precepts.'[2] And Mathathias, mindful of this precept and its force, killed him who had approached the altar to sacrifice.[3] But if before the coming of Christ these precepts were kept with regard to the worship of God and the spurning of idols, how much more should they be kept after Christ's coming; since He came and exhorted us not with words but with deeds, suffering also and being crucified after all injuries and insults, that by His example He might teach us to suffer and to die, that man might have no excuse for not suffering for Him, since He suffered for us; and that, since He suffered for the sins of others, much more ought each one to suffer for his own sins. And so He threatens in the Gospel, and says: 'Everyone who acknowledges me before men, I also will acknowledge him before my Father who is in heaven. But whoever disowns me before men, I in turn will disown before my Father who is in heaven.'[4] Likewise the Apostle Paul says: 'For if we die with Him, we shall also live with Him; if we endure, we shall also reign with Him; if we disown Him, He will also disown us.'[5] Also John: "He who disowns the Son does not have the Father, he who confesses the Son has both the Father and the Son.'[6] Therefore, the Lord urges us to contempt of death, and strengthens us by saying: 'Do not be afraid of those who kill the body, but cannot kill the soul. But rather be afraid of him who is able to destroy both the soul and body in hell.'[7] And again: 'He who loves this life

---

2 Cf. Deut. 13.12-18.
3 Cf. 1 Mach. 2.24.
4 Matt. 10.32,33.
5 2 Tim. 2.11.
6 1 John 2.23.
7 Matt. 10.28.

shall lose; and he who hates his life in this world, shall keep it unto life everlasting.'[8]

VI. That we who have been redeemed and quickened by the blood of Christ should place nothing before Christ.

The Lord speaks in the Gospel and says: 'He who loves father or mother more than me is not worthy of me; and he who loves son or daughter more than me is not worthy of me; and he who does not take up his cross and follow me is not my disciple.'[1] As it is written in Deuteronomy: 'Who say to their father and to their mother: "I know you not," and have not known their own sons, these have guarded thy precepts and kept thy covenant.'[2] Likewise the Apostle Paul says: 'Who shall separate us from the love of Christ? Shall tribulation, or distress, or persecution, or hunger, or nakedness, or danger, or the sword? Even as it is written: 'For thy sake we are put to death all the day long. We are regarded as sheep for the slaughter. But in all these things we overcome because of Him who loved us.'[3] And again: 'You are not your own; for you have been bought at a great price. Glorify God and bear him in your body.'[4] And again: 'Christ died for all, so that they who are alive may live no longer for themselves, but for him who died for them and rose again.'[5]

VII. That those who have been snatched from the jaws

---

8 John 12.25.

---

1 Matt. 10.37,38.
2 Cf. Deut. 33.9.
3 Rom. 8.35-37.
4 1 Cor. 6.19,20.
5 2 Cor. 5.15.

of the devil and freed from the snares of the world should not return anew to the world lest they lose the benefit of having escaped.

In Exodus the Jewish people prefigured in our shadow and image, when, with God as their guardian and avenger, they escaped the very severe slavery of Pharao and Egypt, that is, of the devil and the world, faithless and ungrateful with regard to God, looking back upon the troubles of the desert and of their labor, murmured also against Moses; and, not understanding the divine benefits of freedom and salvation, they sought even to return to the slavery of Egypt, that is, to the slavery of the world, from which they had been withdrawn, when they should rather have had faith and belief in God, since He who liberates His people from the devil and the world protects them when liberated. 'Why have you done this to us," they say, by throwing us out of Egypt? It was better for us to serve the Egyptians than to die in this desert. And Moses said to the people: "Trust and stand and see the salvation which is from the Lord, which he will do today for us. The Lord will fight for you and you will hold your peace."[1] The Lord warning us of this in His Gospel, lest we return to the devil again and to the world, which we have renounced, and from which we have escaped, says: 'No one having put this hand to the plow and looking back is fit for the kingdom of God.'[2] And again: 'And let him who is in the field not turn back. Remember Lot's wife.'[3] And lest anyone, either because of some desire for wealth or by the charm of his own be regarded from following Christ,

1 Exod. 14.11-14.
2 Luke 9.62.
3 Luke 17.31,32.

He added saying: 'He who does not renounce all that he possesses, cannot be my disciple.'[4]

VIII. We must press on and persevere in the faith and virtue, and in the consummation of heavenly and spiritual grace, that we may be able to arrive at the palm and the crown.

In Paralipomenon: 'The Lord is with you, as long as you are with him. But if you forsake him, he will forsake you.'[1] Likewise in Ezechiel: 'The justice of the just shall not deliver him, in what day soever he shall sin.'[2] Again in the Gospel the Lord speaks and says: 'He who has persevered to the end, will be saved.'[3] And again: 'If you abide in my word, you shall be my disciple indeed, and you shall know the truth, and the truth shall make you free.'[4] Forewarning also that we should always be prepared and stand firmly equipped for battle, He added, saying: 'Let your loins be girt about and your lamps burning, and you yourselves like to men waiting for their master's return from the wedding, so that when he comes and knocks, they may open to him. Blessed are those servants whom the master of his return, shall find watching.'[5] Likewise the blessed Apostle Paul, that our faith may prosper and increase and attain the highest, exhorts and says: 'Do you know that those who run in a race, all indeed run, but one receives the prize? So run as to obtain it. And they indeed to receive a perishable crown, but we an imperishable?'[6] And again: 'No one serving as God's

---

4 Luke 14.33.

1 Cf. Par. 15.2.
2 Ezech. 33.12.
3 Matt. 10.22.
4 John 8.31,32.
5 Luke 12.35-37.
6 1 Cor. 9.24,25.

soldier entangles himself in worldly affairs, that he may please Him whose approval he has secured. And again one who enters a contest is not crowned unless he has competed lawfully.'[7] And again: 'I exhort you, therefore, brethren, by the mercy of God, to present your bodies as a sacrifice, living, holy, pleasing to God. And be not conformed to this world, but be transformed in the newness of your mind, that you may discern what is the good and acceptable and perfect will of God.'[8] And again: 'We are sons of God. But if sons, then we are heirs also, joint heirs with Christ, if indeed we suffer with Him, that we may also be glorified with him.'[9] And in Apocalypse the same exhortation of the divine preaching speaks and says: 'Hold fast what thou hast, that no one receive thy crown.'[10] This example of perseverance and persistence is pointed out in Exodus, where Moses, to overcome Amalech, who bore the figure of the devil, raised his outspread hands in the sign and sacrament of the cross, and he was unable to overcome his adversary except after he had persevered steadfastly in the sign with hands raised continuously. 'And it came to pass,' it says, 'when Moses lifted up his hands, Israel prevailed, but when he let them down Amalec overcame. So they took a stone and put it under him, and he sat upon it. And Aaron and Hur stayed up his hands on both sides. And the hands of Moses were made firm even to sunset. And Josue put Amalec and all his people to flight. And the Lord said to Moses: "Write this that it may be a memorial in a book, and deliver it to the ears of Josue,

---

7 Cf. 2 Tim. 2.4,5.
8 Rom. 12.1,2.
9 Rom. 8.16,17.
10 Apoc. 3.11.

for I shall destroy utterly the memory of Amalec from under the sun." '[11]

IX. That troubles and persecutions take place for this purpose, that we may be proved.

In Deuteronomy: 'The Lord your God trieth you, that He may know whether you love the Lord your God with all your heart and with all your soul and with all your strength.'[1] And again in Solomon: 'The furnace trieth the potter's vessels, and trial of affliction just men.'[2] Paul also gives like testimony, and speaks saying: 'We glory in the hope of the glory of God. Not only so, but we glory also in tribulations knowing that tribulation works out endurance, and endurance tries virtue, and virtue hope. And hope does not disappoint, because the charity of God is poured forth in our hearts by the Holy Spirit who has been given to us.'[3] And Peter in his Epistle lays it down, saying: 'Beloved, do not be startled at the trial by fire that is happening among you which is happening for your trial, and fail not, as though a strange thing were taking place for you. But rejoice in all things as often as you partake in the sufferings of Christ, that you may rejoice with exultation in the revelation of his glory. If you are upbraided for the name of Christ, blessed are you, because the name of the glory and power of God rests upon you, which indeed according to them is blasphemy, but according to us is an honor.'[4]

---

11 Cf. Exod. 17.11-14.

1 Deut. 13.3.
2 Eccli. 27.6.
3 Rom. 5.2-5.
4 Cf. 1 Peter 4.12-14.

X. That the injuries and punishments of persecutions are not to be feared, because the Lord is greater in protecting than the devil in assaulting.

John in his Epistle approves, saying: 'Greater is he who is in you than he who is in the world.'[1] Likewise in Psalm 117: 'I shall not fear what man does to me; the Lord is my helper.'[2] And again: 'Those are strong in chariots, these in horses, but we, in the name of our God. They with their feet bound have fallen, but we are risen up and stand erect.'[3] And still more strongly the Holy Spirit, teaching and showing that the army of the devil is not to be feared, and, if the enemy should declare war on us, our hope consists rather in that war itself, and that this conflict of the just arrives at the reward of the divine abode and of eternal salvation, lays down in Psalm 26, saying: 'If a camp be pitched against me; my heart shall not fear; if a war shall arise against me, in this do I hope. One thing I have sought of the Lord, this I shall seek after, that I may dwell in the house of the Lord all the days of my life.'[4] Likewise in Exodus holy Scripture declares that we are rather multiplied and increased, saying: 'The more they oppressed them, the more they were multiplied and increased.'[5] And in the Apocalypse divine protection is promised in our sufferings. 'Fear none of these things,' it says, 'that thou art about to suffer.'[6] Nor does any other promise us security and protection than He who speaks through Isaias the prophet saying: 'Fear not, for I have redeemed thee, and called thee by thy name. Thou art mine.

---

1 1 John 4.4.
2 Ps. 117.6,7.
3 Ps. 19.8,9.
4 Ps. 26.3,4.
5 Exod. 1.12.
6 Apoc. 2.10.

When thou shalt pass through the waters, I am with thee, and the rivers shall not cover thee. When thou shalt walk through the fire, thou shalt not be burnt; the flame shall not burn thee. For I am the Lord thy God, the Holy One of Israel who shall save thee.'[7] And He also in the Gospel promises that divine aid will not be lacking to God's servants in persecutions, saying: 'But when they deliver you up, do not be anxious how or what you shall speak; for what you are to speak will be given you in that hour. For it is not you who are speaking, but the Spirit of your Father who speaks through you.'[8] And again: 'Resolve in your hearts not to mediate beforehand to make excuse. For I shall give to you utterance and wisdom which your adversaries shall not be able to resist.'[9] Just as in Exodus God speaks to Moses, when he delays and fears to go to the people, saying: 'Who gave a mouth to man and who made the dumb and the deaf, the seeing and the blind? Did not I the Lord God? Go now, and I shall open thy mouth and I will teach thee what thou shalt speak.'[10] It is not difficult for God to open the mouth of a man devoted to Him, and to inspire constancy and confidence in speaking in one who confesses Him, who in the book of Numbers made even a female ass speak against Balaam, the prophet. Therefore, let no one consider in persecutions what danger the devil brings, but rather let him bear in mind what assistance God affords; and let not the disturbances of men weaken the mind, but let divine protection strengthen the faith, since each one according to the Lord's promises and the merits of his faith, receives so much

---

7 Isa. 43.1-3.
8 Matt. 10.19,20.
9 Luke 21.14,15.
10 Exod. 4.11,12.

of God's help as he thinks he receives, and since there is nothing which the Almighty cannot grant, except if the frail faith of the recipient be deficient.

IX. That it was formerly predicted that the world hold us in hatred, and that it would stir up persecutions against us, and that nothing new happens to the Christians, since from the beginning of the world the good have labored and been oppressed, and the just have been slain by the unjust.

The Lord in the Gospel forewarns and predicts, saying: 'If the world hate you, know that it hates me first. If you were of the world, the world would love what is its own; but since you are not of the world, but I have chosen you out of the world; therefore the world hates you. Remember the word that I have spoken to you: "the servant is not greater than this master." If they have persecuted me, they will persecute you also.'[1] And again: 'The hour will come for anyone who slays you to think that he does God a service. And this they will do because they do not know the Father nor me. But these things I have spoken to you, so that when the time comes for them you may remember that I told you.'[2] And again: 'Amen, amen, I say to you that you shall weep and lament, but the world shall rejoice; and you shall be sorrowful, but your sorrow shall be turned into joy.'[3] And again: 'These things I have spoken to you that in me you may have peace. In the world you will have affliction. But take courage, for I have overcome the world.'[4] But when He was asked by His disciples about a sign of His coming

---

1 John 15.18-20.
2 John 16.2-4.
3 John 16.20.
4 John 16.33.

and of the consummation of the world, He answered and said: 'Take care that no one leads you astray. For many will come in my name, saying: "I am the Christ" and they will lead many astray. Moreover, you shall begin to hear of wars and rumors of wars. Take care that you do not be alarmed; for these things must come to pass, but the end is not yet. For nation will rise against nation and kingdom against kingdom, and there will be famines and earthquakes and pestilence in various places. But all these things are the beginnings of sorrows. Then they will deliver you up to tribulation and will put you to death, and you will be hated by all nations for my name's sake. And then many will fall away and will arise and will lead many astray. And because iniquity will abound, the charity of many will grow cold. But whoever perseveres to the end, he shall be saved. And this gospel of the kingdom shall be preached in the whole world, for a witness to all nations, and then will come the end. Therefore, when you see the abomination of desolation, which was spoken of by Daniel the prophet, standing in the holy place—let him who reads understand—then, let those who are in Judea flee to the mountains; and let him who is on the housetop not come down to take anything from his house; and let him who is in the field not turn back to take his cloak. But woe to those who are with child, or have infants at the breast in those days. But pray that your flight may not be in the winter, or on the sabbath. For then there will be great tribulation such as has not been from the beginning of the world until now, nor will be. And unless those days had been shortened, no living creature would be freed. But for the sake of the elect those days will be shortened. Then if anyone say to you: "Behold, here is the Christ," or, "There he is," do not believe it. For false Christs and false prophets will arise, and will show great signs and wonders, so as to lead astray, if possible, even the elect. But do yet take care. Behold I have told all things to you beforehand. If, therefore, they say to you: "Behold, he is in the desert," do not go forth; "Behold, he is in the inner chamber," do not believe it. For just as the lighting which goes forth from the east and shines even to the west, so also will the coming of the Son of man be. Wherever the body is, there will be gathered together the eagles. But immediately after the tribulation of those days, the sun will be darkened, and the moon will not give her light, and the stars will fall from heaven and the powers of the heavens will be shaken. And then will appear the sign of the Son of man in heaven; and then will all the tribes of the earth mourn and they will see the Son of man coming in the clouds of heaven with great power and majesty. And he will send forth his angels with a great trumpet and they will gather his elect from the four winds, from one end of the heavens to the other.'[5]

And these are not new or sudden things which are now happening to Christians, since the good and the just, who are always devoted to God by the law of innocence and by the fear of the true religion, always walk through afflictions, and injuries, and the severe and manifold punishments of attackers in the difficulty of a narrow road. Thus at the very beginning of the world, the just Abel is the first to be killed by his brother, and Jacob is sent into exile, and Joseph is sold, and King Saul persecutes merciful David, and King Achab tries to oppress Elias who constantly and courageously declares the majesty of God. The priest Zacharias is killed between the temple and the altar, that he himself may become a sacrifice there where he was accustomed to offer sacri-

5 Matt. 24.4-31.

fices to God. Finally so many martyrdoms of the just have
often been celebrated; so many examples of faith and of
virtue have been set forth for posterity. The three youths,
Ananias, Azarias, Misahel, equal in age, harmonious in love,
stable in faith, constant in virtue, stronger than the flames
and punishments that oppressed them, proclaim that they
serve God alone, know Him alone, and worship Him alone,
saying: 'King Nabuchodonosor, we have no occasion to
answer thee concerning this matter. For our God whom we
worship, is able to save us from the furnace of the burning
fire, and to deliver us out of your hands, O King. But if he
will not, be it known to thee, that we will not serve thy gods
and shall not adore the gods and the golden image that you
have set up.'[6] And Daniel, devoted to God and full of the
Holy Spirit, exclaims saying: 'Nothing do I worship except
the Lord my God who made heaven and earth.'[7] Tobias,
although under a royal and tyrannical slavery, yet in feeling
and spirit free, preserves his confession to God, and sublimely
proclaims the divine power and majesty saying: 'In the land
of my captivity I praise him and show forth His power in
a sinful nation.'[8]

Now what as to the seven brothers in Machabees, alike in
their lot of birth and virtues, fulfilling the number seven in
the sacrament of a perfect fulfilment? Thus the seven brothers, united in martyrdom, just as the first seven days in the
divine plan containing seven thousand years; as the seven
spirits and the seven angels who stand and go in and out
before the face of God, and the seven-branched lamp in the
tabernacle of witness, and the seven golden candlesticks in

6 Dan. 3.16-18.
7 Cf. Dan. 14.4.
8 Cf. Tob. 13.7.

the Apocalypse, and the seven columns in Solomon, upon which Wisdom builds her house, thus also here the number of seven brothers embracing in the quantity of its number seven churches, according as we read in the first book of Kings that the barren woman bore seven. And in Isaias seven women lay hold of one man, whose name they demand be invoked upon them. And the Apostle Paul, who is mindful of this lawful and certain number, writes to seven churches. And in the Apocalypse the Lord directs His divine mandates and heavenly precepts to seven churches and their angels. This number is now found here in the brothers, that a lawful consummation may be fulfilled. With the seven children is clearly joined the mother[9] also, their origin and root, who later bore seven churches, herself the first and only one founded by the Lord's voice upon a rock. Nor it is without significance that the mother alone is with her children in their sufferings. For the martyrs, who in their suffering bear witness to themselves as sons of God, are not considered as of any father other than God, just as the Lord teaches in the Gospel saying: 'And you shall call no one your father on earth. One is your Father who is in heaven.'[10]

What proclaimings of confessions have they given forth! How glorious and how great proofs of faith have they furnished! Hostile King Antiochus, rather, antichrist represented in Antiochus, sought to contaminate the mouths of the martyrs, glorious and invincible in the spirit of confession, with the contagion of swine's flesh, and when he had beaten them severely with rods and had been able to move them not at all, he ordered irons to be heated. When these had been heated and made to glow, he ordered him who had been

---

9 The mother referred to here is *Ecclesia Catholica,* the Catholic Church.
10 Matt. 23.9.

the first to speak and had provoked the king the more by the constancy of his virtues and faith to be brought up and to be roasted, after having pulled out and cut off the tongue which had confessed God. And this happened the more gloriously for the martyrs. For the tongue which confessed the name of God ought itself to have proceeded first to God. Then in the second case, when more severe punishments were devised, before he tortured the other members, he tore away the skin of the head with the hair, out of hatred, namely of a certainty on this account: for, since the head of man is Christ, and the head of Christ is God, he who tore the head on a martyr persecuted God and Christ in the head. But trusting in his martyrdom and promising himself the reward of resurrection from God's recompense he exclaimed and said: 'Thou indeed, impotent one, destroyest us out of this present life; but the King of the world will raise up into the resurrection of eternal life us who have died for His laws.'[11] The third, on being ordered, put forth his tongue. For he had now learned from his brother to despise the punishment of having his tongue cut out. He also steadily extended his hands to be cut off, happy with this kind of punishment, whose lot it was to imitate the manner of the Lord's passion. The fourth also with like virtue, despising the torments and replying with the heavenly voice to restrain the king, exclaimed saying: 'It is better, being put to death by men, to look for hope from God, to be raised up again by Him. For, to thee there shall be no resurrection unto life.'[12] The fifth, besides trampling under foot with the vigor of faith the torments of the king and the severe and various tortures, inspired by the Spirit of divinity to prescience also

11 2 Mach. 7.9.
12 2 Mach. 7.14.

and a knowledge of the future, prophesied to the king that God's wrath and vengeance would follow swiftly. He said: 'Whereas thou hast power among men and though you are corruptible, thou dost what thou wilt, but think not that our nation is forsaken by God. But stay and see in what manner his great power will torment thee and thy seed.'[13] What a consolation that was for the martyr! How grand a solace it was not to consider his own torments in his sufferings but to predict the punishments of his tormentors! But in the sixth not virtue alone but also humility is to be proclaimed; that the martyr claimed nothing for himself and did not bring forward the honor of his confession with proud words; rather he ascribed his suffering persecution at the hands of the king to his own sins, but that he would later be avenged he attributed to God. He taught that martyrs are modest, have confidence in their being avenged, and boasted not at all in their passion. He said: 'Be not deceived without cause, for we suffer these things for ourselves in that we sin against our God. But we do not think that thou shalt go unpunished to fight against God.'[14] Admirable also was the mother who, neither broken by the weakness of her sex nor moved by her manifold bereavement, gazed upon her dying children cheerfully and did not compute the punishments of her children but the glories, furnishing as grand a martyrdom to God by virtue of her eyes as her sons had furnished by the torments and sufferings of their limbs. When, after six had been punished and killed, one of the brothers survived, to whom he promised riches and power and many things that his cruelty and fierceness might be favored by the solace of at least one being subdued, and

13 2 Mach. 7.16,17.
14 2 Mach. 7.18,19.

when he asked that the mother also entreat the son to cast himself down with herself, she entreated, but as befitted the mother of martyrs, as befitted one mindful of the law and of God, as befitted one who loved her sons not lightly but strongly. For she entreated, but that he confess God. She entreated that the brother be not separated from his brothers in the communion of praise and glory, then accounting herself the mother of seven sons, if it should happen that she had borne seven sons rather to God, not to the world. So arming him and strengthening and bearing her son then by a happier birth, she said: 'Son, have pity on me who bore you in my womb ten months and gave you suck three years, and nourished you and brought you up unto this age. I beseech thee, my son, look upon heaven and earth and when you have looked upon all things that are in them you may know that from nothing God made them and so the race of men came to be. And do not fear that tormentor, but may you become worthy of your brothers and receive death, that in that mercy I may receive thee with thy brethren.'[15] Great was the praise of the mother in her exhortation to virtue, but greater in her fear of the Lord and in the truth of faith, because she claimed nothing for herself or her son from the honor of six martyrs, nor did she believe that the prayer of the brothers would avail for the salvation of a denier; rather she persuaded him to become a sharer in their suffering, so that on the day of judgment he could be found with his brothers. After this the mother also died with her children; for now nothing else was fitting than that she, who had both borne and made martyrs, should be joined in the companionship of their glory, and that she herself should also follow those whom she had sent on ahead to God.

---

15 2 Mach. 27-29.

And lest anyone, when the occasion has been presented to him of a certificate or something else, whereby he may deceive, embrace the evil role of deceivers, Eleazar must not be passed over in silence. This man, when the opportunity was given him by the servants of the king to take flesh which it was lawful for him to eat and, to circumvent the king, to pretend that he was eating what was handed him from the sacrifices and the forbidden foods, refused to consent to this deception, saying that to do this was becoming neither to his age nor his dignity, for others would be scandalized thereby and led into error, thinking that Eleazar, who was ninety years old, had gone over to the custom of strangers after abandoning and betraying the law of God; that it was not worthwhile so to barter the brief torments of life as to offend God and incur eternal punishments. And, after he had been tormented for a long time and was now at the end of his life, as he died in the midst of lashes and torments, he groaned and said: 'O Lord, who hast the holy knowledge, it is manifest that, although I might be freed from death, I endure most severe pains of the body as I am beaten with stripes, yet I endure these things freely in soul because of fear of thee.'[16] Certainly it was a sincere faith and a sound and quite pure virtue not to have considered King Antiochus but God the judge, and to have realized that it could not profit him for salvation, if he derided and deceived man, when God, who is the judge of our conscience and is alone to be feared, can neither be derided in any way at all or be deceived.

If then we too live dedicated and devoted to God, if we make our way over the very tracks, ancient and holy, of the just, let us proceed though the same evidences of punish-

16 2 Mach. 6.30.

ments, through the same testimonies of sufferings, considering the glory of our time greater by this: that, although your examples are numbered, as the abundance of virtue and faith later comes forth, the Christian martyrs cannot be numbered, as the Apocalypse bears witness, saying: 'After this I saw a great multitude which no man could number out of every nation and out of every tribe and tongue standing in the sight of the throne and of the Lamb; and they were clothed in white robes, and there were palms in their hands, and they were saying with a loud voice: "Salvation belongs to our God who sits upon the throne and to the Lamb." And one of the elders spoke and said to me: "These who are clothed in the white robes, who are they and whence have they come?" And I said to him: "My Lord, you know." And He said to me: "These are they who have come out of the great tribulation and have washed their robes and made them white in the blood of the Lamb. Therefore, they are in the sight of the throne of God, and serve him in his temple." '[17] But if the assembly of the Christian martyrs is shown and proved to be so great, no one should think that it is difficult or hard to become a martyr, when he sees that the people of the martyrs cannot be numbered.

XII. What hope and reward awaits the just and the martyrs after the conflicts and sufferings of this time.

The Holy Spirit shows and predicts through Solomon, saying: 'And though in the sight of men they suffered torments, their hope is full of immortality. Afflicted in few things in many they shall be well rewarded because God hath tried them, and found them worthy of himself. As gold in the furnace he has proved them and as victim of a holocaust

---

17 Apoc. 7.9,10,13-15.

he hath received them, and in time there shall be respect
had to them. They shall judge nations, and rule over peoples,
and their Lord shall reign forever.'[1] Likewise in the same our
vindication is described, and the repentance of those who
persecute and harass us is declared. He says: 'Then shall
the just stand with great constancy against those who have
afflicted them and taken away their labors. These seeing it
shall be troubled with terrible fear, and shall be amazed at
the suddenness of their unexpected salvation, saying within
themselves, repenting and groaning for anguish of spirit.
These are they whom we had some time in derision, and for a
parable of reproach. We fools esteemed their life madness,
and their life without honor. How are they numbered among
the children of God, and their lot is among the saints? Therefore, we have erred from the way of truth, and the light
of justice has not shined on us, and the sun has not risen
upon us. We have wearied ourselves in the way of iniquity
and destruction, and have walked through hard ways, but
the way of the Lord we have not known. What has pride
profited us? Or, what advantage has the boasting of riches
brought us? All those things are passed away like a shadow.'[2]
The price and reward of suffering is likewise indicated in
Psalm 115. It says: 'Precious in the sight of God is the death
of His saints.'[3] Likewise in Psalm 125 the sadness of conflict and the joy of retribution is expressed. It says: 'They
who sow in tears shall reap in joy. Going they went and
wept sowing the seed; but coming they shall come, with
exultation carrying their sheaves.'[4] And again in Psalm 118:

1 Wisd. 3.4-6,8.
2 Wisd. 5.1-9.
3 Ps.. 115.6.
4 Cf. Ps. 125.5,6.

'Blessed are they whose way of life is spotless, who walk in the light of the Lord. Blessed are they who search His testimonies, who seek Him with the whole heart.'[5] Likewise the Lord in the Gospel, Himself the avenger of our persecution and the rewarder of suffering, says: 'Blessed are they who have suffered persecution for justice sake, for theirs is the kingdom of heaven.'[6] And again: 'Blessed shall you be, when man shall hate you and when they shall shut you out and reproach you and shall rewrite your name as evil because of the Son of man. Rejoice in that day, and exult, for behold your reward is great in heaven.'[7] And again: 'He who loses his soul on account of me shall save it.'[8] Nor do the rewards of divine promise await only the persecuted and the slain, but, if the passion be wanting to the faithful, yet if the faith has remained sound and unconquered, and, after forsaking and continuing all his possessions, shows that he follows Christ, he also is honored among the martyrs by Christ, as He Himself promises and says. There is no one who leaves house, or land, or parents, or brothers, or wife or children for the sake of the kingdom of God, who shall not receive much more in the present time, and in the age to come life everlasting.'[9] Likewise in the Apocalypse He says this same thing: 'And I saw the souls of those who had been beheaded because of the name of Jesus and the Word of God.' And when he had put those beheaded in the first place, he added saying: 'And who did not worship the image of the beast, and did not accept his mark upon their foreheads or in their hands.' And all these he joins together as seen by him in

5 Ps. 118.1,2.
6 Matt. 5.10.
7 Luke 6.22,23.
8 Luke 9.24.
9 Luke 18.29,30.

the same place and says: 'And they came to life and reigned with Christ.'[10] He says that all live and reign with Christ, not only those who have been slain, but whoever standing in the firmness of their faith and in the fear of God have not adored the image of a beast and have not consented to his deadly sacrilegious edicts.

XIII. That we receive more as reward of suffering than that which we endure in this world in the suffering itself.

The blessed Apostle Paul proves this, who, on being caught up by the divine esteem, even into the third heaven and into paradise, testifies that he heard unspeakable words, who boasts that with a visible faith that he saw Jesus Christ, who professes that which he both learned and saw with the truth of a greater conscience. He says: 'The sufferings of the present time are not worthy to be compared with the glory to come that will be revealed in us.'[1] Who then does not labor in every way to arrive at such a glory as to become a friend of God, as to rejoice at once with Christ, as to receive the divine rewards after earthly torments and punishments? If it is glorious for the soldiers of the world to return to their fatherland triumphant after vanquishing the enemy, how much better and greater is the glory for one, after overcoming the devil, to return to heaven triumphant, and, after laying him low who had formerly deceived us, to bring back the trophies of victory there whence Adam the sinner had been ejected, to offer the Lord the most acceptable gift an incorrupted faith, an unshaken virtue of the mind an illustrious praise of devotion, to accompany Him when He begins

10 Cf. Apoc. 20.4.

1 Rom. 8.18.

to come to receive vengeance on the enemies, to stand at His side when He sits to judge, to become co-heir of Christ, to be made equal to the angels, to rejoice with the patriarchs, with the apostles, with the prophets in the possession of the heavenly kingdom? What persecution can conquer these thoughts, what torments can overcome them? The brave and stable mind founded on religious meditations endures, and the spirit persists unmoved against all the terrors of the devil and the threats of the world, which a certain and strong faith in the future makes strong. The lands are shut off in persecutions, heaven is open; Antichrist threatens, but Christ protects; death is brought on, but immortality follows; the world is snatched from him who has been killed, but paradise is displayed to him who has been restored; temporal life is extinguished, but eternity is exhibited. How great a dignity and, how great a security it is to go forth hence happy, to go forth glorious in the midst of difficulties and affliction, in a moment to shut the eyes with which men and the world were seen, to open them immediately that God and Christ may be seen. How great is the swiftness of so happy a departure! You will be withdrawn suddenly from earth, that you may be replaced in the heavenly kingdom. These things should be grasped by your mind and thinking; these should be meditated upon day and night. If persecution should come upon such a soldier of God, virtue made ready for battle will not be able to be overcome. Or if the summons should come beforehand, the faith which was prepared for martyrdom will not be without its reward; without loss of time with God as judge reward is rendered; in persecution loyal military service, in peace purity of conscience is crowned.

THAT IDOLS
ARE NOT GODS

Translated by

ROY J. DEFERRARI, Ph.D.
The Catholic University of America

THAT IDOLS ARE NOT GODS

THE TITLE, *That Idols Are Not Gods,* is definitely confirmed by the manuscripts, by Jerome in his letter (70.5) *'To Magnus,'* and by Cyprian himself in *To Fortunatus.* Nearly all early editions have the title, *The Vanity of Idols,* but this cannot be supported by evidence. Chronologically, it is closely associated with *To Donatus* and belongs in the period of Cyprian's conversion, probably in the year 247. It is not included in Pontius' list of Cyprian's works. It is largely a compilation from the *Octavius* of Minucius Felix and the *Apologeticum* of Tertullian. There is no longer any question as to its authenticity, although its authorship was long questioned.

Cyprian first argues that the popular divinities are identifiable with historical benefactors. Their work is to 'confound true with false, deceiving and being deceived.' Over against all this confusion rises the glorious truth of the unity of God. This he does not attempt to prove but illustrates, not always happily, from analogy. Then follows an impressive sketch of the history of Judaism, pointing out the exact correspondence of its greatness and dispersion with predictions. Finally, he sets forth the inadequacy of the Roman gods, and the continuous sufferings of believers in attestation of the credibility of Christian truth. These ideas, repeated frequently by later writers, appear to have their origin with Cyprian.

347

This treatise has been called 'the work of a learner, not of a teacher.' In spite of Jerome's praise of its learning, it is a simple compilation, showing little not already presented by Cyprian's Christian predecessors. However, it is quite worthy of Jerome's praise for *brevitas* and *splendor,* although it has none of the literary polish that we find in Cyprian's other works.

THAT IDOLS ARE NOT GODS

Chapter 1

THAT THOSE ARE NOT GODS who are worshipped by the populace is known from the following. There were once kings, who, because of their memory as kings, began later to be worshipped even in death. Thereupon, temples were established for them; thereupon, to retain the features of the dead by an image statues were formed, and men sacrificed victims and celebrated festal days giving them honor. Thereupon, these rites became sacred for posterity, which were taken up as consolations for those first concerned. Let us see whether this truth also holds in individual cases.

Chapter 2

Melicertes[1] and Leucothea are plunged into the sea and later become divinities of the sea; the Casters[2] die alternately

---

1 Melicertes in Greek legend was the son of Ino. When Ino, his mother, was driven mad by Hera, she threw herself with her boy into the sea. Both were then changed into marine deities, Ino becoming Leucothea, and Melicertes Palaemon.

2 That is, Castor and Pollux.

that they may live; Aesculapius[3] is struck by lightning that he may rise into a god; Hercules[4] is consumed by the fires of Oeta that he may put off the man. Apollo[5] tended the flocks of Admetus; Neptune built walls for Laomedon and the unfortunate builder received no wages for his work. The cave of Jupiter is seen in Crete and his tomb is pointed out, and it is clear that Saturn was driven into exile by him; from his hiding place[6] Latium received its name. This one was the first to teach how to print letters and how to stamp coins in Italy. Hence the treasury is called Saturn's. He always was the cultivator of the rustic life, and so he is depicted carrying a sickle. Janus had received him, when driven into exile, in hospitality, from whose name the Janiculum was so called and the month of January was established. He himself is represented with two faces, because, placed in the middle, he appears to the year equally as it begins and as it recedes. The Mauri[7] indeed manifestly worship kings and do not conceal this name by any covering.

---

3 The common story of the later poets make Aesculapius the son of Apollo and Coronis. When Coronis was with child by Apollo, she became enamored of Ischys, an Arcadian. Apollo promptly had her killed, but, when the body was to be burned, he saved the child, Aesculapius, and brought him to Chiron from whom he learned the art of healing and the ways of the hunt. The legend is continued by Pindar that he not only cured all the sick, but called the dead to life again. While he was restoring Glaucus to life, Zeus, fearing lest men might escape death entirely, killed him with a flash of lightning.

4 Hercules or Heracles put on a garment which had been soaked by his wife Deianira out of jealousy in the blood of Nessus. This caused Hercules excruciating pain. He then ascended Mt. Oeta, raised a pile of wood, on which he placed himself, and ordered it to be set on fire. When the pile was burning, a cloud came down from heaven, and amid peals of thunder carried him to Olympus, where he was honored with immortality.

5 Apollo tended the flocks of Admetus, when he was obliged to serve a mortal for a year for having slain the Cyclops.

6 *Latebra.*

7 One of the chief tribes of the Gaetulians who inhabited North Africa west of the Syrtes.

Chapter 3

From this the religion of the gods is variously changed throughout individual nations and provinces, since not one God is worshipped by all, but the cult of its ancestors proper to each is preserved. Alexander the Great wrote to his mother that this is so in a famous volume, saying that because of fear of his power the secret about the gods as men, which was preserved in the memory of ancestors and kings, was revealed to him by a priest. From this the rites of worshipping and sacrificing have developed. But if the gods were born at some time, why are they not born today?—unless perchance Jupiter has grown old or the faculty of bearing in Juno has failed.

Chapter 4

But why do you think that the gods have power in behalf of the Romans, whom you see have availed nothing for their own [worshippers] against their[1] arms? For we know that the gods of the Romans are indigenous. Romulus was made a god when Proculus[2] committed perjury, and Picus and Tiberinus and Pilumnus and Consus whom Romulus wished to be worshipped as the god of fraud as if the god of counsels, after his perfidy resulted in the rape of the Sabine women.

---

1 The Romans.
2 One day, as Romulus was reviewing his people on the Campus Martius, the sun was suddenly eclipsed, darkness spread over the earth, and a dreadful storm dispersed the people. When daylight had returned, Romulus had disappeared, for his father, Mars, had carried him up to heaven in a fiery chariot. Shortly afterwards he appeared in more than mortal beauty to Proculus Julius, and bade him tell the Romans to worship him as their guardian god under the name of Quirinus. This is the older of two legends.

Tatius also invented and worshipped the goddess Cloacina;[3] Hostilius, Pavor and Pallor.[4] Presently Februs[5] was dedicated by someone or other and the harlots Acce and Flora. These are Roman gods. But Mars is Thracian and Jupiter Cretan and Juno either Argur or Samian or Carthaginian and Diana of Taurus, and the mother of gods from Mt. Ida, and Egyptian monsters, not divinities, which surely, if they had had any power, would have saved their own and their people's kingdoms. Plainly there are also among the Romans conquered household gods,[6] whom Aeneas as a fugitive conveyed here. There is also bald Venus, much more disgraced by her baldness here[7] than by being wounded in Homer.

Chapter 5

Moreover kingdoms do not come into existence by merit, but they are varied by chance. Moreover the Syrians and Persians formerly held an empire; and we know that the Greeks and the Egyptians have ruled. Thus, with changes of powers time for ruling fell to the Romans also as well as to others. But if you should go back to their origin, you would blush. A people is gathered together from the vicious and the criminal, and, after an asylum was established, impunity from crime makes a large number; presently that the king himself may have the chief place in crime, Romulus becomes a parricide and, in order to form a marriage, he begins an affair of concord through discord. They steal; they rage; they

---

3 Sewer.
4 Fear and Paleness.
5 Fever.
6 *Penates.*
7 In Rome.

deceive to increase the resources of the state; their marriages
are broken agreements of hospitality and cruel wars with
their fathers-in-law. Also the consulship is the highest step in
Roman honors. So we see that the consulship began as did
the kingdom; Brutus[1] kills his sons that praise for the dignity
may grow from the approval of the crime. Therefore, not
from holy observances nor from auspices or auguries did the
Roman kingdom grow, but it guards its appointed time
with a definite limit. Moreover, Regulus observed the auspices
and was captured, and Mancinus[2] maintained his religion
and was sent under the yoke; Paulus had chickens that fed
and yet at Cannae[3] he was slain; Gaius Caesar spurned the
auguries and the auspices that restrained from sending ships
to Africa before winter, and so much the more easily did he
both sail and conquer.

Chapter 6

Yet in all these affairs there is the principle of misleading
and deceiving and leading the foolish and wasteful people
astray by tricks that becloud the truth. They are impure and
vagrant spirits, which, after they have been immersed in
earthly vices and have receded from heavenly vigor because
of earthly contagion, themselves ruined do not cease to ruin

---

1 After the banishment of the Tarquins, Brutus and Tarquinius Colla-
  tinus were elected the first consuls of Rome. Brutus loved his country
  better than his children, and put to death his two sons, who had
  tried to restore the Tarquins.

2 Proconsul in 137; he had conducted the war against the Numantines
  but was defeated.

3 A village in Apulia, situated in an extensive plain east of the Aufidus
  and north of the small river Vergellus, memorable for the defeat of the
  Romans by Hannibal in 216 B. C.

others, and themselves depraved to infuse the error of depravity in others. These demons the poets also know, and Socrates declared that he was instructed and ruled according to the will of a demon, and thence the Magi have power to cause dangers or mockeries, of whom the chief one, Ostanes, both denies that the form of the true God can be seen and says that true angels stand by His throne. In this also Plato with like reasoning agrees, and, while maintaining one God, calls the rest angels or demons. Hermes Trismegistus[1] speaks of one God, and confesses that He is incomprehensible and impossible of estimation.

Chapter 7

So these spirits lurk under statues and consecrated images; these inspire the hearts of seers with their afflatus; they animate the fibres of entrails; they control the flight of birds; they rule lots; they effect oracles; they always involve falsehood with the truth, for they are both deceived and deceive; they disturb life; they disquiet sleep; also these spirits creeping into bodies stealthily terrify minds; they distort the limbs; they break down health; they provoke diseases, so as to coerce people to worship them, so as to seem, when glutted with the steam from altars and the piles of cattle, by removing what they had constrained, to have affected a cure. This is a cure on their part: the cessation of injury to their worshippers, and they have no other desire than to call men away from God and to turn them from an understanding of the

---

1 The reputed author of a variety of works, some of which are still extant. A vast number of works on philosophy and religion, written by the Neo-Platonists, were ascribed to this Hermes.

true religion to superstition with regard to themselves. Since
they themselves are under punishment, [they have no other
desire than] to seek companions for themselves in punishments,
whom they will make by their error sharers in their own
crime. Yet these [spirits], when adjured by us through the
true God, immediately withdraw and confess and are forced
to go out of the bodies which they have possessed. You may
see them struck with the lashes of the unseen majesty at our
voice and prayer, burned with fire, stretched out with the
increase of a growing punishment, shriek, groan, implore,
confess to their very listeners, who worship them, whence they
come and when they depart, so that they either leap out at
once or vanish gradually, according as the faith of sufferer
gives aid or the grace of the healer draws near. Hence they
force the populace to hate our name, so that men begin to
hate us before they know us, lest they either be able to imitate
us when we are known or not be able to condemn.

Chapter 8

Therefore, one is the Lord of all. For that sublimity cannot
have a peer, since it alone holds all power. Let us borrow
an example for the divine government even from the earth.
When did an alliance of kinship ever either begin with trust
and cease without bloodshed? Thus the brotherhood of the
Thebans was disrupted, discord enduring even in death as
their funeral pyres were in disagreement. And one kingdom
does not take the Roman twins, whom one hospice took to
womb. Pompey and Caesar were related,[1] and yet they did

---

1 In order to cement the union of the first triumvirate more closely,
in 59 B. C. Caesar gave to Pompey his daughter Julia in marriage.

not hold the bond of relationship in the urge for power. And you should not marvel at man, since in this all nature agrees. The bees have one king, and there is one leader among flocks, and one ruler among herds. Much rather is there one ruler of the world, who by His word orders all things, whatever exist, arranges them according to plan, accomplishes them by His power.

Chapter 9

This One cannot be seen, He is too bright to see; cannot be comprehended, He is too pure to grasp; cannot be estimated, He is too great to be imagined. And so we thus estimate God worthily, when we declare Him inestimable. Indeed what temple can God have, whose temple is the whole world? And when I as man dwell far and wide, shall I enclose the power of so great majesty within a small temple? He must be dedicated in our mind; He must be consecrated in our heart. You should not seek a name for God; God is His name. There is need of words there where a multitude is to be distinguished by the appropriate characteristics of designations. To God, who is alone, is the whole name of God. Therefore, He is one even wherever He is diffused. For even the populace naturally confesses God in many things, when the mind and soul of their author and origin are admonished. We hear it frequently said: 'O God' and 'God sees' and 'I commend to God' and 'God will render to me' and 'Whatever God wishes' and 'If God shall grant.' But what a height of sin is this—to be unwilling to acknowledge Him of whom you cannot be ignorant.

Chapter 10

Now that Christ is, and how through Him salvation came to us, this is the plan, this the means. At first the Jews had favor with God. Thus at one time they were just; thus ancestors were obedient to their religious views. Hence the excellence of their kingdom flourished and the greatness of their race advanced. But afterwards having become undisciplined and puffed up with confidence in their fathers, when they contemned the divine precepts, they lost the favor that was granted them. How their lives became profane, what offence to their violated religion was contracted, they themselves also bear witness, who, though silent in voice, confess by their end; dispersed and straggling they wander about; exiles from their soil and climate, they are tossed upon the hospitality of strangers.

Chapter 11

Furthermore, God had predicted before that it would happen that, as the world passed on and the end of the universe was now at hand, God would gather to Himself from every nation and people and place much more faithful worshippers, who would draw from the divine gifts the favor which the Jews had lost by contemning their religious principles, after having received it. Therefore, as the ruler and master of this grace and teaching, the Word and the Son of God is sent, who is proclaimed through all the prophets as the Enlightener and Teacher of the human race. He is the power of God; He is the reason; He is His wisdom and glory; He enters into a virgin; the Holy Spirit put on flesh; God mingles

with man. This is our God; this our Christ who, as mediator
of the two, puts on man, to lead him to the Father. Christ
wished to be what man is, that man might be able to be what
Christ is.

Chapter 12

The Jews too knew that Christ would come, for He was
always being announced to them by the admonishment of the
prophets. But since His advent was signified as twofold, the
one which would perform the office and example of man, the
other which would confess God, not understanding the first
advent which preceded hidden in the passion, they believe
only the one which will be manifest in His power. Moreover,
that the people of the Jews were unable to understand this
was the desert of their sins; they were so punished for the
blindness of wisdom and intelligence, that those who were
unworthy of life had life before their eyes and saw it not.

Chapter 13

So when Christ Jesus according to the former predictions
of the prophets by His word and the command of His voice
drove demons out of man, released paralytics, cleansed the
leprous, illuminated the blind, gave the power to walk to the
halt, brought life back to the dead, compelled the elements
to be servants unto Him, the winds to serve Him, the seas
to obey Him, those of the lower regions to yield to Him,
the Jews who had believed Him only a man from the
humility of His flesh and body, thought Him a sorcerer from
the freedom of His power. Hence their masters and leaders,

that is those whom He surpassed in teaching and wisdom were so inflamed with anger and roused with indignation that they finally seized Him and handed Him over to Pontius Pilate who at that time was procurator of Syria for the Romans, and demanded His crucifixion and death by violent and stubborn approbations.

Chapter 14

He himself also had predicted that these would do this, and the testimony of all the prophets had thus preceded, that He should suffer, not that He might feel death, but that He might conquer it, and that, when He had suffered, He should return again to heaven to show the force of divine majesty. Thus the course of events fulfilled the prophecy. For when He had been crucified, forestalling the office of the executioner He of His own accord gave up His spirit, and on the third day of His own accord He rose again from the dead. He appeared to His disciples just as He had been; He offered Himself to be recognized to those who looked on and had been joined with Him, and conspicuous by the firmness of His corporeal substance He tarried for forty days, that they might be instructed by Him according to the precepts of life and learn what they should teach. Then, when a cloud had spread about Him he was raised up into heaven, that as victor He might bring to the Father the man whom He loved, whom He put on, whom He protected from death, soon to come from heaven for the punishment of the devil and the judgment of the human race with the strength of an avenger and the power of a judge; but the disciples scattered over the world, with their Master and God advising, gave out precepts for salvation, led man from the error of darkness to the way of light, endowed the blind and ignorant with eyes to recognize the truth.

Chapter 15

And that the proof might not be the less solid and the confession of Christ not be a matter of pleasure, they are tried by torments, by crosses, by many kinds of punishments. Pain, which is the witness of truth, is applied, so that Christ, the son of God, who is believed to have been given to man for life, might be proclaimed not only by the proclamation of the voice but by the testimony of suffering. Therefore, we accompany Him, we follow Him, we hold Him the Leader of our journey, the Source of light, the Author of salvation, as He promises heaven as well as the Father to those who seek and believe. What Christ is, we Christians will be, if we follow Christ.

INDEX

Apology, of Tertullian, 164
Apostle, 40, 45, 67, 98, (Paul),
102, 104, 105, 109, 111, (the
blessed) 117, 118, 136, 142,
144, 148, 156, 209, 216, 217,
235, 237, 250, 264, 271, 276,
278, 287, 299, 301, 303, 305,
323, 324, 326, 343
Apostles, 66, 87, 98, 99, 117, 120,
133, 251, 269, 292
Apulia, 353 n.
Arnobius, 163
Asia Minor, 258
Aufidus, river, 353 n.
Augustine, St., xii; the Confessions 5; De doctrina Christiana, 5 n., 25 and n.; 30, 125,
263, 257 n., 258 n., 260
Author of salvation, 360
avarice, 177
Avenger, 286
Azarias, 84, 114, 334

Babylon, 149
Balaam, 330
baptism, 228, 316
Bardenhewer, 26 n.
bees, 178, 356
Benson, E. W., xiii
betrayer, 269
Bible, Latin versions of, 311
Book of Kings, first, 322
Bread of Heaven, 268
Brunner, F. A., 277
Brutus, 353 and n.

Caesar, Gaius, 353, 355
Cain, 109, 148, 213, 281, 296,
301, 308
Callistus, Pope, 61 n.
Campus Martius, 351 n.
Cannae, 353
Canticle of Canticles, 99
Carthage, conditions in, 212 n.,
225, councils in, 258, 313
Cassiodorus, 30, 257 n.
Castor, 349 n.
Cestus, 68
Chapman, Dom, 92
Charity, 109, 277, 278, 328
Cheltenham list, 291
Chiron, 350 n.
Christ, 38, 50 58, 61 62, 64, 65,
66, 67, tribunal of, 72, 81, 82,
83, 96, 97, 98, 99, 100, 101,
102, 103, 116, 118, 119, 121,
126, 134, 138, 140, 141, 142,
143, 147, 149, 158, 159, 182,
187, 188, 191, 199, 201, 202;
teacher 203, 204, 216, 217, 221,
227, 228, 232, 234, 235, 238,
240, 241, 242, 243, 245, 247,
248, 250, 252, 262, 264, 268,
270, 271, 279, 281, 282, 283,
292, 297, 301, 302, 304, 305,
306, 307, 308, 311, 313, 315,
316, 317, 323, 324, 327, 328,
332, 3336, 342, 343, 344, 357,
358, 360
Christianity, 262
Christians, 38, 98, 158, 163, 164,

364

Isaac, 138, 213, 250, 272
Isaias, 36, 42, 135, 151, 156, 230, 285, 320, 330
Ischys, an Arcadian, 350 n.
Israel, 76, 102, 135, 151, 174, 320, 330
Italy, 350

Jacob, 76, 138, 149, 213, 230, 250, 272, 296, 333
Janiculum, 350
Jannus, 112
January, 350
Janus, 350
Jealousy and Envy, 291-308
Jeremias, 32, 74, 130, 320, 321
Jeroboam, 102
Jerome, St., v, vi, 29, 257 n., 347, 348
Jerusalem, 102, 149, 187, 200 n.
Jews, 134, 135, 138, 159; Jewish people, 207, 211, 269, 270, 279, 282, 283, 297, 325, 357, 358
Job, 74, 150, 206, 244, 280, 281, 321
John 37, (Apostle) 110, 139, 146, 218, 229, 271, 287, 301, 323, 329
Joseph, 272, 296, 333
Josue, 327
Jubaianus, Bishop of Maureta-nia, 260
Judaism, history of, 347
Judas, 117, 149, 269

Judea, 332
Judge, 16, 72, 80, 137, 241, 285, 286
judgment, day of, 64, 248, 266, 319, 359
Julia, daughter of Caesar, 355 n.
Jungmann, J. A., 277
Juno, 351, 352
Jupiter, cave of, 350, 351, 352
justice, 140

Kings, Book of, 242, 335; kings, 349
Koch, H., 27 n., 291, 311

Lactantius, xii, 163, 164
Lamb, 340
Laomedon, 350
Lapsed, The, 55-88, 115
lapsi, vii, 196
Latebra, 350 n.
Latium, 350
Leclercq, H., 277
LeMoyne, Dom Jean, 93
Leucothea, 349
libellatici, vii, 56, 196
libelli, vii
Lot's wife, 325
Lucius, 261 n.

Machabees, 334
Magi, 354
Magnus, 259; To Magnus, 347
maidens, of Christ, 39
Malachias, 285

Synnada, Council of, 258 n.
Syrians, 352
Syrtes, 350 n.

Tabitha, 232, 233
Tatius, 352
Teacher, of peace, 132; of our life, 233
Tertullian, 28, 55, 61 n., 125, 163, 258 n., 262, 347
Testament, New, 230
Testament, Old, 230, 291
Thebans, 355
Thornton, C., xiii
Tiberinus, 351
Tobias, 206, 246, 281, 334
toga, 16, 16 n.
Trinity, 157
Tucce, bishop of, 313 n.
twelve tables, 15

Valerian, Emperor, ix, 126; persecution, 261
Valerius, 311

van den Eynde, D., 93
Venus, 352
Vergellus, 353
virginity, 34, 48, 50, 51
virgins, the Dress of Virgins, 25-52; of Christ, 39, 42, 44, 46, 48, 50, 58, 211, 283
Volusianus, 195, 261
Von Hartel, W., xiii
Vanity of Idols, 347
vow, of chastity, 27; of poverty, 27; of obedience, 27

Wallis, E., xiii
widows, 44, 48, 232, 233, 241, 283
Wisdom, 335
witnesses, 73 n.
Word of God, 270
Works and Almsgiving, 225-253

Zachaeus, 234
Zacharias, 333
Zeus, 350 n.

THE FATHERS
OF THE CHURCH

(A series of approximately 100 volumes when completed)

translated by L. Schopp
The Magnitude of the Soul
   translated by J. McMahon
On Music
   translated by R. Taliaferro
The Advantage of Believing
   translated by L. Meagher
On Faith in Things Unseen
   translated by R. Deferrari, M–F. McDonald

OCLC 856032

Volume 5:   **SAINT AUGUSTINE**   (1948)
The Happy Life
   translated by L. Schopp
Answer to Skeptics *(Contra Academicos)*
   translated by D. Kavanagh
Divine Providence and the Problem of Evil
   translated by R. Russell
The Soliloquies
   translated by T. Gilligan

OCLC 728405

Volume 6:   **WRITINGS OF SAINT JUSTIN MARTYR**   (1948)
The First Apology
The Second Apology
The Dialogue with Trypho
Exhortation to the Greeks
Discourse to the Greeks
The Monarchy or Rule of God
   translated by T. Falls

OCLC 807077

Volume 7:   **NICETA OF REMESIANA**   (1949)
Writings of Niceta of Remesiana
   translated by G. Walsh
Prosper of Aquitaine: Grace and Free Will
   translated by J. O'Donnell
Writings of Sulpicius Severus
   translated by B. Peebles
Vincent of Lerins: The Commonitories
   translated by R. Morris

OCLC 807068

Volume 8:   **SAINT AUGUSTINE**   (1950)

Life of St. Cyprian by Pontius
    translated by M. M. Mueller, R. Deferrari
Life of St. Epiphanius by Ennodius
    translated by G. Cook
Life of St. Paul the First Hermit
Life of St. Hilarion by St. Jerome
Life of Malchus by St. Jerome
    translated by L. Ewald
Life of St. Anthony by St. Athanasius
    translated by E. Keenan
A Sermon on the Life of St. Honoratus by St. Hilary
    translated by R. Deferrari

                                        OCLC 806775

Volume 16:   SAINT AUGUSTINE   (1952)
    The Christian Life
    Lying
    The Work of Monks
    The Usefulness of Fasting
        translated by S. Muldowney
    Against Lying
        translated by H. Jaffe
    Continence
        translated by M–F. McDonald
    Patience
        translated by L. Meagher
    The Excellence of Widowhood
        translated by C. Eagan
    The Eight Questions of Dulcitius
        translated by M. Deferrari

                                        OCLC 806731

Volume 17:   SAINT PETER CHRYSOLOGUS   (1953)
    Selected Sermons
    Letter to Eutyches
                SAINT VALERIAN
    Homilies
    Letter to the Monks
        translated by G. Ganss

                                        OCLC 806783

Volume 18:   SAINT AUGUSTINE   (1953)

Letters (83–130)
> *translated by W. Parsons*

OCLC 807061

Volume 19:   **EUSEBIUS PAMPHILI**   (1953)
Ecclesiastical History (books 1–5)
> *translated by R. Deferrari*

OCLC 708651

Volume 20:   **SAINT AUGUSTINE**   (1953)
Letters (131–164)
> *translated by W. Parsons*

OCLC 807061

Volume 21:   **SAINT AUGUSTINE**   (1953)
Confessions
> *translated by V. Bourke*

OCLC 2210845

Volume 22:   **FUNERAL ORATIONS**   (1953)
Saint Gregory Nazianzen: Four Funeral Orations
> *translated by L. McCauley*
Saint Ambrose: On the Death of His Brother Satyrus I & II
> *translated by J. Sullivan, M. McGuire*
Saint Ambrose: Consolation on the Death of Emperor
Valentinian
Funeral Oration on the Death of Emperor Theodosius
> *translated by R. Deferrari*

OCLC 806797

Volume 23:   **CLEMENT OF ALEXANDRIA**   (1954)
Christ the Educator
> *translated by S. Wood*

OCLC 2200024

Volume 24:   **SAINT AUGUSTINE**   (1954)
The City of God (books 17-22)
> *translated by G. Walsh, D. Honan*

OCLC 807084

Volume 25:   **SAINT HILARY OF POITIERS**   (1954)
The Trinity
> *translated by S. McKenna*

OCLC 806781

Volume 26:   **SAINT AMBROSE**   (1954)

Letters (204–270)
  translated by W. Parsons

OCLC 807061

Volume 33:   SAINT JOHN CHRYSOSTOM (1957)
Commentary on St. John The Apostle and Evangelist
Homilies (1–47)
  translated by T. Goggin

OCLC 2210926

Volume 34:   SAINT LEO THE GREAT (1957)
Letters
  translated by E. Hunt

OCLC 825765

Volume 35:   SAINT AUGUSTINE (1957)
Against Julian
  translated by M. Schumacher

OCLC 3255620

Volume 36:   SAINT CYPRIAN (1958)
To Donatus
The Lapsed
The Unity of the Church
The Lord's Prayer
To Demetrian
Mortality
Works and Almsgiving
Jealousy and Envy
Exhortation to Martyrdom to Fortunatus
That Idols Are Not Gods
  translated by R. Deferrari
The Dress of Virgins
  translated by A. Keenan
The Good of Patience
  translated by G. Conway

OCLC 3894637

Volume 37:   SAINT JOHN OF DAMASCUS (1958)
The Fount of Knowledge
On Heresies
The Orthodox Faith (4 books)
  translated by F. Chase, Jr.

OCLC 810002

Rule for the Monastery of Compludo
General Rule for Monasteries
Pact
Monastic Agreement
translated by C. Barlow

OCLC 718095

Volume 64:　　　THE WORKS OF SAINT CYRIL　　　(1970)
OF JERUSALEM II
Lenten Lectures (Catcheses) 13—18
translated by L. McCauley
The Mystagogical Lectures
Sermon on the Paralytic
Letter to Constantius
translated by A. Stephenson

OCLC 21885

Volume 65　　　　　　SAINT AMBROSE　　　　　　(1972)
Seven Exegetical Works
Isaac or the Soul
Death as a Good
Jacob and the Happy Life
Joseph
The Patriarchs
Flight from the World
The Prayer of Job and David
translated by M. McHugh

OCLC 314148

Volume 66:　　　SAINT CAESARIUS OF ARLES III　　　(1973)
Sermons 187—238
translated by M. M. Mueller

OCLC 1035149; 2494636

Volume 67:　　　　　　　NOVATIAN　　　　　　　(1974)
The Trinity
The Spectacles
Jewish Foods
In Praise of Purity
Letters
translated by R. DeSimone

OCLC 662181